The Debt We Owe

·EX·LIBRIS·

R. I. Johnson

The Founder of the RAF Benevolent Fund, Marshal of the Royal Air Force the Rt. Hon. The Viscount Trenchard GCB, OM, GCVO, DSO, DCL, LL D.

The Debt
We Owe

The
Royal Air Force
Benevolent Fund 1919-1989

Edward Bishop

Airlife
England

By the same author

THE WOODEN WONDER

MOSQUITO

THE BATTLE OF BRITAIN

THEIR FINEST HOUR

THE GUINEA PIG CLUB

BLOOD AND FIRE!

WELLINGTON BOMBER

EMMA, LADY HAMILTON

BETTER TO DIE

HURRICANE

Copyright © Edward Bishop, 1989

First published in the UK in 1989 by
Airlife Publishing Ltd.

British Library Cataloguing in Publication Data available

ISBN 1 85310 079 X

Printed in England by Livesey Ltd., Shrewsbury.

Airlife Publishing Ltd.

101 Longden Road, Shrewsbury, England.

Contents

Foreword

by Sir Arthur Bryant CH, CBE, LLD, MA

Lecturing at the Royal Air Force Apprentices' School at Halton, before the war I made use of a phrase that was more true than I knew. I had been speaking of the close relation — one then forgotten by our leading intellectuals — between the historic British command of the seas and the development, preservation and expansion of our liberties. After outlining the naval occasions by virtue of which it had been won and maintained, I looked up from my notes and, on the spur of the moment, added, 'Gentlemen, it all now depends on you!' Three years later, in the Battle of Britain, the truth of my words was dramatically proved.

'For what we have received', I was taught to say after my meals as a little boy, 'the Lord make us truly thankful!' Every year, when the anniversary of the Battle of Britain comes round, we of our generation recall with thankfulness the men, living and dead, who by their courage, skill and devotion won for our country and the world that salvationary victory. In the epic autumn the Royal Air Force saved this country and, with it, the world's freedom. It did so again in those laborious years of preparation and endurance before the assault on Hitler's western wall, when night after night the crews of Bomber Command went out on their perilous missions, suffering losses in proportion to their strength unparalleled in any sustained successful operation known to history, yet winning by it that stranglehold on the aggressor's production-centres and communications without which D-Day would have been a shambles and a disaster, and London itself would have been slowly destroyed by German rockets and flying bombs.

We can never be sufficiently grateful. The Royal Air Force in its seventy-one years of life has won its place in the English heart beside the Royal Navy for the service it has done in preserving all we love and value. The strains of Walford Davies's noble Royal Air Force March arouse something of the same association and emotions as the noble air of 'Sunset' played by the Royal Marines band at the highest moment of naval ceremony. They remind us, with a sense of pride, pity and tenderness too deep for words, of the valour, sacrifice, unselfishness and imperishable glory of those who, transcending their own human needs and inclinations, laid down all they loved for their country and gave her existence continuance and her beliefs meaning. They commemorate all that was beautiful in those freely-given and dedicated lives, the love of their comrades and dear ones, the hours of life and happiness and preparation that had gone to make them what they were and, in doing so, to serve and save England. And they remind those who hear them that in the service of England there is no finality or discharge, that life for every one of us has a purpose, and that its highest achievement is sacrifice — the key that alone opens the door to the truest and enduring aspirations of men. For, if their sacrifice has meaning, it is that the end of life is not material satisfaction but mastery over self in the cause of something more satisfying and lasting than self.

Such spiritual greatness can only be achieved at a heavy price of intense human suffering, both material and mental, endured both by the giver of the initial sacrifice and by those who love and depend on him. The Royal Air Force Benevolent Fund exists to reduce so far as possible the extent of such unavoidable suffering and loss. Founded in 1919 by Marshal of the Royal Air Force Lord Trenchard, the man who more than any other was responsible for the creation of the service that saved England in 1940, it offers assistance to all Royal Air Force personnel and their dependants who stand in need of it. Anyone commissioned or enlisted in the Royal Air Force or Women's Royal Air Force in whatever capacity is qualified for consideration by the fact of his or her service, past or present.

The work that the Fund performs is of many kinds: grants or loans in time of sickness or convalescence or of great financial stringency, in providing tools and working equipment, in meeting maternity and similar expenses, in redeeming pawned articles and pressing debts incurred by virtue of past services, in the education of children and the provision of housing. The education work of the Fund is among its most important activities. It is the Fund's policy that children whose fathers were killed or died whilst serving should receive education of the standard they would have been given had they not been orphaned. This help is continued from earliest school-days to the university if the child shows promise.

In the last resort, all national security, active or passive, depends on the readiness of men to sacrifice themselves for the defence of their country. That readiness had been shown by the officers and men of the Royal Air Force ever since it came into existence in 1918. The confidence that their countrymen would look after their dependants in the event of their full sacrifice being accepted was, and still is, a most vital factor in the formation and preservation of the service's morale. The Royal Air Force Benevolent Fund is the permanent guarantee that that confidence shall never be misplaced.

Sir Arthur Bryant, the distinguished historian, has since died.

Chapter 1
Into the Nineties

*'The way in which the Fund conducts its relief work through its
independent Grants Committees is the envy of many similar
organisations.'*

Lord Catto, Chairman

Outside the bunkhouse where formerly the firemen slept a coal-black
KC 125 United States Air Force air-to-air refuelling tanker thunders
off the runway and into a scowling sky; a noisy and chilling reminder
that not only does RAF Fairford economically accommodate the
Royal Air Force Benevolent Fund's International Air Tattoo
Organisation, but that operationally it hosts the United States Tanker
Task Force in Europe.

It seems appropriate that the flourishing fund-raising-through-fun
business branch of the Fund should be within yards of present day
operational take-offs and landings; and at an airfield from which
D-Day and Arnhem airborne operations were flown in 1944.

As the tanker climbs, Paul Bowen, IAT's director, picks off on his
fingers the components of the profitable enterprise he has built in
partnership with Tim Prince, the operation's director. In ten years
their air shows, publishing, advertising, and radio ventures and RAF
Massed Bands Festivals of Music at The Royal Albert Hall, have
placed IAT in the front rank of such traditional and conventional
revenue sources as donations, legacies and the serving RAF's half-a-
day's-pay-a-year scheme.

On Bowen's desk the telephone rings. King Hussein, the International Air Tattoo's Patron is calling from Amman. No royal figure-
head, the King of the Hashemite Kingdom of Jordan keeps abreast of
details as each biennial event is planned and executed. He also meets,
encourages and sometimes flies with the disabled men and women for
whom he finances six of the nine annual IAT flying scholarships in
memory of Sir Douglas Bader, the Tattoo's first president. Though,
in accordance with protocol, IAT now designates the post Patron,
Hussein modestly insists that, as with Bader, he is president.

No one is more keen to learn IAT's profits in a Tattoo year. Expected to exceed £500,000 in 1989, the RAF Benevolent Fund's seventieth anniversary year, and bringing IAT's total ten-year contribution to more than £2 million, this commercial enterprise conducted from the firemen's bunkhouse accounts for a healthy percentage of an estimated £8.5 to £9 million likely to be disbursed in 1989 from the Fund's headquarters for the relief of distress.

Fairford sets the progressive tone of the Fund for what remains of the 1980s and as it enters the 1990s. Finely tuned, increasingly computerised, it accepts the need to be aggressive in making and attracting money, careful in conserving its resources, while never stinting its assistance for the alleviation of distress.

With the fiftieth anniversary of the Battle of Britain falling within what promises to be the most costly decade of its existence, the Fund has challenged itself unashamedly not only to repeat but, in comparative terms, to far exceed the success of the Appeal which Marshal of the Royal Air Force Lord Trenchard urged upon it in 1940.

Trenchard, Father of the Royal Air Force, was not in current phraseology a natural communicator, and on this occasion he broke his self-imposed rule of radio silence. In a Battle of Britain broadcast he said:

> 'It is now time to ask this country, as I feel the whole British Empire recognises all that the Royal Air Force has done, to put the Fund on a firm basis. A very large sum will be required for us to carry out our obligations to the airmen, their wives, children and dependants, so that these men may go into battle, feeling that the future of their immediate relations will, anyhow, be secured from want.'

The £53,342 obtained from that appeal, together with £250,000 from Lord Nuffield and £354,530 10s from the chairman, Lord Wakefield's public appeal in the Press, plus other individual donations, provided the Fund with the financial base from which it has gone forward.

Fifty years on, the renewal of Trenchard's appeal at the time of the RAF's 'Finest Hour' coincides with the heaviest call ever on the Fund's resources. Survivors and widows of 1940 are elderly, as indeed is anyone who served in the 1939-45 War, ex-service people of the post-war years do not get any younger and, though this factor tends to be overlooked, families of the present day service are equally entitled to the Fund's assistance.

If, as this history will show, the means of money raising and the needs of beneficiaries have altered radically since the Fund began in 1919, its geographical location and basic organisational structure have remained reassuringly unchanged since it established permanent headquarters at 67 Portland Place in 1945.

Step down west London's Portland Place from the BBC and, passing the Chinese Embassy in the direction of Regent's Park, enter No 67. It is a Tuesday morning which means that the Main Grants Committee is meeting in the spacious Adam room which serves as Council chamber and Controller's office. The chairs at the long table are upholstered in Royal Air Force blue and the walls are hung with photographic studies. Here is Lord Trenchard, who founded the Fund in 1919, and here the Duke of Kent, president since 1969, and whose father was killed on active service with the RAF in 1942 while he was chairman. Here, too, is Princess Marina, the president's mother, president in succession to her husband for twenty-five years. Sir Winston Churchill, wearing RAF wings and the uniform of an Air Commodore, is also here. He was a vice-president from 1919 until he died in 1965. 'Never in the field of human conflict was so much owed by so many to so few' — it seems almost that the phrase in which he immortalised the Few of Fighter Command in 1940 is on his lips. Or is it that memorable phrase from his radio appeal in 1951 on behalf of the Fund when he spoke of 'the debt we owe to the paladins of the Royal Air Force', extending his earlier tribute to embrace air and groundcrew of all Commands and coining a title for this book.

It is ten o'clock and, as Committee members arrive, Air Chief Marshal Sir Thomas Kennedy — Sir Jock, as he is popularly known — moves from his desk in the far corner to greet them. He is executive custodian of the Fund, whose Main Grant and sub-committees disburse its income week by week.

Over the years, inevitably, controllers, committee chairmen and members change, but the week-in-week-out work of the grants committees, the heart pumping the Fund's life-blood to relieve distress, provides continuity. Air Chief Marshal Sir John Aiken takes the chair, and members of the welfare staff led by Air Commodore Robert Barcilon square off the buff folders from which they will present the day's applications.

Sir Jock's predecessors of the past twenty years, Air Marshal Sir William Coles, Air Marshal Sir Denis Crowley-Milling and Air Chief Marshal Sir Alasdair Steedman would recognise the scene. But there familiarity fades. It is immediately apparent that, as the Fund enters its eighth decade, salaried staff and honorary committee members are mostly of the nuclear deterrent generation, while its beneficiaries are increasingly veterans of the 1939-45 war.

Ten years ago Air Chief Marshal Sir David Lee, Director Plans at the Air Ministry during the critical war yeras of 1943-44, had chaired the Main Grants committee since 1971; Crowley-Milling, the Controller, had fought in the Battle of Britain, as had Air Commodore Roy Dutton, his welfare secretary; and Jean Ashton, Dutton's assistant had joined the Fund in wartime as a young girl. Crowley-Milling's successor, Steedman, had been a reconnaissance pilot and Dutton's successor, Air Vice-Marshal Michael Robinson, while just missing the war, flew Beaufighters in a light bomber role during the Malayan Emergency.

Sir Jock Kennedy personifies the change. The first Controller since that War who did not serve in it, he has inspired radical shifts in the Fund's approaches to welfare, appeal and public relations. The Fund has always been fortunate that controllers have been men for their time. It is, therefore, no disrespect to Sir Jock's predecessors that since his arrival at Portland Place in August 1988 he has questioned long held concepts and doctored or excised some former practices. Air Member for Personnel from 1982 until his retirement in 1986, such recent experience of the RAF's serving men and women has been, and will be, of immeasurable value to the Fund's assessment of their needs and enlistment of their support.

While Coles and Crowley-Milling, anticipating the beginning of the 1939-45 War 'bulge' were, in so far as they could be, conserving controllers, Steedman, at No 67 from 1981 to the summer of 1988, coincided with the preliminary pressures of the bulge and spent accordingly. The need was there.

Kennedy, following Steedman, has been confronted with the consequences of deficit, the prospects of an ever inflating bulge and the urgency of securing the Fund's future beyond the turn of the century. His routine measures in the Fund's front-line fields of welfare and appeal will become apparent. Problems, obstacles and as yet unforeseen hurdles will doubtless impede his progress. But with 1990 around the corner he enters this testing period with one exceptional advantage: the fiftieth anniversary of the Battle of Britain and the opportunity this presents to publicise the Fund and increase its capital dramatically. The target for the Battle of Britain Appeal is £20 million.

In cold print this figure may seem unnecessarily ambitious, but placed in context with each Tuesday's Grants Committee outgoings, an estimated overall annual expenditure for 1990 of up to

£9 million and the year-by-year inflationary effects of the bulge, it is realistic.

An introductory glimpse of the Committee in session serves well to establish the central purpose of the Fund. As the Chairman welcomes members, the Welfare Director, a former Lightning fighter pilot, squadron and station commander, and now presenter of the morning's list of applicants, consults foolscap sheets from the top folder. So orderly seem the files that it is easy to imagine a voice from each, offering name, rank and number, though such Service stiffness would be entirely alien to those around the table. Most — including wives of serving officers — have the relaxed approach of senior retired people to age, rank and status, but this in no way diminishes alertness and concentration as they consider cases.

The bulge of the 1939-45 War survivors supplies Barcilon and his staff with all too many cases, numbers of them from Bomber Command which was the 'front line' of the RAF's war. Random selection among cases of the past ten years will turn up innumerable cases of bomber aircrew severely injured when expectation of life was as short as their Brylcreemed haircuts.

One such was that of the Wellington sergeant air-gunner who had miraculously survived heaven knows how many bomber operations over Germany and surgical operations thereafter. Suffering eighty-five per cent burns, repaired by Sir Archibald McIndoe at the Queen Victoria Hospital, East Grinstead, and revitalised through membership of the Guinea Pig Club, he sought a loan for a central heating system to make life more tolerable. As so often when burns are considered, Archie McIndoe's widow, Connie, chairman of a grants sub-committee, or Vanora Marland, also a committee member and daughter by the plastic surgery 'Maestro's' — a Guinea Pig accolade — first wife, are present.

The Chairman turns towards Lady McIndoe. She explains that the Fund's Co-ordinating Committee for the Resettlement of Burns Cases recommends a grant of £500 and a loan of £500. The Chairman looks round the table. 'This man was badly burnt. It has been long accepted that we do everything we can for the Guinea Pig Club. A grant of £1,000?' Approval is unanimous. 'Very well, agreed.'

Many applications concern housing and are regarded as fairly routine. The seventy-year-old widow of a Chief Technician who has died aged seventy-four and was discharged in 1966 after twenty-nine years' service in the Engineering Branch, seeks a loan to settle a mortgage and pay outstanding house repair bills in the Isle of Man. The Committee notes that the house's value of £47,000 in 1987 had risen to £72,000 in 1988, but this does not deter a loan of £7,000 of which £5,000 is to clear the mortgage and £2,000 the repairs.

The Committee hears that a former Leading Aircraftwoman with four years' service has given birth to a mentally handicapped child. The marriage has broken down. She has returned to her home town and obtained a council house which is in a deplorable condition, run down and vandalised. After investigation the Committee decide to buy a house for the benefit of mother and child.

A former Leading Aircraftman, who served throughout the 1939-45 War, has had two legs amputated within the past two years. The Fund purchases an electrically propelled invalid wheelchair and makes it available on permanent loan. It also makes a grant towards winter fuel bills, general needs and comforts and provides a weekly maintenance allowance.

The morning moves on. As successive members of the Welfare Director's staff present his or her share of the week's applications, it is manifest how closely each has indentified with the range of domestic, social and financial problems the cases represent. Inevitably, given the nature of emotive cases, some submissions are made in terms of warm advocacy which can only come from the heart, yet each presenter manages to retain a measure of detachment sufficient to help Committee members to balance their decisions between heartfelt instincts and the written or unwritten observances of the Royal Air Force Benevolent Fund, which must rule their heads when authorising loans, grants or sympathetically refusing assistance.

Some applicants have a long history of need but, whether a folder is fat or thin, investigation of the immediate need has been thorough. Perhaps one of the Fund's 800 voluntary welfare helpers has reported, possibly an associated ex-service welfare organisation, such as the Royal Air Forces Association, the Soldiers', Sailors' and Airmen's Families Association, or the Royal British Legion, has assisted or, as in many instances, a station commander has sought help for one of his people.

The cases are infinite in their variety: a serving airman has been let down by a fraudulent builder; a flight lieutenant who served in Korea has suffered a personality change through a rare disease; the widow of a test pilot whose death was front page news many years ago has insufficient means; the sixty-two-year-old widow of a corporal who became a Baptist minister after a medical discharge in wartime needs help.

Another folder is opened. A thirty-two-year-old corporal is dying of cancer. He has a wife, aged twenty-seven, and children of two and four. Within weeks there will be a widow and two young children. 'She would like to live near Brighton,' the Committee is told. 'She has found a suitable house, but it will be costly when one includes repairs, Value Added Tax and other expenses.' The Chairman gently makes the point that Brighton is an expensive area. 'Well, she has set her heart on it.' There is no further dissent. Agreed. A flight lieutenant has been killed in a Vulcan bomber accident and the required sum is authorised to house his family. In each case the houses will be purchased through and owned by the Royal Air Force Benevolent Fund Housing Trust.

Can this be the same Fund which in 1919 went overboard about the generosity of Mrs M. E. Salting, who presented two Ascot houses which were sold for less than £10,000. Or which felt deeply indebted to the white residents of Swaziland for their contribution of £406, and for £31 11s received from Wei-hai-wei in China? Or the Fund which in 1919 held serious reservations about accepting as a gift Vanbrugh Castle, the home in south-east London of Mr Alexander Duckham who had made a fortune in oil, and which thereafter was to accommodate the Fund's school for almost fifty-five years?

Certainly, Duke of Kent School, which emerged from Vanbrugh's coming together in September 1976 with Woolpit, a preparatory school in Ewhurst in Surrey, and upon which nearly £1 million has been spent, would astonish Trenchard and his contemporaries as would also Princess Marina House, the Fund's convalescent and residential centre at Rustington in Sussex and Alastrean House, an equivalent care home in Scotland.

Any vestige of Vanbrugh has long since disappeared from the Duke of Kent School in the Surrey countryside. The school's gradual development to its present status as a boarding school for fee paying pupils from service and civilian families, as well as the Fund's Foundationers, has been a feature of the past ten years. Since 1980 this transformation has taken place under the headship of Roger Wilson, who came to Duke of Kent after sixteen years at Christ's Hospital, ten of them as a housemaster of Peele A. Although it bore no influence on Wilson's appointment, unless of course it was pre-ordained, Peele A was Sir Barnes Wallis's house as a boy at the Bluecoat school. So many years on, the Fund's RAF Foundationers Trust, part-funded at the start in 1951 by Wallis's £10,000 inventor's award for the bouncing bombs, which breached the Mohne and Eder dams, and for other wartime weapons, continues to educate boys and girls at Christ's Hospital. Happily, the Duke of Kent's Foundationers are particularly eligible.

There have also been marked advances in the past ten years in the Fund's convalescent and residential care arrangements. Princess Marina House at Rustington in West Sussex can now accommodate convalescent and long stay men and women. In Scotland, Alastrean House provides residential care for elderly ex-service people from anywhere, although the north of England and Scotland are important sources. Peacefully rural in Aberdeenshire and deriving from the Fund's favoured relationship with one of its most generous benefactors, The MacRobert Trusts, Alastrean, as will be shown, is a recent acquisition. In Scotland, too, the new Downing House, close to the centre of Moffat, will be a bricks and mortar reminder of the Fund's interdependence in so many directions with the Royal Air Forces Association. For Downing House, a £1 million Fund and RAFA development of St Ninian's, the prep school founded by Lord Dowding's father and where the 'Leader of the Few' was born, is to provide sheltered housing for thirty-eight residents. The original house hs been restored and a wing built to provide a total of twenty-six flats, two of which are adapted for disabled people.

Princess Marina, Alastrean and Downing Houses are prime examples of how far the Fund has come since grants of seventy years ago ran to little more than one shilling for a night's lodging, the redemption of pawning clothing, the purchase of a pair of boots in which to seek work, or provision of a hawker's licence. Comprehension of the present day Royal Air Force Benevolent Fund's humble origins puts such awards in perspective.

Chapter 2
Origins

I bore you on eagles' wings
And brought you unto myself (Exodus 19:4)

Inscription on the Royal Air Force Memorial, Victoria Embankment

When The Royal Air Force Benevolent Fund was founded seventy years ago by Air Marshal Sir Hugh Trenchard, it was named The Royal Air Force Memorial Fund because one of its earliest objects was to raise a memorial to airmen who died in the First World War.

The memorial was completed in 1923. A simple monument in Portland stone, it is surmounted by a gilded eagle and on sunny mornings railway passengers arriving at London's Charing Cross terminal can glimpse it glinting in the sunlight from its riverside position on the Victoria Embankment.

The original intention was for Mr W. Reid Dick's sculpted eagle to face inwards to the embankment road traffic, but Sir Reginald Blomfield, the Fund's consultant architect, altered his design to allow the eagle to face across the river, symbolically to France.

In the summer of 1923 the Memorial was unveiled by a youthful Prince of Wales who spoke prophetically, and heaven knows how when the Royal Air Force was so emaciated, of 'our cloud armies of the future'. When the flags fell away from the memorial a Royal Air Force guard of honour crashed into the 'present arms', and a carefully marshalled contingent of twenty-seven small boys lifted their caps. The boys had come from Vanbrugh Castle, where the Fund had already established a school at Blackheath in south-east London. They were the sons of airmen who had died in the Service.

The Thames embankment might not seem the most appropriate place for a flying men's memorial. This position was not the first choice of the Royal Air Force Memorial Fund. Discarding a proposal to join the Army and the Navy in building a memorial opposite Buckingham Palace, the Royal Air Force Memorial Fund had hoped to raise a Cross on the ground between Westminster Abbey and St.

Margaret's Church; a hope that the Dean of Westminster was unable to approve because he preferred not to consider a memorial for the Royal Air Force alone. In any event, as the Dean explained, the particular piece of ground belonged to St. Margaret's.

In the centuries preceding the Armistice of 1918, a year in which men had sincerely believed that they had fought the war to end war, warfare of the past had so sprinkled Britain with memorials that the selection of places prominent enough to commemorate the dead, as well as to symbolise the end of war, was limited. But sites were found and in village, town and city, on the hills and in the valleys, the stonemasons chipped away until the nation had remembered its dead, sailor for sailor, soldier for soldier, and the new airmen too.

Thus when the Office of Woods and Forests offered the new Royal Air Force a site at the head of the Whitehall Stairs on Victoria Embankment about midway between Charing Cross and Westminster Bridge, the offer was accepted thankfully, though only as a second best.

However, the passage of time has confounded any intention, if such it was, of keeping a somewhat junior Royal Air Force in its place. Seventy years on, and showing honourable scars from bombs in the Second World War, mere accident has placed this discreet monument neatly in view of the Air Force Board at the Ministry of Defence. It is tidy, too, that, as a result in 1956 of the placing of Lord Trenchard's statue in Whitehall Gardens below the windows of the present Ministry of Defence, the Royal Air Force Memorial stands in line of sight from the martial figure who conceived both the Royal Air Force and the Royal Air Force Memorial Fund. Here by the Thames, the man who started it all has, since May 1975, been joined by Marshal of the Royal Air Force Lord Portal, Chief of the Air Staff in the Second World War and Deputy Chairman of the Royal Air Force Benevolent Fund from December 1947 until his death on 22 April 1971.

The winter of 1919-20 provided a raw social and economic climate in which Trenchard, canvassing his Royal Air Force Memorial Fund, said, 'Lots of people will get into trouble and go looking for others to help them, but the finest men and women will not ask.' A pride in self-reliance and a readiness to meet privation and disability uncom-plainingly were national characteristics as yet unwarped by social legislation. Such characteristics had dominated Trenchard's early career and he feared for the welfare of the 'finest men', his men of the Royal Air Force.

The armistice of 11 November 1918 had found the Royal Air

Force, a wartime amalgamation under the Air Force Constitution Act 1917 of the Royal Flying Corps and the Royal Naval Air Service, not quite eight months of age. Lacking the long traditions of the Royal Navy and the Army, the Royal Air Force possessed no strong and influential lobby through which to preserve itself, no memorial by which to be remembered, and no existing charitable fund upon which to call and to build. Indeed, even some years later, it seemed possible that the Royal Air Force, 300,000 strong in war, might disappear altogether, and almost without trace.

But, if the outlook for the new service was bleak, the future welfare of its needy presented an almost hopeless picture. Disillusion was widespread among the demobilised, and particularly so among ex-servicemen of the Royal Air Force.

In war the aviators had been praised to the skies. 'The heavens are their battlefields,' the Prime Minister, Mr Lloyd George, had lyricised in the Commons. 'They are struggling there by day, yea, and by night — and amongst the multitude of heroes we must continually thank the Cavalry of the Air.' But the end of the war had brought the Cavalry of the Air very much down to earth, to bicycles and to buses, to competing with soldiers and sailors for work in the front line of civilian life, soldiers and sailors who held the advantage in that there were established service funds and societies to which they could turn in distress.

Outside such shared service charities as the Forces Help Society and Lord Roberts Workshops, the Soldiers' and Sailors' Families Association and other funds of the time, including the United Services and Flying Services fund, officers and men of the new flying services were unsupported. Neither the Royal Flying Corps, the Royal Naval Air Service, nor their successor, the Royal Air Force, had collected charitable funds of their *own* during the war. With peace their needs were soon apparent. They had suffered more than 16,000 casualties, leaving 2,600 widows and dependants, and 7,500 totally or badly incapacitated officers and men.

It was against this background that Trenchard conceived a charitable fund for the flying services.

Recruiting an Executive Committee of prominent and wealthy people, he persuaded Lord Hugh Cecil MP, who served in the Royal Flying Corps in 1915, to accept the chairmanship and to join the first Viscount Cowdray and himself as the founding trustees of the Royal Air Force Memorial Fund. The treasurer was Sir Charles McLeod and in November 1919 the presidency was accepted by Wing Commander the Duke of York (later to become King George VI). The Executive Committee held its first meeting on 23 October 1919 at 25 Victoria

Street in the office of one of its members, Mr Frank E. Rosher.

Rosher had lost his twenty-two-year-old son, Flight Lieutenant Harold Rosher of the Royal Naval Air Service, in a flying accident at Dover. A pilot's death was, of course, a frequent sorrow in 1914-18, but Flight Lieutenant Rosher had earned what, even in the First World War, was an unusually chivalrous reputation. His prowess had been noticed personally by Mr Winston Churchill, recognition which Arnold Bennett, the author, recorded by way of introduction to a posthumously published collection of the pilot's letters home from Belgium and France. Rosher's name, therefore, was associated publicly with all that had been glorious in wartime flying. When Frank Rosher came to consider a memorial to his son he invited the new Fund to establish itself at his office, and it was this generous and farseeing act that got the Royal Air Force Memorial Fund off the ground.

Concisely, the early objects of the Fund were: to build a memorial, to establish boarding schools for the children of deceased airmen, to assist the education of deceased officers' children, and to relieve distress among officers and men and their dependants, particularly through the provision of medical treatment. Those eligible for commemoration or assistance were United Kingdom or Dominion service people who had served during wartime in the Royal Naval Air Service, the Royal Flying Corps, the Australian Flying Corps, the Royal Air Force and the Women's Royal Air Force.

It is noteworthy that Dame Helen Gwynne-Vaughan, the Commandant of the Women's Royal Air Force of 1918, was a member of the Executive Committee from its inception in 1920, and served the Fund continuously in Committee and Council until her retirement from the deputy chairmanship in 1947. At a Council Meeting in December 1947, Lord Riverdale, the Chairman at that time, paid tribute to the splendid work of Dame Helen, whose exceptional general knowledge had been of the greatest help in solving difficult problems. The Council unanimously approved her election as a Vice-President in recognition of her long and invaluable service.

Dame Helen spent the evening of her life at the Royal Air Forces Association's home at Sussexdown, where she died on 26 August 1967. At a Service of Thanksgiving for her life and work in the Royal Air Force church of St Clement Danes on 2 November 1967, the Deputy Vice-Chancellor of the University of London, Professor C. T. Ingold, paid further tribute to this brilliant contemporary.

Another lady associated with the birth of the Fund was Mrs B. H. Barrington Kennett, a widow whose husband had served in the

Grenadier Guards and the Royal Flying Corps. She attended the first meeting of the Committee in Mr Rosher's office on 23 October 1919, and remained on it until 23 October 1931. She was also an original member of the Vanbrugh Castle School Committee from its inception in 1921 until her retirement.

In 1921, under a resolution of the Executive Committee, benefits were 'to a strictly limited extent' opened to the post-war Royal Air Force in special cases of distress arising from sickness only, where the burden 'was not sufficiently met by the normal provision of medical attendance granted by the rules of the service'. At the time, service personnel in a service hospital were liable to 'hospital stoppages' from their pay.

At first the Executive Committee's main task was to raise money, and although it was well constituted for the purpose its early efforts held little promise of accumulating any very substantial sum. The total of £125,000 received in the first year fell far short of a target of £400,000, and of this sum £95,000 was from official sources, including £50,000 from the Air Council, being part of wartime canteen profits. It is interesting to compare this last figure with the generous sum of £636,000 from NAAFI profits during the Second World War.

When the first annual report was published at the end of 1920, Lord Hugh Cecil commented: 'If the objects of the Fund are to be properly supported the public must show greater liberality.' The fact was that the Royal Air Force Memorial Fund had set itself an ambitious programme for a new service charity of limited resources and an unpredictable future income.

Disappointment at public response was softened, however, by the knowledge that the message was spreading. The Fund had found friends almost everywhere and donations were received from forty different countries, including numerous contributions from places, authorities and individuals redolent of empire. Handsome donations were received from a number of India's ruling princes.

At home, some of the fortune makers of the early part of the century contributed generously, among them Trenchard and Cecil's fellow trustee Cowdray, and Northcliffe, the newspaper and periodical proprietor; while on its own account the Fund profited £550 from its first money-raising event, a ball held at the Ritz Hotel.

In the course of the ball the Fund's recently appointed Secretary, a young and badly wounded Lieutenant in uniform, named McCulloch, was approached by the Colonel-in-Chief of the 16th Lancers who said he wished to make a personal donation. The Colonel-in-Chief, King Alfonso XIII of Spain, promptly disproved the theory that royalty never carry money, for he handed to McCulloch a crackling five-pound note. The Secretary was not caught off balance by this unexpected generosity; he promptly asked King Alfonso to sign the fiver. The following morning the Secretary paid a substitute five-pound note into the Fund, intending to retain the royal autograph. But such was the general insecurity of the time that the Lieutenant was soon obliged to settle an account with Alfonso's fiver, which, unless any reader of this story happens to know of its existence, has disappeared for all time.

In the winter of 1919, at the age of twenty-one, the Secretary shared a room with Rosher's Rumanian clerk at 25 Victoria Street. Lieutenant Derek McCulloch, who was later to become widely loved as Uncle Mac of the British Broadcasting Corporation, was the first employee of the Royal Air Force Memorial Fund and was paid five pounds a week. He was still in uniform through the personal dispensation of Trenchard, who regarded McCulloch's battered appearance as a helpful advertisement.

Fighting at the age of eighteen as a private soldier on the Somme, McCulloch had lost his right eye in 1916 and that side of his face had been sewn up. He carried a bullet in a lung and eleven other wounds. Although released as unfit for further service he had talked himself back into the Army, receiving a commission in the Green Howards and obtaining a transfer to the Royal Flying Corps.

McCulloch's function was to knit together the voluntary work of members of the Fund's distinguished Executive Committee and at first he found it an unnevering experience. The Secretary's business with the Chairman was conducted at Lord Hugh Cecil's breakfast table at 21 Arlington Street, where McCulloch attended regularly with the Fund's papers. Although his broadcasting career was soon to separate him from the Fund's affairs, Derek McCulloch retained an affectionate and helpful interest in them until his death at the age of sixty-nine in May 1967.

Lord Hugh, who later became Lord Quickswood and retired as a Trustee of the Fund in 1944, would have totally disbelieved any prophecy that seventy years afterwards the struggling charity he was running from his breakfast table would own some £20 million of investment and have spent some £83 million on the relief of distress, in the course of making over 740,000 awards.

Chapter 3
Getting Off the Ground

*'Their exploits and undoubted courage have established a tradition for
the new service which our cloud armies of the future, whether in peace
or war, will I feel sure follow with devoted pride.'*

His Royal Highness The Prince of Wales, 1923

In the very first year of the Fund's life two separate acts of generosity
opened the way for the beginning of its educational work. A Mrs M.
E. Salting who lived in Berkeley Square presented the Fund with two
unoccupied houses at Ascot, and Mr Alexander Duckham, who had
made a fortune in oil, offered his former London home, Vanbrugh
Castle, to the Fund.

Unfortunately, the Ascot houses were sold in poor market
conditions. But, producing a total of £9,956 0s 5d after expenses,
they enabled the Fund to establish the first of many educational trust
funds, the Salting Benefaction.

Odd though it may seem at this distance in the light of Vanbrugh's
fine record and the establishment in 1976 of its successor, Duke of
Kent School in the Surrey hills, Vanbrugh Castle was not accepted
as eagerly as was Mrs Salting's gift. After the war, when the house
stood empty, Duckham's brother-in-law, Wing Commander Vernon
Brown, had hinted, 'Trenchard could use Vanbrugh Castle.' Duckham
talked to Trenchard with the result that a special Memorial Fund
Committee was formed to consider the offer. At first the Committee
was inclined to exchange Vanbrugh for cash, subject to Duckham's
agreement, and this step would have been taken but for the vigorous
opposition of the Committee's two Royal Air Force members, Air
Commodore H. R. M. Brooke-Popham and Air Vice-Marshal Sir
John Salmond.

Brooke-Popham proposed and Salmond seconded the experimental
use of the house as a boys' home and his proposal was accepted by
three votes to two, four members of the committee abstaining. At
about the same time that Vanbrugh Castle's future was assured and

the property legally transferred to the Fund in 1921, the Air Council gave the fund £50,000 from canteen profits.

In the light of Duke of Kent School's present role as a boarding school for the sons and daughters of deceased, and in some cases disabled, officers, warrant officers, non-commissioned officers, airmen and airwomen, as well as children of serving personnel, it is noteworthy that as far back as 1920 Vanbrugh Castle was conditionally tied to the education of airmen's children. In no circumstances were officers' children to benefit. But the world moves on and it will be seen how in the 1970s this stipulation was overcome.

To give is better than to receive and, since it is impossible to give if the charitable chest is empty, it is in the natural order of things that much of this account will be about the indispensable substance of money. The first Lord Attlee once said, 'Voluntary effort would always be necessary to humanise the state schemes.' Methods of obtaining money have altered considerably since the receipt of the earliest donation, a fact which reflects the redistribution of wealth and the great social changes which, cantering along between the wars, went into a gallop after 1945. As with the tax-burdened princes of private enterprise, the wealthy and generous potentates of Britain's imperial past no longer proliferate, and minor royalty has either disappeared or finds itself in sadly reduced circumstances. The Emperor of Ethiopia addressed a bag of gold to the Fund during the Second World War, but King Alfonso's fiver was a once-and-for-all.

Within the Fund, the arts of appeal have accorded with prevailing conditions over the years, the exceptions being the constant appeal for legacies and the concept of the Air Display.

The first Royal Air Force air display, or aerial pageant as it was described, took place at Hendon on 3 July 1920. Flight Lieutenant E. B. C. Betts and Air Commodore B. C. H. Drew acted as the secretaries. It was a big success, *Flight* commenting that it put pre-war aerial race meetings 'in the shade'. The Fund reported: 'For the first time on record the British public were able to witness an exhibition of almost every phase of modern aerial warfare . . . a sausage kite balloon was brought down in flames, trenches were bombed from the air and aerial duels between British and captured Boche machines were displayed.' Mr Heath Robinson's aeroplane, 'smoke belching from the funnel, nearly took the air'.

The occasion was charmingly period. The 50,000 spectators who witnessed Miss Sylvia Boyden's parachute descent from a Handley-

Page machine accepted it as the courageous highlight of a most daring afternoon.

At the end of the day, the Fund's gate amounted to more than £6,700, a sum large enough to present Air Vice-Marshal Sir John Salmond, who had supervised the pageant, with the immediate problem of what to do with the money.

But Salmond, whose imaginative mind was to benefit the Fund for so many years, provided a characteristically unorthodox solution. Summoning six officers to his tent, he asked them to fetch their wives. Shortly afterwards, the astonished ladies were despatched to their homes, each with more than £1,000 in her custody. 'Put the money under you pillows', Sir John instructed them, 'until I find out what to do with it.'

If Salmond's overnight banking ruse was splendidly unorthodox, the Fund's general finance and legal arrangements were, of course, professionally advised. The Fund's bankers and solicitors, Barclays, Cox's and King's, and Charles Russell and Co., had been appointed at the outset. The auditors were Blackburns, Barton, Mayhew and Co. With the alteration that Barclays now bank for the Insurance Advisory Service and Lloyds Bank, incorporating Cox's and King's, for the Fund generally, these founding arrangements remain.

From the beginning, the chartered accountants, lawyers and bankers have been employed as the paid professional servants of the Fund. All decision has rested with members of the Fund's honorary Committees which, by the year 1922, were the Executive Committee, the Vanbrugh Castle Sub-committee, and the Grants Sub-committee.

In 1922 the Grants Sub-committee was authorised to spend up to £4,800 at the monthly rate of £400. Any proceeds from the annual pageant were received as 'corn in Egypt' and spent as available. Practically, this brought the Fund's spending power to £9,000 for the year, an infinitesimal sum by contrast with at least £8·5 million which is likely to be spent on relief in the seventieth anniversary year.

Looking back from the present when relief lies largely in the realm of home purchase loans for widows and disabled; loans for property maintenance; the resolution of indebtedness that has arisen from circumstances beyond an individual's control; the private education of orphaned or needy service children, and the provision of the smaller comforts and extras which brighten the lives of the disabled and the elderly, some of the Fund's early rates and forms of relief were of necessity comparatively modest. But society has changed. When a man had no boots in which to seek work, or lacked the elementary tools of his trade, such possessions as a home of his own, a car if he was disabled, were beyond all contemplation.

In 1922, benefits, which included sixty-three grants for clothing, twenty cases of redeeming pawned goods, and fifty-six grants for hawker's licences, were necessarily minimal, but on the whole rather better than assistance available from other war charities.

Individual calls for assistance in the 1920s were small and uncomplicated. Small awards were as little as a shilling for a night's lodging at the Young Men's Christian Association huts at Waterloo or Victoria, and such small grants alleviated the distress of large numbers of men out of work or stranded in London. 'Seven days Soldiers' Home', or twenty-one shillings a week and threepence a day pocket money at the Soldiers' Home was an everyday decision.

Modest though such measures were, together with the larger issues of educational assistance and the commemorative centrepiece, the Royal Air Force Memorial, they consumed money. But the Fund was in no mind to preserve capital while distress existed, as is still the case today. In 1922 the Executive Committee was of the opinion that 'the need for assistance in the present bad state of trade and the country's finances generally' was far more acute than it was likely to be in the future. It was considered 'wiser and better to spend now in relieving distress among the deserving who had helped to win the Great War, rather than accumulate capital for posterity'.

The early part of that resolution sounds a familiar note and, as will be seen, subsequent experiences of a 'bad state of trade and the country's finances generally' were to tax the Fund's resources.

But after the 1914-18 War the natural mood and desire was to assist all officers and men who had fought in the flying services, and to raise a memorial to the dead, a place at which to pause, to pray and to remember now that the war belonged to the past. However, as memories of the war receded, the mood began to change, and change introduced concern for the future needs of ex-service people and the immediate troubles of serving officers and airmen or their dependants.

As it happened, the completion and unveiling of the memorial in 1923 separated the two moods as an inscribed stone might mark the boundary between adjoining towns. The Prince of Wales presaged the future course of the Fund when he unveiled the memorial on 16 July 1923. Speaking of the dead, he said:

> 'Their exploits and undoubted courage have established a tradition for the new service which our cloud armies of the future, whether in peace or war, will I feel sure follow with devoted pride; and the nation on whose behalf I am asked to accept this Memorial, and to whom I am to dedicate it, will ever

thankfully remember the gallant lives and great deeds it commemorates.'

The possibility of war again was publicly accepted. Four months after the ceremony, the Executive Committee of the Royal Air Force Memorial Fund resolved to assist the next of kin of serving officers or airmen, bearing in mind that the hazards of peacetime flying caused casualties during training flights.

The raising of the memorial, and the attendant publicity, had played its public relations role in helping to perpetuate the Royal Air Force. Now, it was clear to the Fund that its resources ought to be available to the men who were losing their lives, their limbs and their livelihoods in peacetime service. Henceforth, Air Ministry Weekly Orders announced at the end of 1923, the Fund would offer immediate financial assistance to the next of kin of officers or airmen killed on active service, or who died from accident or disease while serving. The object was to bridge the gap between death and the issue of a pension of gratuity.

The Fund's resolution to accept responsibility for serving families was an important milestone on its journey, even though the resources to support it were limited. Relief expenditure had risen from £919 in 1920 to £9,861 in 1923; and, with 1923 donations tailing off to £1,554, income from all sources totalled £17,783. But the milestone marked rather more than the broadening of the Fund's scope. It indicated a dawning appreciation of the Fund's potential value as a first-rate morale factor throughout the Royal Air Force.

For the moment, however, the outlook was gloomy. In 1924 the maximum grant of £100 was suspended and in the following year public donations fell to £2,043. Without the aerial pageant which had become an annual event, and subsequently the Royal Tournament, the Fund would have been in peril of collapse. Memories of the flying services' wartime exploits were fading and, apart from a momentary interest in the pageant and the Royal Tournament and the publicity given to record-breaking flights, crashes and casualties, the public was largely unaware of the mostly distant and little publicised day-to-day activities of the Royal Air Force.

It was a critical period for the nation's future as an air power, a period in which the Royal Air Force Memorial Fund had its contribution to make by staying the course with the Royal Air Force and the fledgling aircraft industry.

Losing support from such exotic quarters of the Empire as the princely states of India and the white citizens of Swaziland, the Fund grew more conscious of the potential value of such modest contributors as the struggling aircraft companies, and the Royal Air Force stations themselves: Biggin Hill in 1926, ten shillings. An airfield's mite, but it reflected an awakening concern within the Service and such contributions were to place the Fund's subscriptions' account on a more durable basis for the future. Fourteen years separated Biggin Hill from the Battle of Britain and 1926 found the Royal Air Force, the aircraft manufacturers and the Fund stumbling forward under the most frustrating conditions. Fortunately, the Royal Air Force and the British aircraft industry persevered and donations flowed into the fund in thanksgiving during and after the touch-and-go events of 1940.

Organisationally, the Fund was developing in the mid-1920s. There was now very much more paperwork than could be shuffled at breakfast, while the Secretary and the staff of four had outgrown the shared room with Frank Rosher's clerk. The Fund occupied three rooms at Iddesleigh House, Westminster, where Lieutenant-Colonel W. S. Burch had succeeded Lieutenant Derek McCulloch. There were also an Assistant Secretary, Mr J. P. Cunninghame, who remained a Fund Helper and Education Adviser for many years, and two shorthand typists, one of whom, Mrs Grace Inglis, was promoted a Relief Secretary and spent forty years with the Fund, retiring in 1965. She was awarded the MBE for her long and devoted service.

The small staff worked long hours and on Saturday mornings. Administrative expenditure was kept to a minimum. Such economy was only possible because of the Fund's inspired founding principle of co-operation with other interservice organisations such as the Forces Help Society and Lord Roberts Workshops, the Soldiers', Sailors' and Airmen's Families Association, and the British Legion, a principle that has remained fundamental to the Fund's relief work for seventy years. In 1921, for example, the Fund reimbursed the Officers' Association £200 per month for its work with ex-Royal Air Force officers and such an arrangement continued by which the Officers' Association accepted responsibility for veterans of the First World War, with no service after August 1921, subject to an upper limit, until the Royal Air Force Benevolent Fund took over responsibility. Nowadays the Fund also works very closely with the Royal Air Forces Association.

Early co-operation with other organisations for the investigation of cases, and financial sharing in the work of sympathetic societies, reduced outgoings and fostered many connections for the future. Aided from the outset by the Executive Committee's self-adjuration to beware 'mischievous overlapping', this process was greatly advanced when Earl Haig invited two of that committee's members, Lieutenant-Commander H. E. Perrin and Mrs L. M. K. Pratt-Barlow, to join his Services Funds Advisory Council.

Chapter 4
Between the Two World Wars

'After church they lectured us in the cinema on savings certificates, telling us we'd be glad of the money when we left the service and faced civil life.'

Aircraftman T. E. Shaw (Lawrence of Arabia)

From the 1920s to the early 1930s the Royal Air Force was busy justifying its post-war reprieve in the developing role of an airborne imperial constabulary. Whitehall had learned the economy of patrolling troublesome people from the air, and Royal Air Force squadrons were replacing the marching, ambushed, waterless columns of imperial experience.

Trenchard, supported by Colonel T. E. Lawrence at the 1922 Cairo conference, had first urged this new role upon the Colonial Secretary, Mr Winston Churchill. It was accepted and the Royal Air Force was stationed thinly across the British Empire, far removed from the headquarters of the Royal Air Force Memorial Fund, but by no means out of mind.

In 1924 the Fund paid £200 to the Air Ministry to enable commanding officers in Malta, Palestine, India and the Middle East, excluding Iraq, to give immediate help to families distressed by the death of an officer or an airman. Iraq was excluded because Royal Air Force families were not then permitted in that country. Happily, though, the restriction did not deter units stationed in Iraq from supporting the Fund. Indeed, they could scarcely do otherwise. The Air Officer Commanding was Sir John Salmond, who had vacated the chair of the Vanbrugh Castle Sub-committee upon appointment.

In its formative years the Fund was fortunate that members of the immediate generation of Royal Air Force leaders had involved themselves with its ideals and aspirations from the start. The Air Officers Commanding carried their enthusiasm for the Fund to their commands overseas with encouraging results, the Salmond brothers being exceptionally successful. Sir John and Sir Geoffrey Salmond pulled off an excellent family double in 1927. While Sir John collected 10,000 rupees at an aerial pageant in Delhi, Sir Geoffrey raised £8,006 4s 7d on his brother's old pitch at Hendon.

The interchange of the Salmonds' appointments suited the Fund admirably, and for their part the brothers enjoyed competing with one another to raise money. It was in the nature of things, therefore, that after Sir Geoffrey's return from Egypt in 1921 he should have succeeded his brother as Chairman of the Vanbrugh Castle Sub-committee.

The Fund's acceptance of responsibility towards serving members of the Air Force applied at Vanbrugh too, and in 1926 the castle gates were opened to the sons of serving airmen, in addition to the sons of men who died in the service, but the fatherless boys were still given priority. The addition of a new dormitory for twelve boys increased Vanbrugh's numbers from twenty-seven boys between the ages of five and school-leaving age in 1923 to thirty-nine boys in 1926.

Although Vanbrugh was already known as Vanbrugh Castle School, no teaching took place there except of the very youngest boys. During Vanbrugh's earliest months the boys attended a local elementary school. But from the summer of 1922 the Fund had paid grammar school fees for boys able to pass the entrance examination.

From the outset the Fund held that 'the future of the boys lies to a large extent with themselves and is greatly dependent upon their own abilities'. The reality of this raw opportunity amounted to a roof, a bed, and the institutional care of a superintendent and a matron, Captain and Mrs G. A. R. Slimming.

Vanbrugh boys were not obliged to enter the Royal Air Force but the Fund hoped that, partly by environment and partly by training, the boys might desire to join their fathers' service, thus 'furnishing', as the Fund phrased it, 'the service with a supply of men whose upbringing from boyhood has been in the very closest touch with its best traditions'. In 1926 the entry of two boys as aircraft apprentices at the Royal Air Force School of Technical Training, Halton — their fathers had died in the war — launched a tradition through which many Vanbrugh boys have volunteered for a service career.

In that year too, Mrs F. Vesey Holt, a young Royal Air Force bride, joined the Grants Committee and Appeals Committee. She was also on the Council. Not retiring until 1973, she was the longest-serving Committee Member of the Fund in her day.

In its early life the Royal Air Force Benevolent Fund made poor financial progress. When Sir Charles McLeod, the Honorary Treasurer, succeeded Lord Hugh Cecil as Chairman in 1929, only

£195,000 of the target £400,000 had been reached. The very conditions which demanded the Fund's existence drained its resources and conflicted with its chances of support.

It was recognised that of the total income the excellent proceeds from the Air Display and the Royal Tournament were unhealthily top-heavy items, but economic conditions seemed to defy the attainment of a balance between these receipts and other donations. For example, in 1926 £6,905 6s 4d and £1,700 were received in respect of the display and the Royal Tournament against £2,599 8s 7d from all other sources.

Unfortunately, for all Biggin Hill's ten shillings in 1926, the Fund lacked any consistent subscription support from the Royal Air Force, where it was widely, if erroneously, held that the Fund possessed ample means.

There was, however, one serving airman who knew this was not so. He was better informed about the Fund than most of his fellows because he happened to know Trenchard personally. He also had the disconcerting practice of calling at Iddesleigh House to inquire for himself how things were going. But this supporter extraordinary was serving in India when the Fund learned that he had arranged (with later supplements) a £20,000 trust known as the Anonymous Educational Fund, to provide an income for the education of the children of deceased or disabled officers.

If the facts have not already disclosed this airman's identity, then possibly a quotation will unmask him: 'Our hut is a microcosm of unemployed England, not of unemployable England for the strict Royal Air Force standards refuse the last levels of the social structure.'

No serving member of the Royal Air Force could have been more conscious at this time of the value of the Fund to the service than Lawrence of Arabia. Colonel Lawrence, who had re-entered the Royal Air Force in 1925 as Aircraftman T. E. Shaw following the discovery of his identity as A. C. John Hume Ross, and a brief intervening spell in the Army, observed the distress in others at first hand and brought cases personally to the notice of Colonel Burch. He wrote, too, of cases known to him in and out of barracks. Two of his letters have survived the Fund's periodical disposal of waste paper:

August 25, 1932

A. C. Shaw, Myrtle Cottage,
Hythe, Southampton

Dear Colonel Burch,

This is a private letter to ask you to be good enough to advise on procedure. Some friends of the late Flt. Lt. J . . . of Tangmere (he died at Halton this year, of cancer, after twenty-two years service) have asked me how his widow can be helped in the matter of educating her daughter. Her son goes to Halton as an aircraft apprentice this next entry. The girl is seventeen and apt for a business career, if she can receive some preliminary training. I suppose a single grant of some forty or fifty pounds would cover the whole affair, and this you can probably easily arrange, when approached on the proper lines. For an airman applications are made through* . . . last C.O., I believe. How about widows of officers: Mrs J's . . . address is . . . She does not know about . . . I expect, and I hope she won't.

Will you deal either direct with Mrs J . . . if proper, or tell me to my address how the . . . should be presented? I am very sorry for troubling . . . In writing will you let me know if . . . income tax problem upon your education fund . . . solved yet? I am holding up the . . . of a lump sum to provide instalments for Mrs H . . . our Mountbatten sergeant's widow, until I hear that the tax question is settled: and meanwhile the station is paying her £5 a quarter, which is not easy for so small a strength to raise.

Yours sincerely,

6.IX.32

338171 A. C. Shaw
Royal Air Force,
Mountbatten,
Plymouth.

Dear Colonel Burch,

You will note that I am returning to my Plymouth address in a day or two. Please forget the Hythe one.

Mrs J . . . is definitely not interested in the interview arranged by a lady offering help with D. H. Evans for her daughter. The girl is described as intelligent and bookish, far more cut out for secretarial work than for the sales department. Only her father's death has taken the family by surprise, and so she is untrained. Her mother's means is only about a pound a week, insufficient to maintain them while her daughter is being trained, and to pay the training fees into the bargain. So it is clearly a case in which a grant for commercial-educational-training should be applied for. Will you please let Mrs J . . .

---

* Breaks indicate where letter torn and illegible.

know (your AMS 1061) how she is to apply for this grant? Her friends are quite definite in their statements to me, after having seen your letter and discussed it with the widow.

Lawrence had earned the money with his pen. His story of his wartime exploits, *Revolt in the Desert*, was a best-seller; Bernard Shaw had named it a masterpiece and its author a genius. But the author was earning airmen's pay in India when he completed his astonishing act of self-denial. As 338171, A. C. Shaw endured the prickly heat and Noël Coward addressed him, 'Dear 338171, may I call you 338?' Lawrence laboured in the knowledge that he was educating ten or more children of Royal Air Force officers.

When Lawrence died in 1935 his trust had paid £4,142 towards school fees and he was educating thirteen children in that year. He was buried in the Dorset village of Moreton on 22 May 1935 in the presence of a small private group of mourners. Amid them stopped the tall figure of Marshal of the Royal Air Force Sir John Salmond who felt simply that 'someone from the top ought to be there'. Mr and Mrs Winston Churchill were present too.

Perhaps the oddest turn in this strange episode was Lawrence's decision to benefit only officers' children at a time when he knew that airmen, falling prey to their natural suspicions, believed the Fund was mainly concerned with the relief of officers and their families.

Communication between the Fund and the barrack room was almost non-existent. Airmen did not generally appreciate that in its formative years the Fund had consistently striven to keep a fair balance between officers and airmen. Because of the high ratio of officers to airmen, and because flying was mostly carried out by officers, casualties among officers were disproportionately large and the Fund was closely exercised to achieve fairness. Of course there was always the possibility that at any moment disaster might tip the balance, and this happened at Quetta in 1935.

Out of 358 British servicemen in No. 3 (Indian) Wing, fifty-five were killed and 130 injured in that historic earthquake. 'The Royal Air Force Station, Quetta, looks like Ypres in 1917,' the Wing Commander wrote to Group Captain G. I Carmichael, who had recently succeeded Colonel Burch as secretary. The Wing Commander reported that fifty-two of the fifty-five men killed were Royal Air Force non-commissioned officers and airmen, adding, 'Some of my own records are still buried and I have not a complete list.' A baptism, indeed, in Benevolent Fund affairs for Wing Commander J. C. Slessor, who was to serve with such distinction during the Second World War and who, in the rank of Marshal of the Royal Air Force, was to maintain his association with the Fund as a Vice-President, until his death on 12 July 1979.

Quetta gave rise to forty-nine cases in Britain, twenty of which required financial assistance. There was, for instance, the case of the airman with nine years' service who was killed at Quetta, leaving a wife and two children. As it happened the Fund was already in touch with the family because of illness and medical expenses. After the earthquake the widow was helped to take her children to Australia, where she had been offered a home and a job. It was, incidentally, an example of co-operation with other organisations, the Fund paying the emigration expenses in conjunction with the Royal Patriotic Fund, the Salvation Army and the Society for the Overseas Settlement of British Women.

Quetta had come at the tail end of an exceptionally difficult period. The trouble was that the national economic depression had so increased requests for assistance and so lowered the Fund's income that in 1933, for example, expenditure had exceeded income by £455. Even those financial buttresses, the Air Display and the Royal Tournament, were shadows of their former glory.

In this worrying situation the Fund stated its duty clearly:

To take money out of capital might be thought to afford a temporary solution of the problem but would be definitely wrong because the Fund does not exist to tide over the temporary problem of helping wartime cases. It must continue to work for all time for the benefit of the post-war Royal Air Force. The Fund must not be allowed to die out through the expenditure of capital, but must be preserved and indeed the capital increased. The Council, therefore, have reluctantly decided that until there is a greater response to the needs of the Fund, both from the service and the public, there is no alternative but to reduce grants.

On the Benevolent Fund of the Service that fights in the air, the needs of the disabled and the dependants of those killed flying must always be a first charge, and a large measure of the help available must be directed towards the assistance of widows and the education of their children.

Other casualties, disability, sickness, and general distress will continue to present many cases and the Fund will meet, as far as means permit, appeals not only from those who left the service years ago, but from those who are leaving in present times and from serving personnel whose needs are beyond station resources.

Thus, fifteen years after the Armistice and in the year as it happened that Hitler and his National Socialist Party came to power in Germany, the Fund readjusted its sights. Several years were to elapse before the Fund was in a position, during the 1939-45 War to change to the policy, which it has followed ever since, of using capital whenever income is insufficient.

Since inception to 5 December 1933 the Royal Air Force Memorial Fund had made 18,608 grants involving, wih the £30,000 maintenance of Vanbrugh Castle, an expenditure of £150,000. The Memorial phase was over and, now that 'benevolent' was thought to be more descriptive of its purpose and qualified it for tax relief, the Fund in December 1933 restyled itself the Royal Air Force Benevolent Fund, an alteration of name that was followed by a change of Chairman. Sir Charles McLeod, Honorary Treasurer since the Fund's inception and Chairman since 1928, resigned at the end of 1934. He was succeeded as Treasurer by Mr Walter S. Field, also a founder member of the 1919 Executive Committee and Chairman of the Grants Committee. The new Chairman was Lord Wakefield.

At this time of change Lord Wakefield brought the Royal Air Force Benevolent Fund precisely what it needed: a wealthy friend who had the right connections and his heart in the Service.

Welcomed to the Fund as 'the man to whom British aviation owes so much', Wakefield, who was seventy-four, soon demonstrated that when a man's heart and enthusiasm are spiritedly engaged, neither his age nor his period will restrain him. Some of Wakefield's contemporaries, born around the time of the Indian Mutiny and already in their forties at the beginning of the century, were content in the depressed and dangerous 1930s to grumble themselves to the grave. But not so C. C. Wakefield. Son of a Liverpool customs official, he had seized upon the combination of the new motor car and of castor oil as a means to a fortune, giving birth to and marketing from this clever marriage the internationally renowned lubricant, Castrol.

After making his money on the roads, Wakefield spent it liberally in the air, coaxing, encouraging the development of speed, comfort and design in the manufacture of aircraft and the growth of skill among the pioneer aviators of the 1920s and 1930s.

One of his earlier actions as Chairman of the Royal Air Force Benevolent Fund was to establish the Viscount Wakefield Benefaction with a gift of £10,000. Since 1936 the income from this trust has provided for the academic or technical training of young officers or airmen who have left the service, and paid for the further education of Royal Air Force children after leaving school.

At this time of change the Royal Air Force Benevolent Fund also restyled and reorganised its executive structure. Detail was removed from the Executive Committee to a freshly constituted Finance and General Purposes Committee, while the Executive Committee raised itself to the status of a policy-making Council. The significance of this reform, however, lay not so much in style as in the reconstruction of the Council which followed. Hitherto, membership of the Executive Committee had evolved as a mixture of business and service leaders with additional members able to bring humanitarian and common-sense judgement to its meetings. On the whole this had been satisfactory but, now that the Royal Air Force Benevolent Fund was as permanent as the Royal Air Force itself, there was a need to regularise its composition and in particular service and ex-service representation. Late in 1934 eligibility for membership of the Council was defined to include:

The Air Officer Commanding-in-Chief, Air Defence of Great Britain; the Air Member for Personnel; the Air Officer Commanding Coastal Area; two members, not serving personnel, nominated by the Air Council; representatives of the Comrades of the Royal Air Forces Association and any other similar air bodies approved by the Air Council, six members nominated by the Council of the Fund.

An early and important result of the reformation was the appointment to the Council of Air Marshal Sir Hugh Dowding in his capacity as Air Officer Commanding-in-Chief Fighter Command. Dowding, of course, in his efforts to prepare the fighter defence of the realm was engaged elsewhere on more urgent work, but he quickly saw how badly the Fund needed money and what ought to be done to get it. Joining the Council, he was dismayed to find some members much in favour of launching a major public appeal. It was not that he was against a future appeal in principle but that he thought it was wrong to seek help outside before asking and getting the Royal Air Force to do more for itself. He said: 'It is right and proper that serving personnel should be the principal contributors and they can do very much more than they are now doing.' He was supported by Air Vice-Marshal Sir Philip Game, who suggested that regular annual subscriptions, as in the Royal Artillery, would be felt by no one.

The time was approaching, too, as Dowding well knew, when the Fund would lose the income from the annual Air Display for the reason that new aircraft types were outgrowing the small Hendon airfield.

Thus in the early spring of 1936 Dowding and Game had set the

Council thinking about an idea which was eventually to transform the Fund's financial prospect. But it was not to happen yet because the Air Council was neither prepared to back an appeal to the public, nor to ask the Royal Air Force for increased support. It was, however, no unusual experience for Dowding to plant ideas which were slow to take root and more than a year passed before his proposal began to gather support.

It was only a postponement of better times but it was a delay the Fund could little afford. Certainly the improved trade conditions of 1936 had resulted in a reduction of minor cases of distress but the Fund was feeling the cumulative effect of casualties in the service and among ex-members of the Royal Air Force in civil aviation.

Relief expenditure in 1936 was £18,825, of which post-war casualties among serving and reserve personnel accounted for £3,607. Education absorbed £7,335, including the maintenance of Vanbrugh Castle where there were now forty-two boys in residence.

By 1936, of the boys who had passed through Vanbrugh receiving their education at local schools, notably the Roan Grammar School, nineteen boys had entered the Royal Air Force Apprentice Training Establishments at Halton and Cranwell.

The successes of Vanbrugh boys who had volunteered for the service greatly pleased Lord Wakefield, who enlarged the school by presenting an adjacent house at a cost of some £3,000. This Wakefield Wing accommodated twenty-five boys and raised Vanbrugh's capacity from forty-two to sixty-seven boys. The wing was ceremonially opened in May 1939 by Lady Newall, wife of the Chief of the Air Staff.

In Council in the summer of 1937 the Commanders-in-Chief of Bomber and Coastal Commands, Air Chief Marshal Sir John Steel and Air Marshal Sir Philip Joubert, returned warmly to the subject of voluntary subscription from the service. Sir John urged: 'The situation whereby the Royal Air Force practically lives on outside charity with only a very small contribution by Royal Air Force personnel should not be allowed to continue.' It was the Air Marshal's opinion that the Royal Air Force ought to put its house in order before there was any question of going to the public. But still the Council remained chary of committing itself to a general service appeal.

However, when the Fund finally introduced the half-a-day's-pay-a-year scheme late in 1938 it was an immediate success, reaping £11,111 through unit pay ledgers and officers' mess bills. At one stroke Dowding's idea had eliminated the old reliance on the Royal

Tournament and the Air Display. It was as well, because in 1938, as Dowding had warned, the Air Display was withdrawn.

Aerial pageantry had paid much of the Fund's way for nearly twenty years. When it passed into history, Hendon, and from 1934 the annual Empire Air Day, had produced almost £200,000 between them. But every penny of this sum had been spent on the relief of distress, leaving the capital outlook as bleak as ever.

War, it was assumed, would break the Fund and war was coming. The pilots and crews of the Royal Air Force, the Auxiliary Air Force and the Royal Air Force Volunteer Reserve were training for war and the Fund now covered them all.

As Germany invaded Poland the Fund's secretary, Group Captain G. I. Carmichael, insisted upon returning to active service, leaving his assistant, Squadron Leader V. S. Erskine-Lindop, in charge. Required to evacuate London, Erskine-Lindop packed his wife, three female clerks and a parcel of current files into his car and drove down to the coast.

Chapter 5
The Second World War

*'Never in the field of human conflict was
so much owed by so many to so few.'*

Winston Churchill, 1940

War came again on 3 September 1939, and on the very day of its
declaration the air-raid sirens sounded on the roof tops below the
Royal Air Force balloons which were already flying over London.
Any 'cloud armies' forecast by the Prince of Wales at the unveiling of
the Royal Air Force Memorial sixteen years earlier were on the
airfields of the enemy.

If, however, the Royal Air Force was inadequately equipped and
undermanned, the very existence of the Royal Air Force Benevolent
Fund, however meagre its resources, placed its families at an
advantage over their predecessors of the First World War. Yet
warfare had changed radically since the building of the Thames-side
memorial. The Council, only too aware that this was going to be an
air war, anxiously considered the prospect of massive need.

For the moment, though, the Royal Air Force Benevolent Fund
could do little more than issue a calm reminder of intent before, as
the Council expected, the crisis came. The Annual Report for the
year 1939 seemed the right place to do this and there the Fund
repeated its creed:

> The general policy of the Fund is controlled by the Council
> and put into effect through the Grants, the Vanbrugh Castle
> School and the Finance Committees. There are no hard and fast
> rules as to the kind of cases which may be helped or as to the
> amount of financial assistance which may be given. The only
> limitations are those prescribed by the dictates of commonsense
> and by the money available. Within these limits the aim of the
> Fund is to provide relief quickly and to provide adequate relief.
> In short the Fund endeavours to enable dependants to carry on
> in some semblance of the life to which they have been

accustomed, and to help children into the careers that their
fathers might reasonably have expected them to follow. The
Fund being a service fund must take into account not only the
human side but service given. Casualty cases are normally more
lasting and if adequate relief is to be given it must be more
expensive than those of temporary distress through sickness or
unemployment.

The 'phoney war' of the winter of 1939-40 postponed the awaited
avalanche. Equally it was not dramatic enough to stir public
generosity.

Although obsolescent twin-engined aircraft of Bomber Command
were attacking enemy rival naval installations in daylight and
sustaining heavy losses, such raids coupled with the leaflet 'attacks'
failed to stimulate any more donations than the meagre sums
received between the wars. It helped, all the same, that Lord
Wakefield diverted his £1,500 prize money for the cancelled King's
Cup air races to the Fund and that the Duke of Bedford sent a cheque
for £1,000 in token of the unsuccessful search by the Royal Air Force
for his wife after the celebrated flying duchess had disappeared on
a solo flight.

Among the Fund's old friends there were those who, remembering
1914-18, feared that the lull would not last, and foremost among the
old friends stood Alexander Duckham, whose gift of Vanbrugh
Castle had so greatly assisted the Fund's education efforts for
eighteen years. For the second time in his life Alexander Duckham
offered his home for the use of Royal Air Force children. Duckham
was now living at Rooks Hill House, a country mansion high in the
Weald of Kent near Sevenoaks and surrounded by 200 acres of land.
Moving to a cottage in the grounds, Mr Duckham made a gift of
Rooks Hill to the Fund together with a settlement of £1,000 a year
towards upkeep and maintenance of the estate.

It was Duckham's wish that Rooks Hill should shelter the very
young children of officer and non-commissioned pilots killed in
action or in flying accidents, and for the greater part of 1940 fifteen
boys and girls between the ages of two and seven were accommodated
as his guests. But Sevenoaks lay amid the fighter defences of south-
east England and along the bomber lane to London. At the end of
August 1940, at the height of the Battle of Britain, Rooks Hill was
closed and the children were returned to their families.

Because of its nearness to London's dockland, Vanbrugh Castle
had been closed too. Both Rooks Hill and Vanbrugh were damaged
by enemy action and neither school was to reopen until the end of the

war. Vanbrugh boys who had been attending the Roan Grammar School locally were evacuated with that school to the country.

For all its reluctance to appeal to the public or even to the Royal Air Force, the main reason why the Fund was so short of capital between the wars is traceable to its late start in 1919. Had the Fund been introduced while Lloyd George was praising the 'Cavalry of the Air', while London was threatened by Zeppelin attack and the Royal Flying Corps and the Royal Naval Air Service were producing a new breed of hero, public response must surely have created a good round sum of capital. But as Churchill later remarked: 'We are a Nation of short memories.'

Between 1914 and 1918 this chance had been missed and as the 'phoney war' passed from 1939 into 1940 it began to look as if the new war might fail to produce a second opportunity. Then, after the spring blitzkrieg of 1940 had placed Germany on the Channel coast, the Battle of Britain, which altered so much, completely changed the comparatively unimportant fortunes of the Royal Air Force Benevolent Fund.

It is rare that a battle's place in the full perspective of history can be seen while it is still being fought, but such was the case of the Battle of Britain.

Wakefield, the motor-oil opportunist of the early century, whose encouragement of weekend flying was now being justified in many a dogfight overhead, was not the Chairman to let this chance slip.

On 30 August 1940, as the Battle of Britain was fought over southern England, he wrote to *The Times*:

The wonderful achievements of the Royal Air Force in these critical weeks of the second Great War of our time have naturally led to various suggestions being made as to the best way in which we can give expression to our gratitude. In the deepest sense, there is no way in which the heroism and sacrifices of our airmen can be assessed or our debt to them in any way liquidated.

As there is, nevertheless, the desire to express the nation's thanks in tangible form, let it be devoted in part to some constructive aim, some cause that can be shown to be solely and entirely for the permanent benefit of all ranks and their dependants. I venture to submit as the most appropriate object of our generosity, The Royal Air Force Benevolent Fund, which exactly fulfils these conditions.

This Fund, founded in 1919 by Viscount Trenchard, in

addition to assisting airmen in various circumstances of special need and difficulty undertakes the education of children of Royal Air Force parentage and helps to establish them in careers that their fathers would be proud for them to follow.

Up to now the funds of the Royal Air Force Benevolent Fund have been raised without any public appeal, largely by contributions from members of the Royal Air Force. It is only too sadly obvious that in the near future there must be heavy calls upon the Fund, to an extent not at present calculable. With the gallant heroism of officers and men of the Royal Air Force before us day by day, I am confident that as a tribute to their ceaseless fight for the cause of freedom, many will wish to support their cause.

Contributions will be gladly acknowledged if sent to me at Eaton House, Eaton Road, Hove, Sussex.

Public response to Wakefield's appeal was more generous than Erskine-Lindop and his small staff, by then established in the former Air Training Corps headquarters at Hove, had dared to hope. They were overwhelmed, donations being received in every mail and mounting magnificently to a total of £354,530 10s 0d.

Among the many who had been stirred by Wakefield's letter was Lord Nuffield, who let it be known that he wished to support the appeal. This was enough for Wakefield who, at eighty years of age, called immediately on Nuffield, the pioneer Morris motor manufacturer, leaving with a cheque for £250,000 in his pocket. Normally a Morris might be said to depend considerably on Castrol, but in this neat reversal of form Lord Nuffield had given Castrol good cause to be thankful for Morris.

Shortly after Wakefield's letter had appeared in *The Times*, the founder of the Fund, Lord Trenchard, relaxed his self-imposed rule of radio silence and spoke to the nation, he said:

This is the first time I have ever broadcast. I had intended never to broadcast, but when it was pointed out to me that it was on behalf of the Royal Air Force Benevolent Fund, and all that that means, I felt it was a duty — and indeed an honour — and I hope, therefore you will bear with me.

Many years ago, at the end of the last war, it was my privilege to start the Royal Air Force Benevolent Fund in 1919 for all the dependants of those wonderful Air Force men of the 1914-18 War — those great men who had covered themselves with glory and thought of nothing except to work for others. Many were lost in those days and it was our duty to help their relations. It is tragic to think that, twenty years later, the Royal Air Force would again be in the forefront of a still greater war and this time surely we can never pay a better tribute than was paid to them by our Prime Minister: "Never in the field of human conflict was so much owed by so many to so few." How true this is. They kept off the German hordes at a very critical time of the history of the fight. They won their fight — and have won many — an they will win many more . . .

It is now time to ask this country, as I feel the whole British Empire recognises all that the Royal Air Force has done, to put the Fund on a firm basis. A very large sum will be required for us to carry out our obligations to the airmen, their wives, children and dependants, so that these men may go into battle, feeling that the future of their immediate relations will, anyhow, be secured from want.

Sometime ago we thought of appealing to the public, but we all considered it was not right to broadcast an appeal for this Fund only, until the Royal Air Force could feel that such great causes as the Air Raid Distress Fund and others were in a better position financially. A short appeal, however, by our chairman, Lord Wakefield, which appeared in *The Times* a few months ago, showed that the public would like to help and that very few people had realised that this Fund was in existence.

Trenchard's broadcast reaped a record £53,342. It was a high figure for a broadcast appeal in wartime Britain.

Perhaps the Fund *had* been too quiet about its existence for all those years, but if this was so, then it was a fault that reacted in the Fund's favour when finally it decided to drop its general disapproval of appeal. The Fund became appeal-minded at precisely the right moment. Departed were the drowsy summer days of aerial pageantry, of dog-fight make-believe, and in their place the Luftwaffe had provided an air display for almost any day of the great weeks of the Battle of Britain. It was not exactly Hendon, but it was quite a show; and when the enemy was defeated, as of course he always was in the mock dogfights of pre-war air displays, the public showered money on the Fund, a free will 'gate' given out of sheer gratitude for the national deliverance.

Wakefield had seen the opportunity in 1940 and he had acted. Shortly after the Battle of Britain had enforced enemy abandonment of *Operation Sealion*, the invasion of Britain, he died. As the Council of the Royal Air Force Benevolent Fund understated in its message of sympathy to Lady Wakefield, the Chairman had given 'a wise lead in the extension of the Fund in war'.

Chapter 6
Royal Patronage

*'Wings for Victory now and good homes
and employment in peace time are inseparable.'*

Her Royal Highness The Duchess of Kent, 1943

From inception in 1919 and the unveiling of the Memorial by the Prince of Wales in 1923 the Fund had engaged the active and sympathetic interest of the Royal Family. King George VI, Patron from 1936, had previously followed the Fund's fortunes closely since, as Wing Commander the Duke of York, a serving officer, he had accepted the Presidency in 1919, while at the time of Wakefield's death the King's brother, the Duke of Gloucester, was President. However, as was customary, neither the King nor his brother exercised any executive authority in their appointments and it would have been inappropriate for the Council to invite a royal duke to accept the chairmanship.

It was only after a short list had been prepared of prospective chairmen to succeed Lord Wakefield that the Council learned with surprise and delight of Air Commodore the Duke of Kent's offer to take the chair. The list was scrapped and the Duke became Chairman of the Royal Air Force Benevolent Fund in April 1941. Unhappily, the Duke was not spared to lead the Fund through the war and into peace. He was killed on active service in August 1942 when an operational Sunderland of No. 228 Squadron, flying from Scotland to Iceland, crashed into a Scottish hillside, killing all but the tail gunner.

Thus, little more than a year after her husband's election as Chairman, the Duchess of Kent was herself a Royal Air Force widow. She asked immediately what she might do to preserve the family connection with the Fund and in March 1943 the Duchess accepted the Presidency of the Royal Air Force Benevolent Fund. Princess Marina, who served the Fund for twenty-five years until her death in 1968, never failed to attend an annual meeting of the Council. In the Fund's seventieth anniversary year the family tradition continues through the Presidency of the Duke of Kent, who succeeded his mother.

Making her inaugural address, the Duchess said:

> I consider it a very great honour to become President of the Royal Air Force Benevolent Fund, as my husband, who was Chairman, was so deeply interested in it. From him I learnt something of your excellent work. The least we can do is to look after the welfare of the men of the Royal Air Force and women of the Auxiliary Air Force, and their families, if they need help. They do not ask for more than this, and by subscribing to the Fund, all people can pay their tribute to them. I shall follow closely the work of the Council, and feel sure that it will never lack the means to carry out its important work. Much has already been done, but there will be still more to do in the future, on which all have set their hopes. Let us, for our part, see that they are not disappointed.

The Duke's death had rendered the chair vacant for the second time in two years and the Fund was faced again with the election of a leader. Now there was an obvious choice in Lord Riverdale, who had joined the Fund as Vice-Chairman in January 1941 and was Chairman of the recently formed Appeals Committee.

Arthur Balfour, first Baron Riverdale, Sheffield industrialist, past Master Cutler, had already made an enormous success of appeals. Honoured by the Air Council with the appointment as Honorary Air Commodore of No. 601 (County of London) Squadron, Riverdale enjoyed an altogether very special relationship with the Royal Air Force, having negotiated the Empire Air Training Scheme in which most wartime aircrew were trained in the safe and clear skies of Canada, Australia, Rhodesia, South Africa, New Zealand and the British West Indies. Vastly successful in the steel industry, Riverdale was a particularly good picker of men and a great deal of his success as Chairman of the Appeals Committee and of the Fund can be ascribed to his part in the recruitment of a certain Bertram Rumble.

During the Second World War, when Air Vice-Marshal Sir John Cordingley was in charge of Manning, he lived at the Royal Thames Yacht Club and Rumble lived there also from Monday to Friday. Rumble, during the early stages of the war, repeatedly said he wanted to serve in some capacity but he was being turned down all the time on account of age. When Riverdale and Cordingley decided that the Fund required an individual of a particular type to run the appeals, Riverdale invited Rumble to dinner. That night Rumble received the run of Riverdale's cellar. 'It drinks well, yes, it certainly drinks well — yes, I'll do it providing you arrange things so I don't get paid.' Riverdale had recognised his man, corralled him in the cellar and won his acceptance of the all-important post of Appeals Secretary. Bertram Rumble refused a salary and established himself at the invitation of Barclays Bank in rooms above its premises at 1 Sloane Street.

Setting themselves to maintain Wakefield's impetus, Riverdale and Rumble had raised £1,250,000 within two years and had greatly broadened the Fund's scope of appeal, an achievement much aided by their inexhaustible ally Alexander Duckham. Beyond his gift of Rooks Hill, Duckham personally raised £100,000 from industry.

Riverdale, Rumble and Duckham were a magnificent team and with their ranging business interests and connections they were ideally suited for the task which, in Trenchard's words, was that of putting the Fund on a firm basis. Of the trio, Duckham did not live to see victory although when he died in 1944 it was clear that was asssured. He knew too that out of fifty-six Vanbrugh old boys, forty-nine were in the armed forces, of whom forty-four had followed their fathers into the Royal Air Force, four serving as commissioned officers, four as flight sergeants, ten as sergeants, twelve as corporals, nine as leading aircraftmen and five as aircraftmen.

Meanwhile, the Fund's appeal activities were attracting the notice of some of the great institutions which, in gratitude for the deliverance of 1940, had been making charitable collections of their own. In particular there were the initiatives of the Auctioneers' and Estate Agents' Institute — subsequently 'Chartered' — and of Lloyd's of London.

In 1943 the Auctioneers' and Estate Agents' Institute entered a long association with the Royal Air Force Benevolent Fund, instigated by Mr S. Linney and Mr F. C. Hawkes, their President and Secretary, as a result of which the Fund benefited directly with £221,084 to create the Pilots and Crews Fund, to be expended within twenty-five years. In addition the Fund benefited indirectly from the use of Headley Court, Epsom, originally given to the Secretary of State for Air as a rehabilitation centre for aircrew and now a Royal Air Force medical rehabilitation unit for the armed services and civilians. The Fund also benefited from a wealth of professional advice, especially that of Mr W. Wallace Withers who joined the Grants Committee in 1943, was elected to the Council and Finance and General Purposes Committee in 1948, and whose firm, Debenham Tewson and Chinnocks, advises the Fund on property matters to this day.

It was in 1943, also that the Corporation and Members of Lloyd's made the Fund a gift of £50,000. Loyal to its sea traditions, Lloyd's accepted the Fund's suggestion to devote the money to officers and airmen of Coastal Command and to the dependants of the large number who lost their lives in that Command.

As with the property men's gifts, the Lloyd's gesture has meant more than money to the Fund. It introduced, among many new friends, Mr Ernest de Rougemont who became Lloyd's representative on the Council and a member of the Finance and General Purposes Committee from 1958 to 1975, and also as a member of the Christ's Hospital Selection Committee.

'Wings for victory now and good homes and employment in peacetime are inseparable.' With this expressive phrase the Duchess of Kent, as President, identified the central theme of the Fund's mid-war philosophy; and it was open to all to subscribe to this philosophy in a very modest way because the Ministry of Aircraft Production decided that two-fifths of every donation to the Spitfire Fund should be allotted to the Royal Air Force Benevolent Fund.

Few people, however, were wealthy and generous enough to be troubled by the choice between buying a complete fighter or bomber or presenting the equivalent purchase price to the Fund. Lady Rosalind Davidson of Huntly paid £20,000 for four Spitfires between November 1940 and September 1941, and was then undecided as to a bomber or the Benevolent Fund. As an interim gesture she offered her *estancia* in Argentina to the Minister of Aircraft Production, who passed her offer on to the Fund. But wartime administrative, legal and communication difficulties decided the Fund against property development down South America way and Lady Rosalind, dropping her plan to buy a bomber, made the Fund a gift of £30,000.

At about this time too, the daily postbag was as exciting as a lucky dip and Lord Riverdale received an extraordinary package. It contained 100 ounces of gold from Emperor Haile Selassie of Ethiopia. A later message said: 'His Imperial Majesty greatly appreciates the formidable task that the Royal Air Force had to put up in the great fight, and it is hoped that the war will soon be won with complete victory for the allies.' The Emperor's gift had arrived unsolicited but the Council was fully alive to the need to attract donations while the public memory of Royal Air Force exploits remained fresh. For instance, there was the story of the East End of London publican for whom a Lancaster crew had signed the label of a bottle of whisky. When the bomber failed to return from operations, the publican presented the bottle to the Fund and it was auctioned in the Isle of Man for £100.

Generally, however, it was unnecessary to guide the protected or the defended towards an acknowledgement of their debt. One such instance was perhaps unique in that it related to a specific air action during which the defended made a collection for the dependants of those who were at that very moment losing their lives.

This splendid gesture was made by United States troops on passage eastwards through the Mediterranean in HMT *Karoa*. When the troopship came under attack two Royal Air Force officers died in her defence, but as it happened neither family wished to accept financial help. Very well, please pass the collection to the dependants as a gift, Royal Air Force Middle East instructed the Fund. There being no question of distress the Fund could only act as an unofficial intermediary and divided nearly £900 between the families.

Complying with the *Karoa* request was a comparatively simple matter for the Fund's hard-pressed wartime staff and it was but one of shoals of weekly requests that poured into Erskine-Lindop's seaside headquarters at Hove.

When the staff of four had left London for Sussex-by-the-sea in 1939 the Fund's total annual expenditure on relief was £22,921. Between 1940 and 1943 it had risen from £27,766 to £89,495, involving 12,824 cases in 1943, the administrative details of every one of which had been handled at Hove.

Certainly the Appeals Department and, from early 1943, a newly created Disablement Branch under Air Commodore E. Digby-Johnson, were self-contained at 1 Sloane Street and relieved some of the pressure. But liaison with the bereaved and the preparation of cases for presentation to the Grants Committee were usually more exacting and time-consuming by their nature.

Although wartime meetings of the Council, of the Finance and General Purposes Committee and of the Grants Committee took place at the Air Ministry in London, the volume of work being handled at Hove did not pass unrecognised. After visiting head-quarters early in 1943 with Bertram Rumble, Lord Riverdale paid a warm tribute to Erskine-Lindop, his wartime joint secretary, Group Captain C. G. Murray, their retired officer assistants and the locally recruited staff of young girls, one of whom, Miss Jean Ashton, long since appointed MBE, served the Fund until 1988 when she retired as Deputy Director Welfare, after nearly forty-four years of devoted service. The Chairman said in Council, 'I met all members of the staff and found them all working like a happy family. I examined the

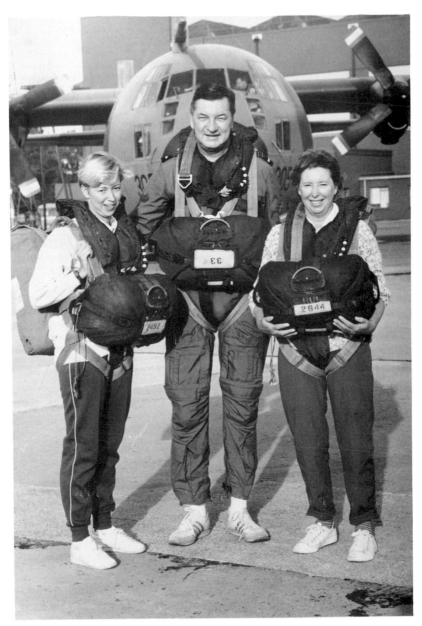

Giving the Fund's 1990 Battle of Britain 50th Anniversary £20 million appeal a daring send-off, Air Chief Marshal Sir Peter Harding, Chief of the Air Staff, Lady Harding and their daughter, Kate, raised £50,000 with a parachute jump from an RAF Hercules into the English Channel off Dorset on 6 September 1989, the Fund's 70th anniversary year.

The RAF Memorial at Victoria Embankment which was unveiled by the Prince of Wales on 16 July 1923.

The Royal Patrons of the Fund: King George VI (right), who as Prince Albert, Duke of York, had been President of the Fund since its inception in October 1919, conferred Royal Patronage on the Fund in May 1936. He is with his father King George V and his brother King Edward VIII.

Sir Winston Churchill, whose BBC appeal on the theme of 'The Debt We Owe', broadcast on Battle of Britain Sunday in September 1951, suggested the title of this book. A Vice-President from 1919 until he died in 1965, this portrait of the wartime Prime Minister, wearing the uniform of Air Commodore, hangs in the Council chamber.

Air Vice-Marshal Sir Hazelton Nicholl, Controller 1944-47.

Air Vice-Marshal Sir John W. Cordingley, Controller 1947-62.

Air Marshal Sir John Whitley, Controller 1962-68.

Air Marshal Sir William Coles, Controller 1968-75.

Air Marshal Sir Denis Crowley-Milling, Controller 1975-81.

Air Chief Marshal Sir Alasdair Steedman, Controller 1981-88.

Air Chief Marshal Sir Thomas Kennedy, Controller 1988 to date.

The Lord Catto of Cairncatto, Chairman of the Fund since May 1978.

The Council in session in May 1976, during the Controllership of Air Marshal Sir Denis Crowley-Milling. The President, HRH The Duke of Kent and on his left, the Chairman, Sir Harald Peake, listen attentively as Sir Denis delivers his annual report.

After business the annual Council meeting offers an opportunity for an informal get-together of old friends as when the President, the Duke of Kent, talked with the Chairman, Lord Catto (facing) the then Controller, Air Chief Marshal Sir Alasdair Steedman (left) and his two surviving predecessors, Air Marshal Sir John Whitley (centre) and Air Marshal Sir Denis Crowley-Milling.

books and their methods of dealing with cases and I am glad to say that the organisation is perfect and quite as good as any industrial concern I am connected with.'

The President, Princess Marina, personally recognised Erskine-Lindop's great devotion and dedication when she presented him with her late husband's cuff-links; a gift deeply appreciated by the Squadron Leader, who retained a keen interest in the Fund's progress until his death in April 1978 denied his hopes of participating in the Diamond Jubilee celebrations ten years ago.

Chapter 7
Grants Policy after the Second World War

'I'd like to feel that no one who is, or has been in the Service need ever be without someone to turn to if they have bad luck.'

Marshal of the Royal Air Force Viscount Portal, 1945

The avalanche which had been expected in 1939, and had not fallen, landed on Erskine-Lindop and Murray and their staff in mid-war. As fighter sweeps began to prepare the way for a return to France and the Low Countries, as Bomber and Coastal Command operations intensified against Germany and in the Atlantic respectively, and as the Royal Air Force helped to hold the Mediterranean and supported the armies in North Africa and Burma, so casualties mounted and lights burned late behind the Benevolent Fund's blackout — to midnight and beyond.

In figures, grants made and cases assisted ran:

    1943   £89,495 covering 12,824 cases
    1944   £163,679 covering 17,780 cases
    1945   £326,697 covering 28,591 cases

Sir Arthur Bryant, writing in the *Illustrated London News*, described the heroism and sacrifice which gave rise to so much need:

> It is the Fund's policy that children whose fathers were killed or died whilst serving with the Royal Air Force should receive education of the standard they would have been given had they not been orphaned.

> This help is continued from earliest schooldays to the university if the child shows real promise. Among those benefiting from it at the present time — and I see him every term — is a boy whose father, formerly an apprentice at the great Royal Air Force Apprentices' School at Halton, to which he had gone, like some many of its members, from a fine provincial Grammar School, fought as a sergeant-pilot in the Battle of Britain and won the Distinguished Flying Medal in its course.

Later this gallant young pilot was commissioned, rose to the rank of Flight Lieutenant and won the Distinguished Flying Cross. He was killed towards the end of the war flying Mosquitos.

He left behind a widow and two children, a boy and a girl, as well as a devoted mother and father whose only son he was — the latter himself a most faithful servant of England who had served in all three Services, as a Regular soldier before 1914, as a Naval Chief Petty Officer during and after the First World War, and, at an advanced age, as a technical Sergeant Instructor in the Royal Air Force during part of the late war.

During the Battle of Britain the hero of this story — one of many similar ones which together helped to change the course of human destiny — was shot down in flames and left unconscious, covered in oil, near his aircraft.

He was subsequently retrieved and found to be suffering from severe shock and bruises but not, by some miracle, seriously wounded. In the stress of that time, instead of being taken to hospital, he was sent to his parents on convalescent leave to recover. After twenty-four hours at home, deeply grateful for the peace and rest and love by which he found himself surrounded, he quietly told his father and mother that his comrades were fighting the Battle of Britain without him and that he must return.

Next day, though anything but fit, he reported for duty and insisted on resuming operational flying. It is to repay some small part of the debt we owe to such men that the Royal Air Force Benevolent Fund exists, and that its support is a permanent duty of all who love their country.

And there were many smaller grants, comparatively minor in monetary terms but totally disproportionate in value to the relief they brought. A sergeant with sixteen years' service had a wife whose leg had to be amputated. All his savings had gone in paying for her medical treatment. The Fund stepped in and bought the artificial limb. A squadron leader and his wife were returning from India. The ship was torpedoed and sunk and the husband drowned. The Fund maintained the widow, reclothed her and returned the financial value of her lost belongings.

But what, it will be reasonably asked, was the State doing? Certainly not as much as more recent legislation enables it to do. War pensions were not on a generous scale.

The Fund explained in a wartime appeal letter:

Nowadays the State has a very large number of citizens of this country to look after. Few, if any, nations of the world have a better system of social legislation and social insurance than Great Britain, but government funds are not unlimited. What money it has the State divides to the best of its ability. It seeks to provide the dry bread without which continued existence is impossible. But no one can live on bread alone and it is funds such as the Royal Air Force Benevolent Fund which exist to find the butter, and if possible, the jam.

However, this considerate approach to the ever-present problem of the demarcation between government and charitable responsibility should not be taken to imply that the Fund was not prepared to press for at least a scraping of margarine where it believed the government was failing in its duty.

Throughout its seventy years the Fund has kept careful watch on this wobbly line of demarcation and there have been numerous occasions when Grants Committees had remonstrated vigorously that the government was attempting to evade its responsibilities. There have been occasions when the Fund has been compelled to render a beneficiary ineligible for State help in order to bring the beneficiary to a standard which the Fund regards as a minimum.

Generally this question arises from the much disputed interpretation of the all-disclaiming tag of 'non-attributable', a tag which, as may be imagined, ignited some especially heated comment in a wartime atmosphere, as in 1943 when Air Vice-Marshal Sir Charles Longcroft raised the matter in Council.

Sir Charles said that the Grants Committee of which he was Chairman felt very strongly that some 'non-attributable' cases were not a fair burden on the Fund and should be the responsibility of the government. Such cases, Sir Charles explained, were typified by that of a flying officer killed in a car accident in Canada and leaving a widow and two children, aged two-and-a-half and one-and-a-half. In another case an airman had been killed in a cycling accident, leaving three children and a widow. Neither of these men would have been at the scene of the accidents had not their service taken them there.

Nevertheless, successive governments have consistently refused to accept responsibility in such cases and to this day the often disputable suffix 'non-attributable' appears all to frequently after the cause of death and involves the Fund in considerable expense.

Morally the Fund has always felt obliged to assist such cases and it has always done so subject to Grants Committee acceptance of distress.

Of all the Fund's seemingly limitless wartime responsibilities there was one which in mid-war assumed an important priority: the assistance of disabled men and in particular of aircrew. Here, the Disablement Branch established early in 1943 soon came into its own and from 1943 onwards service people were assisted right through their hospital life and whenever necessary into new or suitable civil careers, often with the co-operation and advice of the Resettlement Branch of the Air Ministry.

A number of parents who had lost sons in air operations against the enemy offered to help individuals so far as they could, and among these generous, sad-hearted actions that of Mr Charles P. Ackers is especially noteworthy. Ackers arranged a forestry training scheme for ex-officers and airmen on his Gloucestershire estate, helping the scheme with a £1,000-a-year Deed of Covenant in memory of his son, Flying Officer Robert David Ackers, who had been killed over Normandy shortly after D-Day.

Had the Royal Air Force Benevolent Fund glanced momentarily into a mirror at this time, as the war in Europe turned into the home stretch, it might have perceived a prosperous if weary countenance, and smiled wanly as it remembered that lean and hungry look of 1939.

To 1944, £397,823 had been distributed in wartime relief and capital stood at £4,807,673. The Fund could afford to smile and congratulate itself. But there was at least one member of the Council and the Finance and General Purposes Committee and Grants Committee who was convinced that the Fund's most testing time lay in the years ahead.

As Royal Air Force Director-General of Manning throughout the war, Air Vice-Marshal Sir John Cordingley was apprehensive about the future welfare of some one-and-three-quarter million men, women and their families. He therefore proposed to Lord Riverdale that the Fund should prepare carefully for the problems of peace and appoint a general Controller of administrative ability and standing. In October 1944 Air Vice-Marshal Sir Hazelton Nicholl, who had flown as a bomber pilot in the First World War and had been in charge of administration at Fighter Command during the Battle of Britain, became the first Controller of the Royal Air Force Benevolent Fund.

The appointment was of material assistance to Squadron Leader Erskine-Lindop, who had then reached the stage when his head was just beginning to appear above the avalanche. Erskine-Lindop continued to serve as Secretary until his retirement in 1958. At that year's Annual Council Meeting the Air Member for Personnel, Air

Marshal Sir John Whitley, expressed the Air Council's particular thanks to Squadron Leader Erskine-Lindop for his outstanding services to the Fund.

It was evident, even before the war ended with victory over Japan in September 1945, that money might again become the problem it had been between the two world wars. The wartime scale of generosity was drying up. In the last year of hostilities the Fund received £948,959, of which £250,000 was accounted for by a final wartime windfall.

A gift from the people of South Africa, the cheque for £250,000 was received in October 1945, by the Duchess of Kent from the hands of Mrs Jean Hamilton in the presence of the High Commissioner for South Africa, Mr G. Heaton Nicholls. This generous gift owed much to Field Marshal Jan C. Smuts's interest in the Royal Air Force and to the Fund's untiring and voluntary representative in South Africa, Mrs A. C. Haswell, who had lost her son in the air.

In a letter to the President, Field Marshal Smuts, South Africa's Prime Minister — whose recommendation to the British Cabinet in 1917 had resulted in the creation of the Royal Air Force as a separate service — wrote:

> The people of South Africa are sending in the person of Mrs Jean Hamilton, a mission which you have graciously consented to receive.
>
> It is a small tangible expression of South Africa's recognition of the immense debt which our nation, amongst others of the United Nations, owes to the men of the Royal Air Force, who during the Battle of Britain itself, saved the whole civilised world and later played so magnificent a part in achieving victory. It is a tribute of gratitude, of admiration and of pride.
>
> We in South Africa have had the privilege and the pleasure of having as our guests during training many of the gallant young men who have upheld the prestige of the Royal Air Force in the greatest human trial in history, and it is the measure of the affection we have felt for them that, when we came to provide funds for assisting our men of the South African Air Force, it was decided to appeal also for the men of the Royal Air Force, and to send more than half the total collection for the relief of distress among dependants of the latter service.
>
> In asking you graciously to accept on behalf of the Royal Air Force Benevolent Fund this gift from the people of South Africa, I would ask your Royal Highness to convey to the men of the Royal Air Force this expression of South Africa's thanks and admiration.

Smuts' message belongs already to that other age when the British Commonwealth was an Empire, before the wind of change began to blow through Africa. Today it is a message that seems as archaic as Lloyd George's exaltation of the 'Cavalry of the Air' in the First World War. Yet it was delivered as the Royal Air Force was basking in the admiration of the Allied world, just as in its own time the Royal Flying Corps had been praised to the skies.

Now, as in 1918-19, the airmen were due to come down to earth with a bump, to the necessity of facing the problems of civilian life in peacetime austerity: to finding somewhere to live, to learning a job and getting it, and to educating children.

Widows were left to face it all — alone.

Making a timely broadcast in the early autumn of 1945, Lord Portal, then Sir Charles, put the Royal Air Force Benevolent Fund's seal on the war. The wartime Chief of the Air Staff said:

> Exactly six years ago, on this first Sunday in September 1939, 126 young men took off in Wellingtons and Hampdens to strike at the German Fleet. This was the first offensive operation of the Royal Air Force in this war. And now, thank God, they've done their last, and it's all over, and we've won.
>
> Well, it's been a long story, much too long to go over it all, but one mustn't forget the beginning of it, how our squadrons fought to help France and the Low Countries and Norway. They did all they could, but it was impossible to achieve anything much except glory.
>
> You remember too the desperate days of Dunkirk and the Battle of Britain: almost miracles they seemed at the time. Then Greece and Burma and Singapore — impossible odds again. They never had a hope, but they went down fighting for the honour of our country.
>
> Then slowly we began to grow stronger and the Americans — bless them — began to come over in strength. We had North Africa and Malta and all the time that grim Battle of the Atlantic. And so from Alamein on to Berlin and now at last to full victory over Japan . . .
>
> Perhaps we owe the biggest debt of all to our bomber crews. Night after night and night after night again, hammering away at Germany; and those long journeys home over the North Sea — for the lucky ones. Do you know our Bomber Command alone won 19,000 decorations for gallantry, and lost 47,000 killed.
>
> The war's over, but I'm afraid this Fund's got years of urgent work ahead of it.

Now, I know some people think that this sort of thing shouldn't be necessary. Well, I'm here to assure you it *is*. The government does all it can, but there's still an urgent need for personal help. That's the great thing. The Fund's personal; it's quick to act; it doesn't wait to be asked. I wouldn't ask for your support if I didn't feel strongly about it. *I'd like to feel that no one who is, or has been, in the service need ever be without someone to turn to if they have bad luck . . .*

May I read you a bit of a letter from the wife of an airman. This is what she says, 'If it hadn't been for the Fund I often wonder what would have happened to us. My baby was only three days old when my husband died. Sir, may I say you have done the best thing that could be done with the money.'

By God's grace we've won a great victory and tonight I ask you to give thanks by helping this Fund and so helping those of my Service for whom the end of the war may not be the end of suffering or distress.

The broadcast brought in £12,890, but the future implications of Portal's message were every bit as important as the flow of money which resulted from it.

Chapter 8
Management and Relief

'For a time I didn't even want to live. That is what despair does. The
Royal Air Force Benevolent Fund convinced me that I could start
again in a life of my own choosing and assisted me with means to do it.'

Battle of Britain Hurricane Pilot

In the autumn of 1945, the Fund moved back to London where a
973-year lease had been acquired on very favourable terms of a
period building at 67 Portland Place. Removed from its Hove villa,
the Royal Air Force Benevolent Fund was wholly unrecognisable
from the evacuee which Erskine-Lindop had packed into his car in
1940.

Relief expenditure had risen from £22,919 in 1939 to £323,233 in
1945. Total relief expenditure in the war years had amounted to
£724,520 and the Fund entered peace and Portland Place with capital
of £5,542,616.

On paper and behind its imposing facade the Fund appeared well
breeched to meet the demands of peace. Certainly it understood the
reaction of the man who, intending to arrange a £2,000 legacy, turned
on his heel in Portland Place and wrote instead, 'You don't need my
money'. But the Royal Air Force Benevolent Fund has never been
persuaded by that particular comment, or by any similar criticism to
conceal itself in the suburbs.

For some forty-five years the accessibility of 67 Portland Place has
facilitated Council and Committee work, simplified liaison with the
Royal Air Force and the Air Ministry or the Ministry of Defence, and
provided reasonable working conditions for staff, honorary representatives and visitors. Another, if incidental, gain has been the lease
itself. Purchased for £35,000 at a ground rental of £500 a year,
generously reduced to £200 by the ground landlord, Lord Howard de
Walden, it has proved an excellent investment.

Re-established in London, the Royal Air Force Benevolent Fund
bore no outward resemblance to its pre-war self in four rooms at

Iddesleigh House, Westminster, and the end of the war found it a world apart from the modest start in 1919.

Now a memorial existed, standing out into the Thames on the Victoria Embankment and awaiting the addition of a 1939-45 inscription on its bomb-scarred surface. Now, demobilised air and groundcrew could return to civil life supported by a charitable accumulation mountainous by comparison with 1919.

Whereas in that year Trenchard had feared for his new airmen, 'the finest men', because unlike soldiers or sailors they had no fund of their own, 1945 found the circumstances reversed. The Royal Air Force Benevolent Fund had outpaced all comparable service charitable organisations. The generosity with which the world had responded to the exploits of the Royal Air Force in war had placed the Fund in this enviable condition and left it pondering its future responsibilities.

Clearly, therefore, now that Sir Hazelton Nicholl was contemplating retirement, the future executive direction of the Royal Air Force Benevolent Fund would call for an exceptional man possessing an almost impossible combination of qualities: a good heart, an inflexible purpose, a record of administrative achievement, a close appreciation of human nature, a flair for publicity and a working knowledge both of the Fund and of the Royal Air Force.

Extraordinarily, there happened to be at hand a paragon of these virtues, and of many others besides. Air Vice-Marshal Sir John Cordingley, who had served the Fund in Council or Committee for more than ten years, assumed salaried office as Controller of the Royal Air Force Benevolent Fund on 1 May 1947.

A few days later the Duchess of Kent addressed the Council. The President said:

> Though we are still in a position to meet all demands and money continues to come in, the peak of subscriptions and donations may be said to have been reached and passed.
>
> In these very difficult and disturbing days one cannot expect people to be so lavish with their gifts as formerly, though in the public eye the Royal Air Force Benevolent Fund holds a unique position, and we continue to be by far the largest service benevolent fund.

The President's allusion to future income inspired one of Cordingley's earliest actions as Controller. No one was more aware than the wartime Director-General of Manning of the Royal Air Force that, while the balance sheet looked fairly healthy, the future promised unprecedented demand upon the Fund's resources. He knew that several million men and women and members of their families were privileged to call upon the Fund should need arise. If the peak of public subscriptions and donations had been reached then action must be taken to improve support from within the service. Consequently, one of Sir John's first moves was to sharpen up the half-a-day's-pay-a-year voluntary subscription scheme, particularly among officers.

The introduction of this scheme in 1938 had restored the Fund's fortunes most effectively after the withdrawal of the Hendon Air Display, and between 1938 and 1946 the Fund received £562,350 from this source. Learning in 1947 that only fifty per cent of serving officers were contributors, the Controller began to sell the scheme more aggressively. He adopted mail order tactics.

With the co-operation of the Air Ministry, the Controller wrote personally to every newly commissioned officer. Where this failed, and in the cases of previously commissioned officers who were not subscribing, he arranged to send a reminder letter at every promotion in an officer's career. It should also be acknowledged that the co-operation of the Royal Air Force Agents, Lloyds, Cox's and King's and Glyn Mills, in agreeing to collect subscriptions from officers, and of the Royal Air Force itself in permitting the men's subscriptions to be paid through the pay ledgers, contributed greatly to the success of the half-a-day's-pay scheme. These mail shots met with increasing success and, when the Controller retired in 1962, over ninety per cent of serving officers and airmen were subscribers.

Another matter to which the Fund gave priority early in 1947-48 was the implementation of decisions recently taken towards constitutional reform. Arrangements which had developed out of such early and rudimentary decisions as may have been taken at Lord Hugh Cecil's breakfast table were no longer suitable for the Royal Air Force Benevolent Fund in its altogether changed and better circumstances. Certain financial formalities had, for example, become operationally impractical, as Lord Trenchard knew only too well. 'We're getting old and being chased by paper,' the founder had commented on the chores of the Trustees.

One problem was that the signatures of Trenchard and his fellow trustee, Lord Weir, were required on every stock market transaction in the post-war £5-6 million investment portfolio.

Therefore a scheme was needed which would vest any funds or property of the Charity in the hands of a Custodian Trustee, allowing the Royal Air Force Benevolent Fund managerial control of monies required from time to time for the relief of distress and for administration.

Such a scheme was prepared under the guidance of Mr John Fletcher, a senior partner of the Fund's solicitors, Charles Russell and Co., and approved by Mr Justice Harman in the High Court on 21 July 1948. In effect the Deed of Trust appointing Lloyds Bank as the Custodian Trustee rendered the Royal Air Force Benevolent Fund answerable only to the law officers of the Crown. It conferred powers wider than usual, either before or after the execution. Indeed, the new constitution anticipated by twelve years the general legislation which was to unshackle charities from their traditional low yield investment obligations.

The new trust became operative on 1 January 1949, allowing the retirement of Trenchard and Weir, who had served as trustees since 1920 and 1929 respectively.

Constitutionally fit, potentially free under the new trust deed to invest more adventurously, the Fund embarked in the late 1940s and early 1950s on a varied and costly programme of relief.

Grants to resettle or establish a man or woman in civil life, help over education and housing — these were the chief calls the Fund had to meet.

Inevitably, since a large charitable capital was involved, there were criticisms that the Fund was either spending too much or too little. To which the Controller replied, 'Not a penny too much, not a penny too little. The Fund is constituted to relieve distress. Why give half the help really needed and then fail to relieve the distress?'

In fact the Fund was not only giving but lending. The making of loans as distinct from grants held advantages when so many 1939-45 service people were young enough to start or return to civilian careers and repay loans in part or in full. Loans in suitable cases can completely relieve distress and in certain instances preserve self-respect.

In 1946, 1947 and 1948, a total of £166,666 was paid out in business grants and loans, assistance that was amply justified when repayments began to provide money for recirculation. Sometimes there were profits, as in the example of the flying officer who received a loan on his release leave to buy and stock a cycle, electrical and toy shop. After repaying the loan in monthly instalments the beneficiary wrote four years later:

> May I thank you from the bottom of my heart for the help you so generously gave me when I was released from the Royal Air Force . . . Without that help I could not have started up in business; yet because of it the small business I bought then is today worth several thousands of pounds . . . I have confirmed

the cancellation of the Banker's Order after next month's payment as your loan to me, being free of interest, is then repaid in full. I would, however, wish you to send me a further Banker's Order form, as it is my wish as a token of appreciation of your help, to make a donation of £10 each Christmas Eve for as long as I live, or if hard times should come, for as long as I can afford it!

Although Grants Committees considered carefully whether a man was capable of building his own business, if there was doubt they inclined to the generous view. Not every post-war business the Fund helped to finance was as successful as the flying officer's cycle shop, but for every failure there were many success stories, and the Fund remains thankful that in the high streets and industrial estates of Britain there are numerous undertakings which owe everything to an initial interest-free push from 67 Portland Place.

The successful outcome of many of these business loans was attributable to the practical assistance received from established businessmen. One such was Mr A. E. Scotcher, who offered to arrange for applications for assistance to establish small businesses to be investigated by an experienced representative whose advice and recommendation were available to the Grants Committee when they considered each individual request.

So many businesses were launched in this period that it would be repetitive to quote further examples, but just occasionally there was a loan with a difference, and such a loan was that made to a badly burned Battle of Britain pilot who needed capital to establish himself as headmaster of a preparatory school for boys. The Fund, always as opportunist as any individual venturer it has helped, made the fighter pilot a loan under a mutually advantageous agreement. In repayment the Royal Air Force Benevolent Fund obtained the board and education of three boys at any one time, and at eighty per cent of the headmaster's current school fees.

Some years later this arrangement produced a richly rewarding sequel when the headmaster collected a £10,000 postbag following his Battle of Britain Sunday broadcast appeal on behalf of the Fund. He said:

Fifteen years ago I was in hospital. My Hurricane had crashed in flames a few days before. Now my job is teaching. I am not giving you my name as the Royal Air Force Benevolent Fund will not make public the names of those it has helped.

It is the link across those fifteen years — from a Hurricane cockpit to a classroom — that I want to talk about tonight. That link — it was more of a lifeline — brought me through a period of my life that I could not have faced alone. For I am one of the many thousands helped back to worthwhile life by the Fund.

You may think that is not so remarkable: perhaps you are wondering why I am broadcasting rather than some famous person. Well — as one of 'The Few' — I am speaking not only for myself, but for more than a quarter of a million others, men, women and children — all having reason to be grateful to this wonderful Fund.

Forgive just a few words about myself. The Battle of Britain meant my facing the fact that I should never use my hands again, that I was burned and scarred for life. For a time I didn't even want to live. That is what despair does. The Royal Air Force Benevolent Fund convinced me that I could start again in a life of my own choosing and assisted me with means to do it. So I am speaking with first-hand knowledge.

Of course, as you know, the State gives assistance to the disabled and dependants, but there are a hundred and one ways in which the Fund is helping over and above this. When my friends and I realise what it has done, and will do for the widows and children of those who were killed, we don't hesitate to seek support for it.

What of the future? Will the Fund carry on? It will and it must. The Royal Air Force Fund's work will undoubtedly increase. Men who fought in the Battle of Britain and afterwards will need assistance in their old age. Many will meet bad luck and trouble for the first time.

Casualties happen in peacetime too, and for younger men still flying it is wonderful to know that, if anything should go wrong, their dependants will be looked after, and their children educated in the same way as they had planned.

It was Sir Archibald McIndoe, the great plastic surgeon, who in the 1940s drew the Fund's attention to the needs of badly burned members of aircrew — his guinea pigs, as the Consultant in Plastic Surgery to the Royal Air Force called them. A special Grants Sub-committee including Archie McIndoe's widow, Connie, was set up, and still meets regularly, to consider assistance for ageing guinea pigs. Was it really so long ago that Archie asked: 'When their bodies are whole again we also rebuild something of their lives?'

The Fund is also fortunate in having Honorary Consultants to whom it can refer other complicated or difficult medical cases for advice and guidance.

After business loans and grants, housing and furniture accounted for the next highest expenditure on relief, totalling £298,713 in the immediate post-war years of 1946, 1947 and 1948. While the greater part of this sum was distributed among individual applicants the Fund also maintained its practice of co-operating with other organisations, provided Royal Air Force families were guaranteed to benefit. The following are examples:

Under an agreement with the Housing Association for Officers' Families, £24,000 was provided to build twelve houses at Morden named Trenchard Court in honour of the founder. A similar arrangement was made with the British Legion Haig Homes to build eighteen houses for airmen's families on their estates at Morden, named Rhodes-Moorhouse Court in honour of the first VC of the air; also to build houses at Leicester and Cardiff at an estimated £29,000, and at Leckhampton £19,000.

The sum of £1,800 was given to the Thistle Foundation for a Royal Air Force house. In addition, £10,000 was contributed towards the Officers' Association's purchase and equipment of Frimley Park House, Camberley, now removed to Huntly, Bishopsteignton, Devon, as a home for aged and infirm officers of the three services; the Fund agreed to pay £1,000 a year towards upkeep for fifteen years, twenty-five per cent of the accommodation being reserved for RAF officers; £3,700 was given to provide two Royal Air Force houses on the Haig Homes Seacroft Estate, Leeds; £9,000 towards two British Legion country houses for aged and incapacitated ex-servicemen; £2,800 for two houses at the Scottish Veterans Garden City . . . some examples from one year's list, and representative of the Fund's annual participation in ex-service projects throughout Britain.

Chapter 9
Education after the War

'The Council of the Fund realised many years ago that money spent on the education of children is one of the most valuable and fruitful investments that the Fund can make.'

Lord Wolfenden, 1954

As VJ Day receded, the Fund's resettlement liabilities gradually declined. Housing remained a perennial problem, but by 1949 education at £86,597 had emerged as the most costly item on the books.

In this broad and varied field the Fund needed advice and in 1949, on the recommendation of the Education Advisory Committee, which had been set up two years earlier, a national panel of educational advisers was appointed, known as the Education Advisory Panel. Together, the new panel and the Education Advisory Committee presented a formidable front line of learning. But it was necessarily so if the Fund was to continue to fulfil its fundamental promise to provide the children of deceased and disabled officers or airmen with the education the fathers had wished for their sons and daughters.

In the post-war competition for places in preparatory and public schools and in the universities, the Fund needed all the specialist advice and liaison it could muster by employing the knowledge and connections of members of the Education Advisory Committee. The Honorary Secretary of the Education Advisory Committee from its inception in 1947 and for many years was Mr Peter du Sautoy, who served in the Royal Air Force during the Second World War and subsequently became the Chairman of Faber & Faber, the publishers.

The function of each member of the Education Advisory Panel at the time was that of personal adviser to parent or guardian. There were some two hundred panelists geographically distributed to give guidance wherever an education case occurred, it being an adviser's delicate task to suggest an education suitable to each child's individual need. Lord Wolfenden who sat on the Education Advisory Committee summed up the panel's value in human terms:

> One of the first and deepest anxieties of a widow is the education of her children. Sheer information and advice are often the first need. And this the Fund takes great care to supply. For it sometimes happens that a widow, simply not knowing what is best for her children in this rather specialised sphere, and not knowing what opportunities are available, embarks on a course which turns out to be mistaken, misleading and unduly expensive.

The education opportunities available through the Royal Air Force Benevolent Fund are numerous and varied enough to exercise the most knowledgeable educationist. A parent or guardian, unescorted by a member of the Education Advisory Panel, might become inextricably lost in the maze of educational opportunity, although it has not been constructed, of course, to bewilder the uninitiated. The success of the Scheme owes everything to the Fund's long-established principle of co-operating with outside bodies rather than running its own establishment.

Vanbrugh Castle School and Rooks Hill House Nursery School near Sevenoaks were exceptions to this general policy because they had been presented to the Fund by Mr Alexander Duckham for specific purposes. Rooks Hill had to be closed during the Battle of Britain but reopened in May 1946 with twenty aircrew children of from two to seven years of age. It was run by a committee of well-wishers, mostly with Royal Air Force connections, who lived nearby. For many years the Chairman was Lady Babington, the wife of Air Marshal Sir Philip Babington, a former Air Member for Personnel and subsequently Chairman of the Fund's Grants Committee. She was succeeded as Chairman by Squadron Leader Harold Pound.

The Nursery School was closed in July 1957 partly because the demand had decreased since the advent of safer jet aircraft and partly because it was difficult to staff on account of its inaccessibility in the country.

Vanbrugh Castle School, its war damage repaired, reopened in April 1947, with twenty-five boys between the ages of seven and fourteen years and able to accommodate fifty boys. Shortly after reopening the school fell under the Controller's scrutiny. In accordance with pre-war practice the boys were attending the local schools, including the Roan Grammar School, Charlton Secondary and Royal Hill Elementary Schools, with the difference that Roan was no longer fee-paying, entrance depending upon examination, report and selection. The Controller was much impressed by the fact that at each outside school Vanbrugh boys were distinctly identifiable by their smart appearance, a tribute to the lasting influence of the late matron, Mrs Slimming, and to the discipline of her husband, Captain G. A. R. Slimming who, excepting wartime employment at Hove, had been in charge at the School since 1921. Nevertheless, for all the good order and discipline at Vanbrugh itself, there had been complaints from some mothers about the manners and behaviour of their sons during the holidays. It was plain, therefore, that there was a risk that certain boys might deteriorate in character, possibly as a result of some of the company they kept outside the Castle.

It deeply concerned the Controller that, as the sons of deceased airmen, Vanbrugh boys were entitled morally and financially to the Fund's protection. When he visited the outside schools with Wing Commander J. F. Burnet MA, a member of the Education Advisory Committee and Bursar of Magdalene College, Cambridge, they were disturbed by conditions generally and the size of classes. There was the point, too, that in no sense did the Fund wish to fall short of its cherished promise to provide Royal Air Force children with those same opportunities they might have enjoyed if their fathers had lived.

In April 1950, rather than accept this risk, the Fund transformed Vanbrugh into a boarding school for boys between the ages of seven and eleven, while older boys up to the age of eighteen continued to attend local schools.

That year, as it happened, Captain Slimming was due to retire after thirty years' service and Mr J. W. Webb-Jones MA was appointed headmaster. Previously headmaster of St George's School, Windsor, Webb-Jones had served in the Royal Air Force during the war as an Education Officer.

Thus when the Duchess of Kent visited Vanbrugh Castle in 1951 she found the embryo of a boys' preparatory school. Although Vanbrugh Castle School was recognised by the Ministry of Education as an efficient Primary School in 1950, it did not attain the status of a recognised boarding preparatory school for boys between the ages of eight and thirteen until the early 1960s.

Some schools welcome Royal Air Force children at reduced fees, others receive them on varying terms because of past and present Air Ministry or Royal Air Force Benevolent Fund support. There are also numerous scholarships and endowments arising out of two world wars. Coming under the heading of bursaries, foundations, nominations, presentations and scholarships, they commemorate individual or corporate acts of sacrifice and bravery and, in one instance, perhaps the most celebrated bomber operation in Royal Air Force history.

The story of The Dam Busters is one of the best known single Royal Air Force operations of the Second World War. The Lancaster bomber crews and the inventor who figure in it have been immortalised in Paul Brickhill's book and in a film. But the breaching of the Mohne and Eder dams in 1943 by a force of Lancasters of No. 617 Squadron, led by Wing Commander Guy Gibson, using the bouncing 'ducks and drakes' bombs devised by Dr Barnes Wallis, had a sequel which is not so widely known.

After the war when the government was making awards to inventors whose genius had contributed so vitally towards victory, a grateful nation gave £10,000 to Dr Barnes Neville Wallis, who was knighted in 1968. It so happened that when Wallis received his award the Controller was trying to charm Christ's Hospital, the Bluecoat School, into accepting boys nominated from the Fund. As Sir John Cordingley explained, 'few boys had been put down for public schools by their fathers and I was scratching around for nominations at schools at prices one felt were reasonable'. The Fund was particularly attracted to Christ's Hospital by its magnificent record and because it had places for boys *and* girls.

Mr Ernest de Rougemont, a member of the Fund Council and an Almoner of Christ's Hospital, had placed at the disposal of the Fund his Donation Governorship, normally covering in succession the education of three children. Air Marshal Sir Aubrey Ellwood had done likewise in memory of his son, Flying Officer A. J. A. Ellwood, who was killed flying, and Mrs Gregory, the widow of Air Commodore A. L. Gregory, had offered the Fund two presentations.

In 1949 the Fund purchased a single Donation Governor's Presentation at Christ's Hospital. For many years the Governor was Mr Paul Cutting, Secretary (Administration), who exchanged letters every month with the child he had nominated on behalf of the Fund. Having got one presentation, the Controller recalled, 'I said: please could we have some more, but was told that would be most unusual as Christ's Hospital didn't really do this for corporate bodies.' When he persisted, 'The Fund would like nineteen more', his request was refused as contrary to policy.

It was at this stage that Barnes Wallis, who had been educated at Christ's Hospital and was then a member of the Court of Almoners, approached the Fund. Dr Wallis told the Controller that he knew the Fund had been refused presentations and would like to help. The upshot was the creation between Dr Wallis and the Royal Air Force

Benevolent Fund in 1951 of a £20,000 Royal Air Force Foundationers Trust at Christ's Hospital, the Fund to match Wallis's £10,000 inventor's award with £10,000, plus a contribution of one-third of the cost of Foundationers whose fathers were dead or disabled. Five years later the Trust was increased by nearly £11,000, consisting of £911 3s 1d from the Associated British Picture Corporation's première of *The Dam Busters* and £10,000 from the Royal Air Forces Association, being part of cinema foyer collections made by Royal Air Forces Association branches during the showing of the film.

The Royal Air Force Foundationers Trust provides annual studentships at Christ's Hospital in perpetuity — on average three for boys and one for a girl — for the education, maintenance and clothing of boys and girls whose fathers of any rank, and whether or not they have since died, are serving or have served in the Royal Air Force, the Royal Auxiliary Air Force or the Royal Air Force Reserves, and who need help in educating their children.

The following extracts from the Trust Deed record in Sir Barnes Wallis's own words his wishes concerning the selection of candidates:

> In no case should selection be made by means of a competitive examination. That is to say, I earnestly desire selection to be based on the service record of the father, as being a man who has shown himself in the words of Cecil Rhodes, to be a man of 'truth, courage, devotion to duty and sympathy for and protection of the weak', and secondly one who has exhibited during his service days 'moral force of character and an instinct to lead and to take an interest in other men . . .' In addition, the character of the child should of course be taken into account, in that he or she must be of a type that will, as far as can be judged by experienced people, benefit in an outstanding manner by a public school education, and one who has shown, as far as a child of tender years can be expected to show, a desire to serve others rather than themselves.

Some of the Foundationers have since shown signs of emulating the noble character of their fathers and on completion of their education at Christ's Hospital have joined the Royal Air Force, the other armed services, the Police Force, and teachers' training colleges, and most of them have gone to university.

Lord Wolfenden, in an article in *The Times Educational Supplement* on 18 June 1954 wrote:

> The Council of the Fund realized many years ago that money spent on the education of children is one of the most valuable and fruitful investments that the Fund can made. And through-

out the whole range of possible ages and possible types of school this policy is faithfully pursued by the committee and staff.

The essence of the policy can be simply stated. It is that when a member of the Royal Air Force is killed his children should be able to have the kind of education which he could reasonably have hoped to provide for them if he had lived. It is no part of the Fund's duty to provide, automatically or capriciously, an education more expensive or more prolonged than would have been provided by a father who had continued to serve in the Royal Air Force. Nor is it part of the Fund's practice to expend money in such a way as will relieve public funds. The statutory provision made by the Ministry of Pensions, by local authorities, or by other grant-aiding bodies is mobilised in the first instance often as a result of advice proffered by the officials of the Fund itself.

At several schools, notably Christ's Hospital and Wellington College, there are Royal Air Force foundationerships, established either by private generosity or by gifts from the Royal Air Force Central Fund or the Royal Air Force Prize Fund. Other schools, including the Royal Wolverhampton, Reed's School, the Royal Alexandra and Albert School, and the Gordon Boys School (now Gordon's School), have given tremendous assistance to the Fund since the Second World War by educating hundreds of Royal Air Force children under the most favourable terms. Another school, St Edward's, Oxford, produced a large number of gallant men for the Royal Air Force, so much so that the Air Ministry endowed the Guy Gibson Scholarship at the school and paid for a commemorative library window. In addition, both the Fund and the Royal Air Forces Association donated bursaries at this school for sons of deceased and disabled officers and airmen.

From the end of the Second World War to 31 December 1968, some thirty-six thousand educational awards were made and expenditure, including the Fund's own schools at Vanbrugh Castle and Rooks Hill House, amounted to £3,435,702.

The following letter from the orphan son of a fighter pilot summarises the usefulness of the Fund's assistance with education:

I recently [1963] read in the Press that the Royal Air Force Benevolent Fund is having to spend well over half a million pounds each year to relieve distress amongst past and present members of the Royal Air Force and their families, widows and orphans.

As one who has benefited immeasurably from this Fund, I feel that merely to see this sum of £500,000 printed in cold black and white does not give any indication of the constructiveness of the help given to myself and many others.

My father was a fighter pilot in the Royal Air Force during the Second World War. Both he and my mother were killed during the war when I was less than a year old. It was left to my grandparents to bring me up. Soon after I started going to school my grandfather was taken ill and was bed-ridden for five years, until he died. All our family's income went on giving him proper medical care and treatment.

But thanks to this Fund I was still able to receive the first-class education my father would have given me. Because of my grandfather's state of health it was vital that I should go to a boarding school and the Fund helped to finance this. Not only did I receive this aid, but the Fund also helped me to live as normal a life as possible by sending clothing grants, so that I was not obliged to wear my school uniform all the time, and even money to help with holidays.

Nor did I ever feel that the Fund consisted of a bunch of impersonal 'do-gooders'. A keen interest was always taken in everything I did (and still is) and I never found any unwillingness to try to help with every sort of problem. But I am sure that the most important thing I received from this organisation was a sense, throughout the days of my childhood and adolescence, of being quite secure. I honestly feel that as a result of the work of this Fund I had as happy and useful a childhood as any child with parents.

Of one thing I am quite certain. Without this help I should never have been able to gain a University education, as I have done, and the whole course of my life would have been radically different.

May I close by saying that I hope, and indeed I am sure, that other applicants are as grateful to the Royal Air Force Benevolent Fund as I am myself.

Chapter 10
The Conscience of the Nation

'The Royal Air Force Benevolent Fund is part of the conscience of the British nation. A nation without a conscience is a nation without a soul. A nation without a soul is a nation that cannot live.'

Winston Churchill, 1951

'Not a penny too much, not a penny too little.' The Fund had worked faithfully to the Controller's creed and weakened its capital position in the process. Relief expenditure rose steeply to £668,656 in 1948 and to £711,829 in 1949. There were reasons. In many cases wartime savings, gratuities or terminal benefits had been spent. Children were growing up and reaching the expensive age for clothing, maintenance and education. True, recent social legislation, in particular the welfare state and education acts, had partially relieved the pressure but the Fund existed to provide Royal Air Force families with a better future than government assistance alone could offer them.

There was the case, for instance, in which a flying officer had been killed in the First World War before he was able to marry the mother of his child. Between the wars the mother became a teacher, refusing to allow the father's family to educate her son. The boy went to college, passed out as an outstanding young Royal Air Force officer and was killed in 1940 during the Battle of Britain. As the mother became elderly, the Fund heard that she needed assistance and accepted responsibility for her future care.

One case, picked at random. But which cases are to be quoted out of the many thousands of buff folders which pack the basements at Portland Place? Perhaps this one. A Royal Air Force reserve officer died ferrying aircraft in 1945 in the Air Transport Auxiliary. His daughter, after taking a scholarship to university with the object of graduating as a teacher, contracted polio and was paralysed from the neck downwards. She spent six months in an iron lung. Later, assisted by the Fund, she entered a specialist's private nursing home and after that a residence for polio victims. Gradually the girl's health improved as a result of all this private and costly care, and in time her scholarship was restored. Yet, in order to make use of it, she needed the attendance of a trained nurse companion, whose salary was paid for by the Fund. Thus assisted, the pilot's daughter took her degree and became a teacher — a happy ending to a sad story, and it had been achieved as a result of great personal courage on the part of the beneficiary and a considerable sum from the Fund.

However, the cumulative relief of such individual cases was by no means the only cause of the post-war rise of expenditure. At this time, and it merits repetition, substantial sums were paid to outside organisations in accordance with the Fund's old and proven policy of co-operating with kindred bodies. This form of investment was costly at the outset but the annual dividends in educational openings and opportunities, hospital beds, front-door keys, convalescent and many other facilities have amply rewarded each act of faith.

Some further examples, other than the £10,000 contribution towards the Royal Air Force Foundationerships at Christ's Hospital, are: £34,000 for the Royal Star and Garter Home at Richmond for disabled sailors, soldiers, and airmen, endowing six Air Force beds; £60,000 for endowing six beds at the Royal Air Forces Association Home at Sussexdown and contributing towards modernisation of the building; £2,600 to the Papworth Village Settlement to build two houses for pulmonary tuberculosis patients; £3,000 to King Edward VII's Hospital for Officers — Sister Agnes's — to endow a Royal Air Force bed and contribute towards their extension.

In addition, regular donations have been made to such organisations as the Royal Hospital and Home for Incurables, Putney; the Queen Elizabeth Foundation for the Disabled at Exeter; the Queen Alexandra Hospital Home, Gifford House, Worthing; Chaseley Home for the seriously paralysed at Eastbourne; the Ex-Services Mental Welfare Society; the Thistle Foundation, Edinburgh; the Scottish National Institution for the War Blinded; and many others.

Nor were those men forgotten who had travelled from overseas to fight for Britain in the Royal Air Force. Throughout the war men had arrived from many countries to join the Royal Air Force, and after the war the Fund acted to keep open the lines of communication to these men in their home lands.

Within the United Kingdom a Scottish branch had functioned since 1947. For twenty-one years until his retirement in August 1978, Air Marshal Sir Brian Baker, who won the DSO, the AFC and the MC in the First World War. had been the Branch Secretary and as well as supervising the welfare work had been instrumental in raising large donations in Scotland. But the Fund was concerned that neither in Northern Ireland not in the Republic of Ireland was the Fund directly represented. In the war, with the approval of their governments, 10,000 men had joined the Royal Air Force from Northern Ireland, including many who had crossed the border from Eire to enlist; a further 16,000 men had entered the service from Eire. The Controller visited Northern Ireland and the Republic of Ireland in 1948. Finding that 'pawning clothing on Monday and redeeming it on Saturday was a custom, and money-lending was rife', the Fund swiftly established branches in Belfast and Dublin, with the approval of the governments in Northern Ireland and Eire. Sir Basil Goulding has been Chairman of the Republic of Ireland Branch since its inception and Wing Commander J. Higginson the Chairman and Hon. Secretary of the Northern Ireland Branch since 1968. For many years Higginson raised money at Battle of Britain time each September by signing letters of appeal to all the Churches in Northern Ireland.

But, if resettlement was rough for the Irish, the state of the 4,600 Jamaicans and 900 other British West Indians who had served in the Royal Air Force was grievous. The Controller visited Jamaica in 1950 and was appalled by the poverty and living conditions of many of those who had served in the war. So the Fund raised a Committee at Kingston, which was to prove very active under the Chairmanship of Squadron Leader (later Major) H. G. Vyse, to carry on the excellent work of Flight Lieutenant C. S. Williams, who had personally represented the Fund while commanding a small wartime administration unit there.

Between 1948 and 1967 the sum of £38,638 has been spent on all forms of relief in Jamaica but conditions are so wholly different in the West Indies from those in Britain that the Fund makes no claim to dispense relief on equal terms. In the course of his travels the Controller also visited the United States, where he thanked Mrs Edward Antony of New York for the great volume of welfare work she had devoted to the Royal Air Force aircrew trainees whilst in the United States during the war. He also conferred with the organisers of the Air Force Aid Society, the Royal Air Force Benevolent Fund's equivalent organisation, which had been formed during the war after consultation with Riverdale and Cordingley. The Fund was glad in this modest way to be of further service to the Air Force Aid Society of the nation which established a Royal Air Force Benevolent Fund (USA) Inc. in 1940 and contributed generously to the Fund before United States entry into the war.

In South Africa Mrs A. C. Haswell, a former Chairman of the South African Air Force Fund, was appointed the Fund's Honorary Representative in 1949. Applications from ex-members of the Royal Air Force resident in South Africa were referred to her in the first place. For many years Mrs Haswell held an imprest account on behalf of the Royal Air Force Benevolent Fund and as well as dealing with disbursement of assistance she also received loan repayments in that country. Air Vice-Marshal Sir Matthew Frew and Wing Commander W. H. Moyles, who retired from the Royal Air Force and settled in Johannesburg, were also appointed Fund Representatives.

No more branches were established outside Britain but imprest accounts were opened in various localities so that eligible ex-servicemen and women might be assisted in time of need everywhere in the world, except behind the Iron Curtain where investigation is not possible. So great were the outgoings at home and abroad that in 1949 expenditure of £776,942 exceeded the income by £308,855 and resulted in a sale of investments totalling £365,055. Spanning 1948-50 the Fund's expenditure exceeded income by £548,559. The sale of investments was not the happiest of decisions and the Fund had to brace itself to spend capital as well as income. It would have to seek a peacetime income, as it had between the wars, but with the difference that this time it was more experienced and better equipped to do so.

Thus, the burden would ordinarily have fallen squarely on the shoulders of Sir Bertram Rumble, who had been knighted in 1947. Rumble, while retaining his Appeals Secretaryship, and still unpaid, was also Honorary Treasurer, having succeeded Air Commodore B. C. H. Drew in that appointment in 1944. But, sadly, Sir Bertram did not live long enough to meet this new challenge. When he died in 1948 it was calculated that £6 million had been raised during his seven years as Appeals Secretary.

Sir Bertram's successor as Honorary Treasurer was an ex-Air Minister, Sir Archibald Sinclair — later Lord Thurso — who had served the Churchill Government in that office throughout the war. Lord Thurso was the Honorary Treasurer of the Fund from 1949 to 1969. Before his death in 1970 he helped to reshape the financial policy of the Fund. Viscount Ward of Witley, a former Secretary of State for Air, succeeded him. He served until 1987 and died in 1988 after serving the Fund since 1958 when he was appointed a vice-president.

After the end of the Second World War Group Captain J. E. Redding, before becoming a member of the Grants Committee, had given talks about the Fund at every Royal Air Force Station at home and abroad. Some years later a film about the Fund had been shown twice at six-monthly intervals on an equally wide circuit within the Service. But the Service was contracting rapidly and some other source of income was required.

Though Royal Air Force voluntary subscriptions were improving now that sixty-two per cent of serving officers and fifty-four per cent of serving airmen and airwomen were in the scheme, the Finance and General Purposes Committee was soon faced with the prospect of a further and substantial loss of capital. This was temporarily averted by a windfall.

The Royal Air Force is not normally associated with prize money, the traditional perquisite of the Royal Navy, but under the Prize Act of 1948 the Royal Air Force received £1,250,000, a share which was largely due to Coastal Command air operations over the sea.

In naval practice prize money is distributed among officers and ratings, but the Air Ministry, having a smaller sum to divide, established the Royal Air Force Prize Fund for charitable and similar purposes. It was the Air Council's gift of £200,000 from this fund that prevented another sale of Royal Air Force Benevolent Fund investments in 1950. In 1951 a further £100,000 from the Prize Fund was received, to be held in trust for the education of children of deceased service people killed on duty or whose death was attributable to service; a final gift from this source of £14,630 19s 10d being received in 1959.

In the red as the Royal Air Force Benevolent Fund was, where expenditure over income was concerned, the Fund was especially aggrieved in 1948 to be criticised by *The People* Sunday newspaper.

Hesitantly, the Fund had recently engaged the public relations consultancy of F. J. Lyons and was sunning itself in the comforting rays of frequent publication of complimentary news items and feature articles. but now it was to learn the lesson of any publicity seeker: that the retention of good public relations counsel does not indemnify against a critical press. On Sunday 23 May 1948 *The People*, opening a series of articles on service charities, accused the Army Benevolent Fund of hoarding and promised future disclosures about 'the equally amazing state of affairs inside the Royal Air Force Benevolent Fund'.

The phrasing of this trailer came as a thunderclap, but when the article appeared a week later it was clear that the newspaper had assembled a carefully documented argument even if the Fund could not accept its basic premise: that ex-Royal Air Force families went in distress while the Royal Air Force Benevolent Fund sat on its millions.

The newspaper alleged that 30,000 ex-Royal Air Force service people had been helped in 1947 while the appeals of another 30,000 were turned down: 'Every other man or woman who appealed for help was refused, yet there is still nearly £6 million to be spent.'

The Controller's explanation was quoted:

> It is our policy to conserve our Fund. If we answered every call that is made upon us without exercising some sense of responsibility we would very soon run out of money. We have to think of the future . . . In ten years' time there may be another slump like the one we knew in 1931. There are four and a half million people liable to call upon our funds if there is such a slump and we have got to be ready for it. After all it will not be much use making new appeals for war heroes in 1948. The people have too short a memory.

It was emphasised that the Fund had to plan many years ahead for education, especially university education. But in the euphoric atmosphere of post-war welfare and education measures *The People* disputed the need for such prudence. In retrospect it can be fairly observed that the Council's determination to preserve the Fund has been justified many times over since 1948, especially in the late 1950s and the 1960s. But in 1948 when the war had been over for only three years there was a natural demand among some donors and recipients for the immediate use of money that had been given while the enemy was overhead.

The Fund understood this and told *The People*, 'Send us any cases of airmen in need and we will see that they are investigated and every possible help given.'

On 5 December 1948 *The People* announced that it had sent 650 cases to the Fund, of which 367 had never before applied for assistance and 204 had been assisted previously. Readers' letters had resulted in 418 grants totalling £11,925 18s 9d. After this announcement 537 more letters were received, resulting in 332 cases of assistance.

The thunderclap had fallen and had cleared the air with gain to all concerned. The Fund was delighted that the publicity had produced so many new cases — forty-four per cent from ex-servicemen and women or dependants who were apparently unaware the Fund existed — and *The People* could, and did, congratulate itself on a successful campaign.

A few years after *The People* episode another publicity opportunity arose, this time to beat that highly respectable and much sought after broadcast appeal drum, known the world over as the British

Broadcasting Corporation's weekly charity appeal broadcast. Competition is keen among charities for acceptance in this Sunday night 'commercial' and the Fund was obliged to wait six years before receiving its third call to Broadcasting House.

Viscount Trenchard had made the first radio appeal in 1940, and there had been no further broadcast since Viscount Portal's on Battle of Britain Sunday in 1945. The Fund had sought a Week's Good Cause opportunity for some while. When, at last, the Fund was offered Battle of Britain Sunday, 16 September 1951, the Controller knew that there was only one man he wanted for the broadcast. There were problems, however; Winston Churchill, aged seventy-six, was out of office and as Leader of the Opposition was more free to accept an invitation. But the British Broadcasting Corporation warned, 'You'll never get him.' Churchill had made only one previous broadcast appeal, for another charity before the war.

He would have to be won over by strategy and the Controller took up the challenge. There were four factors which had to be considered — Churchill's reputation for personal loyalty, his sense of duty, his impulsive character, and his sense of the fitness of occasion:

1. Loyalty: Well, the Chairman, the Deputy Chairman and the Honorary Treasurer of the Fund had each served handsomely in the war. Riverdale had negotiated the Empire Air Training Scheme; Portal had run the Air Force as Chief of The Air Staff under Churchill's minister, Sir Archibald Sinclair.

2. Duty: The Fund felt that a man who can say 'Never in the field of human conflict was so much owed by so many to so few' must carry some responsibility for saying it.

3. Impulse: The request must be submitted in such a way and at such a moment as to elicit an impulsive 'yes'.

4. Occasion: Imperative for getting that decisive 'yes'. Must be warm and congenial, preferably connected with wartime memories and in wartime company.

The Controller went to work and at the appropriate time he had arranged for Churchill to receive a written invitation to make the broadcast under the signatures of Riverdale, Portal and Sinclair. Moreover, he had the letter delivered on the very day on which Churchill happened to be entertaining the Portals at a family lunch.

Unbeknown to anyone, Princess Marina had also played her part in securing Churchill's agreement to make this broadcast. On 20 July 1951 the Princess wrote privately to Churchill, who was an old friend of hers, to ask for his help in this way; on 26 July he replied as follows:

I thank Your Royal Highness for your letter of the 20 July about the broadcast appeal for the Royal Air Force Benevolent Fund on 'Battle of Britain' Sunday. I am shortly going to be abroad, but I expect to be back in time for this event and will be glad to make this broadcast for the Fund. I am indeed complimented that Your Royal Highness should wish me to do so.

The broadcast took place on Battle of Britain Sunday in September 1951, and, over and above the unique advantage Churchill's name and voice brought to the appeal, the recording provided the nation with a remarkable radio archive. It was the first time that the war leader's immortal tribute to 'The Few' had been heard in public. Much published though the tribute was, it had been spoken in the House of Commons in 1940. Opening his broadcast, Churchill said:

'Never in the field of human conflict was so much owed by so many to so few.'

With those words in 1940 — our darkest and yet our finest hour — I reported to the House of Commons on the progress of the Battle of Britain, whose eleventh anniversary we now celebrate. I repeat my words tonight with pride and gratitude. They spring from our hearts as keenly at this moment as on the day I uttered them. Time dims our memories of many events which, while they are happening, seem tremendous. But the fame of the pilots — a thin blue line indeed — who broke the aerial might of the enemy and saved their native land shines ever more brightly.

Our debt is now not only to 'The Few'. As the Royal Air Force grew larger and larger and the hard years of war unrolled, many thousands of their comrades died so that our Island might live, free and inviolate. By 1945, alas, as our casualty lists told the tale, 'The Few' had become 'The Many'. Had it not been for those young men whose daring and devotion cast a glittering shield between us and our foe, we should none of us be sitting at rest in our homes this Sunday evening, as members of an unconquered — and, as we believe, unconquerable — Nation. Let us all welcome this chance to pay a small measure of *the debt we owe* to the paladins of the Royal Air Force. And I will tell you one thing we can do, and do now.

I am appealing to you tonight on behalf of the Royal Air Force Benevolent Fund. This Fund exists solely to help members of the Royal Air Force — men and women — in time of need, and their families or dependants when they are in trouble. More than two million pounds has been spent in this cause during the last three years alone. The money which has been spent by the Royal Air Force Benevolent Fund has gone beyond the Fund's ordinary income by nearly £600,000. A renewed effort must be made if the future is not to be overclouded.

My friends, I am certain we are all together on this and that we are all agreed upon our purpose. We all rejoice that there is a Royal Air Force Benevolent Fund to give help to the dependants of those undaunted men who lost their lives in the war or have died since, leaving their record behind them. This fine organisation, for which I now appeal, has fortunately up to the present always been able to give at least a measure of aid.

It is our duty now to make sure that the Fund will be able to go on helping, and will not fail as the survivors of the war grow old and feeble. Only thus can the Fund maintain its claim and reputation that no genuine case of distress is ever turned away. The Royal Air Force Benevolent Fund is part of the conscience of the British Nation. A Nation without a conscience is a Nation without a soul. A Nation without a soul is a Nation that cannot live.

Please send whatever you can to Winston Churchill, Royal Air Force Benevolent Fund', 1 Sloane Street, London SW1.

I thank you for listening to me. Goodnight.

Donations ranging from 6d to £1,000 arrived from all over Britain and the world. At the final count £26,460 had been received, including the remainder of the rifled contents of a mail bag recovered from the dark waters of the Serpentine, where it had been tossed by a gang of thieves.

Shortly after the broadcast the Controller was at home one Saturday morning when Winston Churchill came on the line. 'Sir John, how is the appeal? I was going to send you my cheque but I've got a better idea. A film has been made of me. I'll give you that film to show all over the country if you'll give me a quick decision. Korda has the film. Go and see it.'

The Controller went to Sir Alexander Korda's home and saw *The Robin Gets Its Wings*, a charming reel, starring a robin coming closer and closer to Churchill until it fed out of his hand. Cordingley saw at once that the Fund could capitalise on that robin.

By this time Churchill's interest in the idea had been thoroughly aroused. With the assistance of the documentary film producer, Mr Castleton Knight, of the Rank Organisation, a short film was made about the Fund, using the robin sequence as the centrepiece. When the film was ready Churchill, now back in office as Prime Minister, was on his way to the United States and insisted upon seeing it there. Back across the Atlantic came some suggested modifications and the instructions that whatever else was done to the film the robin sequence must remain intact. The commentary of the completed film was supplied by Churchill's appeal broadcast.

With the cheerful co-operation of the cinema industry the film was widely exhibited and, although unfortunately for the Fund it clashed during its run with a King George VI memorial film and the Lord Mayor of London's Flood Relief Fund for the East Coast flood victims, it produced £54,300. Together, Churchill's appeal broadcast and film benefited the Fund by a total of £80,760.

While, thanks to the co-operation of Sir John Davis of the Rank Organisation and Sir Philip Warter of the Associated British Picture Corporation, Churchill and his robin provided the Fund's most spectacular screen result in this period, the Fund is indebted to film producers and cinema exhibitors for their friendship over many years, and after the Churchill film a reception was held at the Ministry of Defence, Whitehall, attended by Princess Marina, members of the Air Council and leaders of the cinema industry.

A flair for quality showmanship, whether in the foyer or on the airfield, had long been one of the Fund's appeal attributes. It was, therefore, not surprising that five years after the war the Fund returned to the air display as a source of income. In 1950 the Fund accepted the Air Council's invitation to make all arrangements, outside the flying programme, for the Royal Air Force's first post-war air display at Farnborough. It took place on 7 and 8 July. Obviously, the revival of the full Royal Air Force air display as a form of appeal raised many problems, including the negotiation of insurance cover against accident. Nevertheless, the Fund, after consultation with the Air Ministry, decided to be its own 'showman' and to organise the display in return for any profits.

With this object, the Royal Air Force Benevolent Fund Development Trust was formed to finance the promotion and presentation of air displays. Approving a grant of £30,000 from the Royal Air Force Central Fund, the Air Council gave this new and separate trust a start in life. At one stage of the preparations the Fund was committed to an expenditure of more than £30,000. Because a weather insurance policy had been rejected on grounds of expense, a bad weather forecast was initially depressing. But the clouds cleared and the two-day event at Farnborough was a great success. The occasion was graced by the presence of King George VI, the Queen, Princess Margaret and Princess Marina. 130,000 people were admitted to the display and the Fund profited by £8,995.

The resumption of the traditional air display, the great coup represented by the Churchill broadcast appeal and the general improvements under Sir John Cordingley's administration are to be especially numbered among the Fund's achievements in the closing days of Lord Riverdale's chairmanship. During his twelve years in office he had done a great amount of entertaining on behalf of the Fund at his own expense. He had introduced, with the concurrence of the National Provincial Bank of which had was a Director, Mr Francis Wilkins, the head of the Bank's Stock and Investment Department, whose advice on investments was of enormous value to the Fund. Riverdale's directorship of the Halifax Building Society had also been most useful when the Fund started to finance mortgages for the beneficiaries. Although often away from London, he kept in close touch, by telephone, with all its affairs.

It should not pass unrecorded that Riverdale's family, like so many he had worked to help, had suffered its loss in war too. Lord Riverdale's son-in-law, Group Captain E. J. L. Hope, had been killed in air operations in 1941, and his memory was perpetuated by Lady Riverdale's £200-a-year Jack Hope Scholarship at Wellington College.

Riverdale was in his eightieth year when in 1952 he announced his wish to retire, and when this became effective on 31 December 1952 he received the following letter from the Private Secretary to The Queen:

Buckingham Palace
12 January 1953

My Dear Lord Riverdale,

I have laid your letter before The Queen.

Her Majesty is indeed sorry to hear that you feel obliged to give up the Chairmanship of the Royal Air Force Benevolent Fund, for she well knows what an incalculable benefit to it your long and devoted service as the Head of its Council has been. It must be a great satisfaction to you to leave the Fund in so flourishing a condition as it now is, and to look back on all the good results it has achieved throughout your twelve years' association with it.

I am to send you The Queen's best wishes for an improvement in your health.

Yours sincerely,
A. Lascelles.

Chapter 11
Policy Reappraisal

'No matter what provision we make there will always be a place for voluntary organisations. For only by voluntary organisation are you able to touch the bottomless reservoir of kindness, humanity and self-sacrifice.'

Aneurin Bevan, 1950

Lord Knollys succeeded Lord Riverdale as Chairman of the Royal Air Force Benevolent Fund in the new year of 1953, Marshal of the Royal Air Force Lord Portal continuing as Deputy Chairman. At Knollys's election Portal reminded the Council: 'We consider that the practice hitherto that the Chairman should be a civilian with wide experience of business life outside the service, and not a retired Royal Air Force officer, is an extremely sound one and should be adhered to.'

Although Lord Portal did not refer to it on this occasion, another practice in the making of the Council's chief appointments is the appointment of a retired senior regular Royal Air Force officer as Chairman of the Grants Committee. The holder of the office was Air Chief Marshal Sir Francis J. Fogarty, a former Air Member for Personnel, who in 1957 succeeded Air Chief Marshal Sir James Robb.

While most of Lord Knollys's working experience had been outside the service — he was a banker by early training — he had been connected with military or civil aviation for much of his life. From the 16th London Regiment in the First World War, he had joined the Royal Flying Corps and had won the Distinguished Flying Cross. Appointed Chairman of British Airways Overseas Corporation in 1943, he had led Britain's overseas airline through the transition from war to peace and in 1956 he was to become, in addition to chairman of a great insurance corporation, chairman of Vickers, an appointment which kept him in touch with the Royal Air Force. In every respect Knollys fulfilled the Fund's preference for a Chairman of 'wide experience of business and life outside the service'. His experience of public service included the Governorship of Bermuda and a senior appointment at the British Embassy in Washington.

Although, as will be recalled, the new constitution approved by Mr Justice Harman in 1948 had sanctioned a more adventurous investment policy than the majority of charities were permitted before the passing of the Trustee Investments Act of 1961, general conditions had frustrated advantage being taken of this remarkable opportunity until shortly before Lord Knollys's arrival.

It was not that the Controller with his bright eye to the opportunity had not keenly sounded the Fund's honorary investment and property advisers, Wilkins of the National Provincial Bank and Wallace Withers of Debenham, Tewson and Chinnocks, but that under Riverdale's leadership the Fund had of necessity picked its way cautiously towards a change. Looking back, no praise can be too high for these two investment consultants who advised the Fund on its first equity and property investments, which nowadays form a substantial and profitable part of the Fund's investment portfolio. Thanks are also due to Sir Ronald Thornton, a Vice-Chairman of Barclays Bank and later a Director of the Bank of England, for his helpful advice.

Nevertheless, at the end of 1951 the Controller, who had been growing increasingly apprehensive about many opportunities that were slipping by, had decided to sound the Chairman, suggesting that the Fund ought perhaps to provide itself with a greater margin of safety against the falling purchasing power of the pound by transferring some of its assets to real estate, property and equity shares. Lord Riverdale's response was not enthusiastic. The Chairman, who had guided the Fund's investments and financial affairs for so long, expressed himself as naturally cautious about any change 'which might leave us open, however slightly, to an allegation that there is a speculative element in our investment policy'. He did agree, however, that the Controller should discuss the matter with Lord Portal in his separate capacities as Deputy Chairman of the Royal Air Force Benevolent Fund and on the Boards of Barclays Bank and Barclays DCO.

It was now very apparent that, if the Fund was to arrest the decline in the book value of its assets and to improve its capital position under peacetime conditions, a somewhat drastic alteration of its investment policy would be required.

By the following May many soundings had been taken of the investment and property worlds as a result of the Chairman's amber light; and the council learned that the Finance and General Purposes Committee had decided, after searching investigation, to consider suitable properties with first-class covenants for investment within a current limit of £250,000 and to invest in carefully selected ordinary stocks and shares to the same limit.

The Chairman was unable to attend this meeting but in his absence it was reported:

> Lord Riverdale considers that the change in the investment policy is necessary in the light of the economic and financial position. He commends it as being in the best interests of the Fund, bearing in mind that inflation affects the Fund in two ways: firstly, by reducing the purchasing value of income and, secondly, by increasing the rate of assistance we have to give.

At the outset of Lord Knollys's Chairmanship, the Fund's appeal side came under scrutiny. Already those of late middle age when the Royal Air Force fought the Battle of Britain were approaching the end of their lives. Memories of the war were fading too.

Inevitably the question arose; where could the Fund look for future support outside such routine sources as the service personnel voluntary subscriptions scheme, Battle of Britain week 'At Homes' at Royal Air Force stations, the Royal Air Forces Association, and other intermittent or incidental appeal activities?

The answer lay in the general public, and a need to strike a balance between reminding the public of its past debt to the Royal Air Force and emphasising that the inheritors of the Air Force's wartime tradition were still occupationally liable to death or disablement.

But the Fund was closely exercised as to the best approach now that the direct, and in retrospect somewhat brash, appeal of wartime could no longer be employed. For in the 1950s it seemed hardly credible that the Fund had actually touched off a big response by mailing this sentiment:

> If it were not for the men of the Royal Air Force, Hitler would be now in Buckingham Palace and Goering swigging Ribbentrop's champagne in the Savoy. You and I and our children would be dead or slaves. Men who have saved us and who are daily saving us from such a fate deserve something more than State help and State support for those whom they love when they fall on evil days.

Very true, but it simply would not do in 1952!

It was plain that what was required was a steady flow of factual publicity. The Controller therefore encouraged F. J. Lyons, its public relations consultant, to increase its activities. For more than thirty years Peter Taylor, a former RAF officer, at first a senior partner of F. J. Lyons and more recently a private consultant, notified newspapers throughout the country of the quarterly and annual relief expenditure of the Fund in every county and and most principal cities of the United Kingdom. Approved news and gifts and legacies and of the money-raising activities of the Charity were prominent in Taylor's output of feature articles and news stories about the Fund. Paid advertising for many years was placed through Dorland Advertising.

The Fund is often remembered in donors' wills, and just occasionally a wealthy man's estate will reveal a windfall, as happened in the magnificent benefaction of the Hattersley bequest. It was puzzling because, in contrast for example with a former colliery-owner, Mr H. Watson-Smith, who left the Fund £30,000 and endowed a scholarship in memory of a son killed in the Royal Air Force, Mr R. E. Hattersley, an industrialist, appeared to have no association with the Royal Air Force.

Hattersley, who died on 2 May 1949, left the residue of his estate to the Fund following the death of his wife. She died on 8 January 1952. This placed almost the entire ordinary share capital of his company, Hattersley (Ormskirk) Limited — since merged with Peglers (Holdings) Limited — in the Trust of the Royal Air Force Benevolent Fund; his total bequest, with other investments, provided the Fund with approximately £320,000 at probate valuation. Subsequently, the Hattersley shares were increased by bonus issues and sales of shares have produced £428,405.

It is known that Hattersley considered that but for the Royal Air Force he would have had nothing to leave and that the Royal Air Force Benevolent Fund was the soundest service charity he could find. It seems fair, therefore, to surmise that the publicised memories of Royal Air Force exploits and post-war publicity of the Fund's activities may have inspired this outstanding legacy, as no doubt they have inspired others.

While, in general, legacies large or small are as uncomplicated as the Hattersley bequest, the Fund is occasionally disappointed where a will has been incorrectly drawn. To take one very substantial example, it had appeared from the will of Mr Philip Hill, a financier, that he had intended to benefit the Fund to the extent of several hundred thousand pounds after his widow's death, but the Courts ruled that the Fund had no claim. However, the Fund was much comforted to learn later that Mr Hill's widow had instructed her trustee to give it especial consideration after her death.

A number of gifts have been directly linked with Royal Air Force exploits. For example, when Herr Barge Moltke-Leth handed the

Fund £4,000 in Copenhagen the gift represented the Danish resistance movement's acknowledgement of the bombing by the Royal Air Force of Gestapo headquarters in Denmark. Presenting the cheque, Herr Moltke-Leth explained that, after the liberation, the Royal Air Force had flown a number of air displays to benefit Danish families which had suffered from their action. After receiving the gift, the Fund transferred £1,000 to the Royal Australian Air Force in respect of two Flying Officers of the Royal Australian Air Force who were killed while taking part in the attack.

Another gift which revived wartime memories came from former British officers, mostly Royal Air Force, who made contributions from their pay to finance escapes and to assist those in need. Under the lead of Group Captain H. M. A. Day, the senior British officer in the Stalag Luft camp, the escapees at the end of the war had a large surplus in Reichmarks against which the Treasury made available £11,000. The Escaping Society, after advertising their intention, entrusted their savings to the Fund, stipulating that the money must help Royal Air Force officers or airmen ex-prisoners-of-war in Europe, or their dependants, with the provision that any capital remaining after twenty-five years be absorbed in the general fund of the charity. The money was finally expended during 1961 after 127 awards had been made.

In 1961 the Executive Committee of the Royal Air Force Church, St Clement Danes, Strand, London, presented an oak table to the church to mark the Royal Air Force Benevolent Fund's work for the Service.

Besides seeking publicity for bequests and its general activities, the Fund has initiated social functions in recent years, some of which have brought the double advantage of income and publicity. But, with a few exceptions, balls, dances and entertainments in London other than film premières generously offered by the cinema industry have been eschewed.

There are more profitable methods of raising money and the Appeals Department has always endeavoured to keep up with the expenditure of the Grants Committee. Neither did Sir John Cordingley spare his own back, because he had no objection to repeating a published description of himself as 'the unbeaten champion beggar of the world, 1956-60'. This tag was in some ways a disservice to his scrupulous ideals but its creator, Air Chief Marshal Sir Hubert Patch, had a point. To encounter the Controller on his social round was a revelation. Lord Mayors with charitable funds at their disposal, great companies of charitable disposition, millionaires, all were assailed. There was the occasion, for instance, when he encountered the late Lord Marks at a St James's Palace party to celebrate the fortieth birthday of the Royal Air Force Benevolent Fund, and Lord Marks promised a donation of £5,000. A cheque for £7,000 was received. Making his retirement address to the Council, in 1962, Sir John reflected: 'Sometimes I blush to think of the extent to which I have bothered some of those people but when begging is one of the principal functions one has to have an element of toughness in the make-up.'

The Controller's approach was equally direct when he broached the highly successful unwanted foreign coins scheme. Lunching opposite Sir Anthony Milward of British European Airways, Sir John Cordingley asked, 'Do you know that your show, when you bend anything, is very expensive to us? Because so many of your aircrew are ex-Air Force the burden falls more heavily on us than it does on you.' The Fund was seeking — and obtained — a page dealing with the unwanted coins scheme in the British European Airways booklet, *About Your Flight*. Between 1955 and 1967 this scheme, through which returning air travellers were invited to drop their 'chicken-feed' coins into airport boxes collected £20,238. Thereafter, it brought in about £1,500 a year for some years. Boxes were provided at more than twelve airports and also some of the Channel crossing ports. The coins were exchanged by Thomas Cook and Son, who found small coins from as many as forty-five countries in one box.

On one occasion an American visitor dropped in a silver dollar by mistake. Reporting that he attached great sentimental value to the coin, the American asked for its return. Cook's found the coin and the Fund was delighted to receive a donation of far greater value from Mr Amory Houghton, former United States Ambassador to France and head of Corning Glass.

The Controller, recalling the origin of this enterprising idea, said:

At the outset we noticed a letter in *The Times* suggesting that charities were missing a good opportunity by not collecting unwanted foreign coins. I sent a letter to *The Times* stating that we were not quite as bad as that because we had explored this means of raising money and were informed that we could not do it as we were not licensed to act as bankers. Mr E. W. Berry, the Foreign Exchange Manager in Thomas Cook's office, rang me and said that Cook's were licensed as bankers and would gladly do the exchanging and banking part of the business, if we organised the collection of the coins. That is how the scheme started and when British Railways refused us permission to install the boxes at the seaports Thomas Cook's came along and said, 'We have a kiosk. You can hang your box on the outside' — which we did.

Another income-producing idea introduced by Rumble was the 'take a little, give a little' lighter fuel scheme, with which almost every smoker in the land will have been familiar. Launched in 1949, the scheme had produced more than £50,000 after payment of all expenses when it was discontinued in its original form in 1964, partly because of the spread of gas lighters.

From time to time the Fund was challenged that its eagerness to put its name to foyer, lighter fuel or foreign coin collections was at variance with its policy not to participate in flag days. In reply the Fund said that there was a distinction between collecting money for a flag and accepting money after giving a service such as the famous Churchill robin film, a drop of lighter fuel, or even relieving the weary traveller of his 'chicken-feed' coins.

Naturally, Battle of Britain week over the years has offered the Fund its best opportunities for publicity, such as the Chairman's annual letter to the press and the gift from Rolls-Royce of the front cover of *Flight*, and to 'earn' money when Royal Air Force stations are 'At Home' to the public. Proceeds from car parking and side-shows are shared with the Royal Air Forces Association, there being no entrance fees. 'At Homes' are the modern counterparts of the Hendon and Empire Air Displays.

Here the Fund has been exceptionally adventurous, producing, originally at the suggestion of the Air Ministry, its own *Battle of Britain Souvenir Book* and co-operating with the Royal Air Forces Association and the Ministry of Defence over its sale and distribution. The *Souvenir Book*, now the *Royal Air Force Yearbook*, has been published annually by the Fund since 1960, to the shared benefit of the Fund and the Royal Air Forces Association.

On Battle of Britain Sunday each year at Westminster Abbey, and in many churches throughout the country, there are special services at which the collections are allotted to the Fund, with the foreknowledge and support of the heads of those churches, who every year draw the attention of their clergy to this observance.

Battle of Britain Week is an annual occurrence but there is one permanent exhibition of benefit to the Fund and this is to be found at Salisbury Hall near St Albans, formerly the home of Mr W. J. Goldsmith, where W 4050, the prototype de Havilland Mosquito, is the centrepiece of the Mosquito Memorial Museum, which houses a wide selection of historic de Havilland aircraft and their engines. This moated pocket manor house, where Nell Gwyn once lived and where Winston Churchill visited and fished as a boy, has become a place of pilgrimage for followers of the Stuarts and lovers of historic aircraft. But with respect to Nell, it is the aircraft that attract the crowds and the money for the Fund.

Visitors learn of the unusual and romantic circumstances in which the first Mosquito was designed in the manor house, assembled alongside the moat and flown from an adjacent field.

The Fund's most glittering annual event takes place indoors. Beginning in 1956 and repeated each April on a night as near as possible to the anniversary of the birth of the Royal Air Force on 1 April 1918, members of the Air Council, or nowadays of the Air Force Board of the Defence Council, and a large attendance of distinguished people at the Royal Festival Hall have joined an audience consisting predominantly of present and past members of the Royal Air Force and their families for the Royal Air Force Anniversary Concert. The concerts were the joint inspiration of Sir John Barbirolli and of the late Kenneth Crickmore, who as Secretary and Director of the Hallé Concerts Society asked the Air Council if it might associate itself publicly with the Royal Air Force for the benefit of the service. Appreciative of the gesture, the Air Council suggested that the Fund should be the beneficiary and be responsible for arrangements.

The opening concert at the Royal Albert Hall on 7 April 1956 was attended by Her Majesty The Queen and His Royal Highness Prince Philip, who also attended the tenth anniversary concert in 1965 at the Royal Festival Hall. Other members of the Royal Family who have attended the concerts include Princess Margaret, Princess Anne, the late Princess Royal, the late Princess Marina, the Duke of Kent, Princess Alexandra and Princess Alice, Countess of Athlone. In 1961 the Queen Mother attended a concert at the Royal Festival Hall in commemoration of the twenty-first anniversary of the Battle of Britain, and returned in April 1978 for the Royal Air Force Diamond Jubilee Concert.

The concert in the Royal Festival Hall on 5 April 1968 in the presence of Princess Marina was given to celebrate the Golden Jubilee of the Royal Air Force.

Since the introduction of concerts in 1956 the orchestras have performed together with the Central Band of the Royal Air Force. Many conductors and soloists have given their services without fee. Conductors who have thus benefited the Fund include Sir John

Barbirolli, Sir Arthur Bliss, Sir Charles Groves, Wing Commander A. E. Sims, Wing Commander J. L. Wallace, Wing Commander R. E. C. Davies, Wing Commander J. Martindale and Wing Commander E. Banks. The soloists have included Agustin Anievas, Gina Bachauer, Peter Frankl, Dame Myra Hess, Jose Iturbi, Eileen Joyce, Julius Katchen, Peter Katin, Malcuzynski, Denis Matthews, Yehudi Menuhin, Henryk Szeryng, Constance Shacklock, Fou Ts'ong, Tamas Vasary and several others. The Royal Air Force Anniversary Concert continues to be one of the chief social occasions in the Fund's diary.

Anniversaries that call for an unadorned and simple act of remembrance are observed at the Royal Air Force Memorial, Victoria Embankment, for which the Fund is responsible. Each year on Battle of Britain Sunday the Chief of the Air Staff places a wreath there on his way to the Thanksgiving Service at Westminster Abbey. On Remembrance Day a very large wreath in the shape of a pilot's brevet with a twelve-foot wingspan is attached to the Memorial at dawn. Some years ago it was found that if a strong breeze happened to be blowing along the Thames the wreath was inclined to take off. The Fund sought suggestions from its friends and the Royal Air Forces Association proposed attaching a symbolic propeller to the Memorial to hold the wreath in place. But the architect disagreed. 'The Memorial', he commented, 'embodies something better than a mere portrayal of the arms and mechanism with which the Royal Flying Corps and Royal Air Force accomplished their noble achievements.' He advised the fitting of inconspicuous lugs faced with the Royal Air Force Badge to which wreaths might be secured and his advice was accepted.

Lord Trenchard, to whose inspiration the Memorial and Fund are due, died on 10 February 1956, a week after his eighty-third birthday. Although towards the end of his life the founder had lost his sight, he insisted on hearing news of the Fund and the Annual Report was read to him. He continued also to promote the Fund, writing to the press, shortly before he died, 'I wonder how many of your readers realise what an important date April 1 is in the history of our Nation. It is the birthday of the Royal Air Force as we know it, for on that day in 1918 the service came into being by Act of Parliament . . . ' Trenchard's letter went on to remind the public about the existence and work of the Fund.

Freshly commissioned Cranwell officers, undertaking to subscribe to the Fund under the half-a-day's-pay-a-year voluntary subscriptions scheme, will find interest in one of Trenchard's favourite observations when Chief of the Air Staff. 'This Air Force', he said, 'will never be complete until a Cranwell cadet sits in my chair.' That wish was fulfilled in the year of Trenchard's death when Air Chief Marshal Sir Dermot Boyle became Chief of the Air Staff. The Marshal of the Royal Air Force is a Vice-President and former Deputy Chairman of the Council of the Fund.

There was also much news from the Fund to cheer Lord Trenchard in his last years, and notably the news of Vanbrugh Castle. There, in 1955, Mr John Corner from King's School, Canterbury, had succeeded Mr Webb-Jones, upon the latter's appointment as headmaster of Wells Cathedral Junior School. Suitable boys were now being coached for entry to the Royal Air Force as cadets as well as apprentices, and Trenchard could, allowably, visualise a former Vanbrugh boy sitting in the Chief of Air Staff's chair.

Two years after Lord Trenchard died the Nation raised his statue in Whitehall Gardens, immediately below the windows of the present Ministry of Defence and in sight of the Royal Air Force Memorial. It is not here, however, that the Fund pays it annual respects to the memory of the founder. Each year he is remembered in the Royal Air Force Chapel at Westminster Abbey. The chapel provides a symbolic setting for this simple act of remembrance and respect, which is held on or around the anniversary of Trenchard's death. Above the company the famous Battle of Britain window incorporates the memorial badges of the sixty-three fighter squadrons which fought and the flags of the nations to which the pilots and aircrew belonged. The stained and painted window by Hugh Easton is dedicated to the memory of 1,495 pilots and aircrew who gave their lives during the summer and autumn weeks of 1940, when the Battle of Britain decided the future of the world. The new window has replaced stained glass shattered by the bomb which destroyed the House of Commons, but a hole made by a bomb just beneath the window in the north corner of the chapel has been allowed to remain, filled by a few square inches of plain glass.

Below the window the Dean of Westminster takes the service in the presence of members of the Trenchard family, the Chief of the Air Staff, Air Force Board and Royal Air Force Benevolent Fund representatives and a thinning company of elderly men who knew and worked with the founder of the Fund, Mr Sidney G. Kemp, General Trenchard's driver in the first world war, and for many years Sir John Cordingley's chauffeur at 67 Portland Place, was a regular attender.

Before the service ends, a Marshal of the Royal Air Force who has been Chief of the Air Staff, the rank and final appointment of Lord Trenchard, places a wreath of Haig poppies in the shape of Royal Air Force pilot's wings on Trenchard's memorial tablet. The company stands in respectful silence and those who know remember that the entire chapel and the great window dominating the scene were made possible by a joint appeal from Trenchard, 'Father of the Royal Air Force', and Dowding, 'Leader of the Few'. Hugely oversubscribed, the appeal produced a surplus £50,000, which Trenchard and Dowding and their Committee presented to the Royal Air Force Benevolent Fund.

Lord Trenchard's death was followed by that of Lord Riverdale, who died in July 1957, at the age of eighty-four — Riverdale, who, succeeding the Duke of Kent as Chairman in 1942, had confidently declared: 'I intend to go on until the financial position of the Fund has been so strengthened as to be able to meet every likely contingency in the future.'

During the first ten years years of Riverdale's chairmanship from 1942 to 1952, the Fund had increased its assets from £680,000 to more than £5 million, notwithstanding an expenditure of £4,869,000 on all forms of relief.

The success of the Riverdale-Rumble money-finding partnership of the past and of Riverdale's guidance of the Fund's investment policy have been noted. His death left a serious void. Thus, shortly afterwards, the Controller negotiated a new arrangement to safeguard and, as it transpired, to strengthen further the financial position in which Riverdale, carrying out his promise, had placed the Fund. He persuaded Sir George Erskine, a partner at Morgan Grenfell, the city bankers, to join the Fund's Finance and General Purposes Committee and, subsequently, Sir George obtained the services of Morgan Grenfell as financial consultants — services which were remunerated nominally as the volume of work increased.

The Fund's portfolio of investments is constantly under review by the Finance and General Purposes Committee and the Controller and Director Finance. In the notoriously difficult investment year of 1966, the Royal Air Force Benevolent Fund, advised by Morgan Grenfell, managed to obtain a stock market yield of 5.7 per cent. With the inclusion of property investments the overall yield reached 6.9 per cent, thanks to the advice which the Fund has received from Mr K. Martyn Sanders of Debenham, Tewson and Chinnocks since the death of Mr Wallace Withers in 1958. Sanders also joined the Grants Committee and served until his retirement in 1989.

When Sir George Erskine retired as Honorary Investment Consultant in 1968, the Fund continued to benefit from his interest as a member of the Council. Meanwhile, the close working relationship with Morgan Grenfell continued through its chairman, Lord Catto, a Mosquito photographic reconnaissance pilot in the Royal Air Force from 1943 to 1947. After the death of Sir Harald Peake in May 1978, Lord Catto accepted the Council's invitation to succeed Sir Harald.

Of all the outside and linked organisations, and all the many thousands of individuals with good cause to be thankful for the financial wisdom and expertise which inspire the Fund's investment decisions, perhaps none holds the Royal Air Force Benevolent Fund in greater veneration than the Guinea Pig Club.

To the end of 1967 the Fund had disbursed more than £70,000 for the resettlement and relief of 367 individual members of this wartime association of badly burned aircrew. Further assistance in the past twenty years underlines that although the Fund does not and cannot have favourites, the Guinea Pigs, after the children of men killed in the service, are in the front line of welfare.

The Guinea Pig Club was founded over a bottle of sherry in 1941 by a small group of badly burned pilots in Ward III, a wooden hut at the rear of East Grinstead's Queen Victoria Cottage Hospital. Thereafter the Club was fostered by Sir Archibald McIndoe who, as consultant in plastic surgery to the Royal Air Force, had hundreds of wartime Guinea Pigs in his care.

With peace, McIndoe, 'the Maestro', as his Pigs called him, was nagged by the question, 'When their bodies are whole again can we also rebuild something from their shattered lives?' In Battle of Britain week, 1958, McIndoe broadcast the BBC's Week's Good Cause and answered that question. He said:

> We could and we did. But we did it only with the help of what I firmly believe to be Britain's most wonderful remedy in time of trouble; the Royal Air Force Benevolent Fund. You know, Sir Winston Churchill called it part of the conscience of the British Nation.
>
> One of my Guinea Pigs was Flight Lieutenant Richard Hillary, who flew again after we had healed his terrible wounds. Later he was to meet his last enemy, death, but before he died he wrote these words, 'I looked down at my hands, and not seeing them, I realised that I had gone blind. So I was going to die. It came to me like that — I was going to die and I was not afraid.'

What is there to say about courage like that? There are no words noble enough to honour such heroism, not enough tears to shed for such a loss.

That gallantry was typical of the young aircrew who gained air supremacy in many theatres of war for six years, and they are still doing it. Some are flying tonight, watching over the western world's uneasy peace.

How can we right the balance of payment? We can't do it personally — the job is too big. But the Royal Air Force Benevolent Fund will do it for us, if you will help.

More than £5,000 was received.

In 1947 the close liaison which had been long kept between the 'Ben Fund', as the Guinea Pigs affectionally call their 'bank', and the Guinea Pig Club was further improved by a Co-ordinating Committee to keep all burns cases under review. The Controller takes the chair and the Committee has included Sir Archibald McIndoe, until his death in 1962; the Chief Guinea Pig, Group Captain T. P. Gleave; the Maestro's widow, Lady McIndoe, who is also on the Grants Committee; 'Blackie', Mr J. E. Blacksell, the Guinea Pig Club's Welfare Officer until his death in 1988; and Dr Russell M. Davies.

The courage displayed by young aircrew, which was so greatly admired by Sir Archibald McIndoe, is exemplified in the following letter published in *The Times* on 18 June 1940 and a copy of which was framed and hangs in the Royal Air Force Club.

April 1940

An Airman's Letter to His Mother

Dear Mother,

Though I feel no premonition at all, events are moving rapidly, and I have instructed that this letter be forwarded to you should I fail to return from one of the raids which we shall shortly be called upon to undertake. You must hope on for a month, but at the end of that time you must accept the fact that I have handed my task over to the extremely capable hands of my comrades of the Royal Air Force, as so many splendid fellows have already done.

First, it will comfort you to know that my role in this war has been of the greatest importance. Our patrols far out over the North Sea have helped to keep the trade routes clear for our convoys and supply ships and on one occasion our information was instrumental in saving the lives of the men in a crippled lighthouse relief ship. Though it will be difficult for you, you will disappoint me if you do not at least try to accept the facts dispassionately, for I shall have done my duty to the utmost of my ability. No man can do more, and no one calling himself a man could do less.

I have always admired your amazing courage in the face of continual setbacks in the way you have given me as good an education and background as anyone in the country; and always kept up appearances without ever losing faith in the future. My death would not mean that your struggle has been in vain, far from it; it means that your sacrifice is as great as mine. Those who serve England must expect nothing from her, we debase ourselves if we regard our country as merely a place in which to eat and sleep.

History resounds with illustrious names who have given all, yet their sacrifice has resulted in the British Empire, where there is a measure of peace, justice and freedom for all and where a higher standard of civilisation has evolved, and is still evolving, than anywhere else. But this is not only concerning our own land. Today we are faced with the greatest organised challenge to Christianity and civilisation that the world has ever seen, and I count myself lucky and honoured to be the right age and fully trained to throw my full weight into the scale. For this I have to thank you, yet there is more work for you to do, the Home Front will still have to stand united for years after the war is won. For all that can be said against it, I still maintain that this war is a good thing; every individual is having the chance to give and dare all for his principle like the martyrs of old. However long time may be, one thing can never be altered. I shall have lived and died an Englishman, nothing else matters one jot, nor can anything ever change it.

You must not grieve for me, for if you really believe in Religion and all that it entails, that would be hypocrisy. I have no fear of death, only a queer elation. I would have it no other way. The Universe is so vast and so ageless that the life of one man can only be justified by the measure of his sacrifice. We are sent to this world to acquire a personality and a character to take with us that can never be taken from us, those who just eat and sleep, prosper and procreate are no better than animals if all their lives they are at peace.

I firmly and absolutely believe that evil things are sent into the world to try us; they are sent deliberately by our Creator to test our mettle, because He knows what is good for us; the Bible is full of cases where the easy way out has been discarded for moral principles.

I count myself fortunate in that I have seen the whole country and known men of every calling. But with the final test of war I consider my character fully developed. Thus at my early age, my earthly mission is already fulfilled and I am prepared to die with just one regret and one only — that I could not devote myself to making your declining years more happy by being with you; but you will live in peace and freedom and I shall have directly contributed to that so here again my life will not have been in vain.

Your ever loving son.

Sir John Cordingley was aged seventy-one when he retired at the end of May 1962. It is no disrespect to the President, the Chairman, members of the Council and Committees or to the staff at Portland Place to write that not only had Sir John served the Fund for fifteen years as Controller after eleven years' membership of Committees and the Council, but that to many people within and without the Fund he was the 'Father of the Royal Air Force Benevolent Fund' and was so described by his successor at the Council meeting in 1968.

He drove, cajoled and charmed the Royal Air Force Benevolent Fund into becoming the universally respected institution that it is, and although he affected a gruff disciplinary manner he drove himself so hard that he received the ungrudging support of those he kept under pressure. Cordingley's car driver, Sidney Kemp, who knew as much about the Controller's working hours as any man, reflected in a British Broadcasting Corporation overseas broadcast:

> The work that man used to do was amazing. I used to take him a bag home every evening. At about 6.30 pm to 7.00 pm he left the office. He'd go home, have his dinner and then he'd work till 10.00 or 11.00 at night; and then on the weekend or Friday evenings, he used to take about three despatch cases and he'd sit all day Saturday and Sunday working and then I'd bring them back on Monday morning. That man used to do some wonderful work for the Royal Air Force Benevolent Fund. It was simply amazing.

Kemp's humble opinion was held in higher quarters. When Sir John retired for the second time the Queen appointed him a Knight Commander of the Victorian Order. It was exceptional for an officer, knighted in his service career, to have his retirement crowned with a KCVO.

At the last Council attended by Sir John as Controller on 22 May 1962, Princess Marina devoted the greater part of her address to expressing her own thanks — and those of the Council — to him in the following words:

> There is not one of us sitting round this table who is not aware of his immense services to the Fund ever since he became Controller in 1947. Throughout all these years he has been largely responsible for the magnificent reputation that the Fund undoubtedly has throughout this country, and not only in this country but in the Commonwealth and in many foreign countries as well. It has been due to his wisdom and skilful administration that the Fund has been in a position, during the period of his office, to expend nearly £9 million in relieving distress and suffering. We are going to miss him, and his great wealth of experience, very much; but perhaps I may say that we are going to miss him even more in the capacity of a friend.

At the same meeting the Controller paid the following tribute to the staff:

> The volume of thanks which could be offered by me on an occasion such as this is tremendous, but time restricts, and I therefore would seek your indulgence to emphasise my thanks and appreciation to all members of the staff. I have had the most loyal support from all members of the staff; a keen, loyal, hard-working and, I do not think it is an exaggeration to say, a team dedicated to their work. The Fund receives thanks and praise for its efficiency, and for the good it does, and this is so very often almost solely due to the magnificent manner in which the staff perform their duties. I cannot take leave of you without emphasising as strongly as possible how much of our success is due to the manner in which the staff carries out your policy.

After retiring Cordingley resumed membership of the Council and was elected a Vice-President in 1975. He died on 5 January 1977 at the age of eighty-six. A crowded Memorial Service, at which Air Marshal Sir William Coles gave the address, was held in St Clement Danes Church on 22 February 1977.

Air Marshal Sir John Whitley succeeded Cordingley on 1 June 1962. It was no easy matter to follow a Controller who had so wholly and personally indentified himself with the office and with the Fund. Where lesser men might have been tempted to put the helm hard over and set a new course, Whitley deliberately kept her steady as she went and sailed the Fund sedately towards its fiftieth birthday.

Inheritor of proven organisation and many years or personal contact with the service, Whitley set out and was more free to renew the knowledge of the Fund throughout the service, a task for which he was ideally suited as the recently retired Inspector General of the Royal Air Force and having been Air Member for Personnel on the Air Council. Moreover, something of Whitley's flying career was known in the service. It brought comfort and confidence that the new feet under the Controller's table in the Council Room at Portland Place had climbed into operational bomber aircraft, had dangled over enemy-occupied France, their owner suspended dangerously by only half a parachute harness.

Early in the war, Whitley, who flew habitually with a civilian suit under his uniform and carrying a self-assembled escape outfit, had evaded capture and returned to Britain in a story-book manner, which is part of the escape lore of the service. Speaking from this background, it went home when Whitley told his Royal Air Force audiences: 'I think you can look on me as someone who has spent a great deal of his life in the service, who has gone into the Benevolent Fund, had a good old nosey around, and can report to the service on what he has found.'

He spoke simply, compellingly, telling officers and airmen wherever he went just how the Fund works. So effective was Whitley's approach that, within the very small margin left to him by his predecessor, he further improved the voluntary subscriptions coverage from eighty-four per cent of service people to ninety-two per cent. By the time of his retirement in the summer of 1968, Sir John Whitley jokingly claimed that he had also reduced the number of 'howlers' in officers' promotion examination papers — such answers to the question 'What does the Fund do?' as 'Builds swimming pools' — 'Helps dependants of RAF wives, who die fighting', 'Provides widows for RAF personnel.'

This is how Sir John Whitley told the story about the Fund:

> The staff who deal with the applications for help are almost entirely people who have served in the Royal Air Force. They have to prepare their cases and put them before a Grants Committee for a decision. The members of the Grants Committees are mostly people who have been connected with the Royal Air Force. The Committees sit once a week and have the cases presented to them by the relief secretaries and they judge the cases purely on their merits.
>
> If the staff want further information about a case, well, if it's a serving case they go back to the Station Commander or his

representative. but, the majority of cases, I find, apply to people who have retired and to widows and dependants of those who have died. Then they get in touch with one of the various organisations up and down the country, like the Royal Air Forces Association, the Soldiers', Sailors' and Airmen's Families Association, the Officers' Association, Red Cross, Royal British Legion, Forces Help Society, and so on.

We have not got our own investigatory service and we avoided setting one up deliberately, because if we did, it would involve us in more administrative overheads. These organisations already have their welfare officers and, after all, they collect money on behalf of the three services. We look upon investigations by these organisations as their contribution to the Royal Air Force. We don't pay them for their services. Of course, a further advantage of doing it this way is that it gives us tremendous coverage throughout the country. For instance, the Soldiers', Sailors' and Airmen's Families Association has something like 12,000 welfare officers, almost one for every village. so if they hear of someone who served in the Royal Air Force who is in distress, they let us know, because in the main, they do not disburse money themselves. If financial help is required, they come to the Benevolent Fund, to 67 Portland Place.

Air Marshal Sir John Whitley retired on 19 August 1968. During his six years as Controller the Fund made over 73,000 awards and the amount spent on the relief of distress totalled nearly £4½ million — a record expenditure for any six years since the Fund's inception. Income (including legacies) during the same period totalled £5,663,954, which was almost £600,000 greater than total expenditure, including administration expenses. An excellent addition to capital in these difficult days. During Sir John's Controllership the Insurance Advisory Service had been most successfully developed, and the Royal Air Force Dependants Fund inaugurated in 1967, in co-operation with the Air Force Board, and accommodated at 67 Portland Place.

No mention of the Fund's work in this period would be complete without a tribute to the devoted services of Squadron Leader Jock Beaton, Personal Assistant to Air Vice-Marshal Sir John Cordingley and to Air Marshal Sir John Whitley during their Controllerships. Squadron Leader Beaton, who had worked with Sir John Cordingley at the Royal Air Force Record Office in pre-war days, put in over twenty years' magnificent work at Portland Place, preceded by twenty-five years in the Royal Air Force and about nine years in the Army. He acquired a positively encyclopaedic knowledge of the Fund's history and activities, which he freely dispensed to younger colleagues. To the entire staff, as well as to his chiefs, he was a guide and philosopher but, above all, friend. When he retired in 1968 he was seventy-two.

Chapter 12
Head Office

'There are no words to thank you for so much. Perhaps the best way I can put it is that although my husband is dead, I cannot regret that he chose to fly with the Royal Air Force.'

An aircrew NCO's widow, 1965

Few service or ex-service people, or their dependants, visit 67 Portland Place, but the front door is always open during business hours by appointment, and any eligible person will receive sympathetic attention. Until Mr Walter J. Chandler retired in January 1977, he had been the Interviewing Secretary for many years and an Assistant Secretary in the Welfare Branch. He was Personal Assistant to the first Controller and during his thirty-two years with the Fund he served under all five Controllers. He is a member of the Goldfish Club, having been shot down over the North Sea during the Second World War. The Head Office staff do a certain amount of personal investigation themselves of nearby cases. Written and telephoned inquiries which are subsequently investigated are more frequent. But, while the cheques are written at Portland Place, investigation and the relief of distress in the field are carried out locally through such organisations as the Royal Air Forces Association, the Soldiers', Sailors' and Airmen's Families Association, the Officers' Association, the British Red Cross Society, the Department of Social Security, the Fund's own Branches, County Representatives, Helpers and Education Advisers, to all of whom the Fund is indebted.

A modest and separate benevolent fund belonging to the Royal Observer Corps is also administered here. The object of the Royal Observer Corps Benevolent Fund is to provide relief to members and ex-members of the Royal Observer Corps and their dependants in necessitous cases arising after the end of the war. Many 'Observers' have not served in the Royal Air Force and thus are ineligible for help from the Royal Air Force Benevolent Fund.

Primarily, Portland Place provides a meeting place for Council and

Committees and is the workshop where cases are prepared for submission to the Grants Committees.

An impression should not be gained, however, that where acute distress exists an applicant must await the decision of a weekly committee. The welfare secretaries, now assistant directors, are authorised to make immediate grants within a limited amount and can seek the Controller's authority to grant or to loan more substantial sums at any time. The splitting of relief cases under three separate headings — main, including house purchase; education and dependants; serving and ex-Royal Air Force — provides the benefits of specialisation and also helps to hasten their arrival in committee. During the peak period after the Second World War seven departments evolved: Main, Education, Dependants, Disablement, Serving, Ex-Royal Air Force and House Purchase.

Generally, unless further investigation is required, the relief staff expect to submit an application to a Grants Committee within a week of receiving it.

At the time of the fiftieth anniversary of the Fund the Secretary (Relief) of the Main Committee was Air Commodore W. H. Hutton, a former Air Officer Administration, Royal Air Force Coastal Command and Director of Manning, Air Ministry. The Branch Secretaries were: Serving and ex-Royal Air Force, Group Captain E. A. Jones, who succeeded the late Group Captain F. J. Taylor in 1967; Dependants and Education, Wing Commander O. E. Simpson, who had recently succeeded Mrs M. Campbell, who had been engaged on relief work since 1946. Their predecessors have included Group Captain H. W. Capener, Wing Commander W. J. Ryan, and Mrs D. Plenderleith.

The work of the welfare department is responsible, pressing, often trying and by its nature normally unpublicised.

The other departments at Portland Place are similarly organised. There are directors for Administration, Finance and Appeals, and a senior executive responsible for the Insurance Advisory Service. The 'admin secretary' at the time of the fiftieth and sixtieth anniversaries was Mr Paul Cutting (Administration), a wartime Squadron Leader who flew with Bomber Command and joined the Fund on release leave in January 1946. He had been Secretary to the Council and to the Finance and General Purposes Committee for many years and took on the task of editing this book. Both he and his assistant, Squadron Leader F. Hawley spent several years on relief work, as did Flight Lieutenant J. A. B. Cairns (Finance), responsible in war for No. 54 Group postings. Cairns came to the Fund on 1 January 1946, the very day of his release from the Royal Air Force, and he was assisted by Mr E. G. Abbott, who has been responsible for keeping the accounts since joining the Fund at Hove in 1945. Group Captain T. J. Arbuthnot (Appeals) joined the staff in 1963, following Group Captains S. J. Bailey and G. P. Woodhouse. Group Captain S. L. Swain (Insurance) succeeded Air Commodore C. V. Mears.

The executive staff is headed by the Controller, who by custom and design, since Air Vice-Marshal Sir Hazelton Nicholl's appointment in 1944, is a retired senior officer. So the desks at Portland Place are customarily 'driven' by experienced aircrew.

Although realistic salaries and wages are paid and there is a staff pension scheme, general administrative costs are pared at Portland Place, where the emphasis is always on economy. Although the Council Room which doubles as the Controller's office was appropriately furnished at an exceedingly low price, the remaining offices were furnished with second-hand items purchased after the war. The anecdote about the Air Commodore who, arriving on his first day, was handed a hammer and a bag of nails to repair a dilapidated desk makes a cheerful canteen topic to impress the visitors!

But when Fund money is spent on furniture, it is in the Grants Committee that such expenditure takes place, substantial assistance being not infrequent in the furnishing of new homes for young widows and disabled applicants with young children.

Apart from the Main Grants Committee and the Education Committee, to which cases requiring substantial financial assistance are referred, the Committees are specialists, considering serving, ex-serving (including disabled), and dependants cases. When a Committee sits, the secretary, who is generally a retired Royal Air Force officer, submits the week's list of applications. The cases are presented with a guide to eligibility, detailing the family and dependants involved; the financial position; and, finally, details of the request for assistance together with the remarks and recommendations of the commanding officer or the local representative. Facts for and against an application are given so that the committee can reach a decision within the Council's policy.

The Fund, being a service fund, must take into account not only the human side but also the service given. Consistent with this policy, it was decided that National Servicemen who entered the Royal Air Force under the peacetime acts between 1 January 1949 and 18 November 1960 were eligible to be considered for assistance from the Fund during their actual period of National Service and for an equivalent period thereafter. Exceptions to this rule are made in cases of death and disability or sickness attributable to or arising from actual service in the Royal Air Force. There are no restrictions on the period of eligibility for National Service officers and airmen who ultimately undertook regular service. Had the Fund accepted liability for all Royal Air Force National Servicemen it would have faced a potential demand from a further 500,000 men and their families. All requests from National Servicemen are considered by the Main Grants Committee. Neither length of service nor where distress exists influences decisions. Committees close on a cheerful note as members read letters received from beneficiaries.

Some cases cover almost as many years as the Fund's existence and originate in the First World War, as in the following examples from the 1960s.

A Royal Flying Corps observer was shot down during the First World War and was taken prisoner. After the war, when flying with his brother, they crashed and he was very badly injured trying to rescue his brother, who was burned to death. He spent eighteen months in hospital before he resumed flying, and he was so grateful to the woman who nursed him through his convalescence that he expended practically all his resources in purchasing a home for her. On another occasion he was being driven in a car over a level crossing when a train hit the car. In 1938 he was again badly injured in another aircraft crash whilst serving abroad and was subsequently invalided with a 100 per cent disability pension. Later on the Fund heard of his difficulties and the Committee approved assistance with house purchase at a time when his wife was suffering from bad health. Two years later the officer had a stroke which rendered him paralysed, blind and speechless. The Fund assisted with sick maintenance and the cost of nursing attendance until he could be admitted to a home, where he remained until he died. His widow occupied the house purchased with the help of the Fund.

Following a long illness, a Royal Flying Corps air mechanic of two years' service had insufficient money to clothe himself for the winter, so the Committee assisted. He wrote, 'I am going to buy an overcoat and winter boots and socks. A nice thought that this winter I shall be warm and have dry feet.'

An ex-warrant officer, aged seventy-three, who served in two wars, was ashamed to go out of doors. His clothes were too shabby. He had not had a holiday for many years and his clothes were too bad for him to be accepted by a home. He was too proud to ask for help but his case had been reported to the Fund. His income was £4 a week. He received an immediate grant for clothing.

A former Royal Flying Corps pilot, decorated for gallantry and aged seventy-two, was as badly off as the warrant officer, although his wardrobe was respectable. Until recently, post-war 'deals' had prospered but now he was down on his luck. He had a large bank overdraft secured by his house. He had local debts. Unable to draw from the bank, he and his wife had a total income quite inadequate for their basic needs. The Committee granted immediate assistance and accepted that 'he would probably be with them until he died'.

Chapter 13
Grants Procedure

'It is really a tremendous inspiration . . . the way the Fund comes to the rescue of the men, particularly amongst the aircrew who marry very young and have no resources and sometimes leave a widow and young children suddenly faced with a new life.'

Air Chief Marshal Sir Harry Broadhurst, 1955

A major disaster such as that of the Hastings aircraft crash in 1965, when thirty Royal Air Force servicemen died, will make the headlines and the Royal Air Force Benevolent Fund does not need to await official confirmation before it acts.

It is, however, routine for the Fund to learn officially of every Royal Air Force officer, airman and airwoman who is killed or missing or who dies while serving; and of the deaths of retired officers and airmen pensioners. Such is the Fund's liaison with the Air Force Department of the Ministry of Defence that within twenty-four hours of notification a relief secretary dispatches a letter to the next of kin, expressing the sympathy of the Fund and asking whether the Fund can help.

From experience, though, the Fund knows that even today some widows and dependants are reluctant to come forward or lack knowledge of how the Fund can help them. There is also the possibility that the Fund's readiness to help will not necessarily register with a bereaved person who is suffering from shock. Whenever practicable, therefore, the next of kin is visited by the station commander or his representative where the next of kin is living in married quarters or locally, or by one of the Fund's Honorary County Representatives or Helpers where the bereaved is living far away.

The Helper sends in a general report about the situation and the Fund can then decide what is the next step to take. If, after some six months, the next of kin has not applied for any help the Fund sends another letter saying, virtually, look, are you still all right? Do remember that if you want help now or in the future the Fund is here to help you.

Fortunately, peacetime disasters on the scale of the Hastings accident are rare but the call this single accident made upon the Fund's resources provides an example of the enormous liability that is never far from the Fund's front door.

When the Hastings crashed on 6 July 1965, forty-one servicemen were killed, of whom thirty were members of the Royal Air Force. There were no survivors. The object of the fifteen-mile flight from Abingdon to Benson in Oxfordshire had been to drop parachutists over an exercise area. Shortly after take-off the pilot reported that there were difficulties and he was returning to Abingdon. Within seconds of that message the aircraft crashed into a field of ripe barley near the village of Dorchester. The thirty Royal Air Force dead comprised six members of the crew, eight instructors, three air quartermasters and thirteen volunteers learning to jump. There were five single and five married officers and five single and fifteen married airmen. In less than a year assistance in twenty-two cases arising from this disaster had cost the Fund more than £40,000, a figure which had reached £60,000 in 1969.

The commitment did not end there. In some cases education was a recurring expense for many years. Since the introduction of education allowances for the services, the practice of educating children at boarding schools has extended greatly, but if a father dies the allowances cease and the Fund, subject to satisfactory investigations, steps in to complete the children's education.

During the decade 1952-61, when the bulk of the children whose Royal Air Force fathers had been killed or disabled in the Second World War reached school age, the Fund made over 20,000 educational awards and spent on this largest item during that period almost £2 million. These figures underline the great and unique achievement of the Fund in the field of education. In 1962 assistance relating to house purchase drew level and from 1963 onwards edged ahead as the most expensive single item in the Fund's budget on relief of distress.

House purchase assistance usually takes the form of a mortgage loan but it is exceedingly long-term because no loan repayment or house surrender is likely in such cases unless a widow's circumstances alter materially, or she dies. Even then the accommodation may have to remain available for any young children who survive her, provided they can be cared for, say, by a relation.

Indefinite 100 per cent house purchase loans in the 1960s were not made indiscriminately. They were normally available only to widows and those seriously disabled, with young children, where death or disability was attributable to service and where rented accommodation proved to be impossible to obtain or beyond the applicant's means. For many years such cases were presented to the Grants Committee by Mrs Ethel Page and now by Mrs Hazel Chapman.

Naturally, numerous considerations qualify the Grants Committee's awards throughout the range of relief and some of these are well demonstrated among the following examples arising out of the Hastings disaster.

Mrs A was living in married quarters when she was widowed and her eight-year-old son was attending a local school. As very often occurs, an officer with whom her husband, Corporal A, had served, offered to assist Mrs A with formalities — assistance which Mrs A gladly accepted because she was a German national by birth with insufficient English. The officer, a flight lieutenant, and the husband had served together in the Jungle Rescue Team of the Far East Air Force and he set out to obtain every possible form of relief for the widow. Thus, when Mrs A received the Fund's routine letter of condolence the flight lieutenant approached the Fund on Mrs A's behalf. He explained that the four worries on Mrs A's mind were a bank overdraft which would swallow up most of her husband's life policy, the future education of her eight-year-old son, house purchase, and a job.

He knew of the existence of Vanbrugh Castle School and it seemed to him the ideal school for her son. Mrs A was not at first persuaded about Vanbrugh, although the Headmaster, after interviewing mother and child, noted 'the boy is above average and acceptable. Excellent for him to come. But mother very weepy and reluctant to part with only child.' However, John Corner had a well-tried remedy for weepy mothers and he applied it to Mrs A, putting her in touch with a previously weepy and by this time appreciative mother who had experienced similar misgivings before allowing her son to board at Vanbrugh.

There can be no more suitable person to speak or write for the virtues of this school than a mother who has been bombarded with Vanbrugh anecdotes in the school holidays . . . 'there's rock-climbing . . . you ought to hear the school band and hear Paddy Purcell in action. He's director of the London Military Band too.' Mr Purcell retired from Vanbrugh Castle in 1968 and died a few years later.

Then there were the visits to Royal Air Force stations at home and abroad, the Christmas party with individual presents, a tradition started in 1948 by Mrs Ackerman, wife of Brigadier-General John B. Ackerman, the then Air Attaché at the United States Embassy, and for many years a much-appreciated annual event. Cricket, football, athletics, swimming, the choir at the Royal Naval College, Greenwich . . .

To all of which, and more besides, John Corner, then Headmaster, would not be human if he had not added with justifiable pride, in the brochure giving facets of life at the Royal Air Force Benevolent Fund's boarding school:

> The boys are taught in small classes and take the Common Entrance Examination at the age of thirteen when they usually transfer under the guidance of the Fund to other boarding schools. Experience has shown that these boys are well up to the standards demanded by other boarding schools, both as regards their scholarship and their general attitude and character.

But it is the appreciative mother who perhaps finally convinces a new and undecided widow, writing:

> I know as the time approaches for my son to leave Vanbrugh he will have a heavy heart. I feel sadness that school years could pass so quickly. I see him so clearly on his first visit to the school wondering what was in store for him, his first holiday at home, and his eagerness to return to Vanbrugh; the time the Headmaster assured me that he would enjoy rock-climbing, how right he was. Above all, he has learnt respect, loyalty and to share the joys and disappointments that a boarding school holds. How lucky to reap a harvest from a very deep sadness. My children have much to be thankful for, and so have I.

Maybe it is needless to add that Mrs A's son was educated at Vanbrugh!

But to return to Mrs A's story. After her husband's affairs had been settled she possessed only a small sum, comprising her husband's gratuity, a gift from a local disaster fund and what was left of her husband's insurance policy after repayment of the bank overdraft. She was receiving a war widow's pension and was still living in married quarters at the dispensation of the station commander, who had also engaged her as a temporary part-time batwoman, raising her income to a moderate figure. Obviously, neither Mrs A nor any Vanbrugh mother was in a position to pay full Vanbrugh fees at the time of £441 a year (£207 tuition plus £234 boarding), but no boy accepted for Vanburgh was prevented from attending because his mother could not afford the fees.

In Mrs A's case the Ministry rejected the application but her Local Education Authority agreed to contribute almost all of the fees, leaving the widow to find a small amount annually, either from her own resources or from the Fund. In this case, Mrs A paid her share of the fees.

With the boy's education arranged, the flight lieutenant turned his attention towards Mrs A's accommodation problem, because she could not remain indefinitely in service quarters. The Fund advised the widow to seek a flatlet in the London area through the Douglas Haig Memorial Homes, but Mrs A had set her heart on a 'front door of her own'. Initially the Fund attempted to deflect her from this dream, suggesting that it might be unwise of Mrs A to take on the expense of her own house when, apart from the school holidays, she would be living alone. Nevertheless, the Grants Committee later consented to consider an application for a house purchase loan sympathetically if Mrs A was prepared to live in a small and modestly priced property.

The Fund wrote:

> In view of the limited capital resources the assistance would take the form of an interest-free loan to cover the full purchase price of the property, subject to survey and valuation, and the survey fee and all legal charges incurred would be added to the loan, which would have to be secured by a first mortgage on the property.
>
> Any assistance sanctioned for furniture would be an extension of this loan and Mrs A would not be required to make any repayments to the Fund while she occupied the property herself and there is no material change in her circumstances, and she does not remarry.

Armed with this splendid news, Mrs A went house-hunting. She was offered a semi-detached by her local council, but preferred a private property at about the same price with a more pleasant outlook. The Fund loaned the money to buy it, adding assistance for furniture.

'This news', the flight lieutenant informed the Fund, 'has been a terrific fillip to her morale and she is a different person.'

Finally, the Fund assisted Mrs A to improve her English sufficiently to obtain work. Her son? 'Good in every way,' reported his Headmaster. 'He is successful, well liked and loyal and can hardly fail to do well'.

Sergeant B who died alongside Corporal A in the accident was an air signaller with nine years' service. He left a widow, two sons aged eleven and four and two daughters aged eight and five.

Mrs B's first visitor was her husband's flight commander and he wrote to the Fund on the widow's behalf. He said Mrs B had met her husband when they attended school together. She had been a very service-minded wife and held no bitterness towards the service at the loss of her husband. She held a small insurance policy on her husband's life but this sum would not be released for some while because of inquest formalities. Apart from this money, Mrs B would only have her pension to support herself and her four children. 'Her most immediate concern', the flight commander wrote, 'is that of housing her family when the time comes to vacate married quarters. She is most concerned that when she has to move from married quarters she is able to settle in one place permanently and will not be involved in a series of temporary moves.'

The flight commander's visit was followed up by the Fund's nearest Helper, who explained to Mrs B how the Fund could assist and in particular that the two boys were eligible for Vanbrugh. The elder boy entered Vanbrugh a few weeks after his father's death. In Mrs B's case a yearly grant of his fees was contributed by the Ministry of Social Security. But, unlike Mrs A, she did not fare so well with the Local Education Authority, where her application for assistance was refused.

As with Mrs A, Mrs B was asked by the Fund to approach her Local Education Authority Committee and the Ministry for assistance with the Vanbrugh fees. At the same time, the Fund assured the widow that, whatever the outcome of her application, her son would be educated at Vanbrugh and that she would only be required to contribute as much as she could reasonably afford. In fact, this generally meant in practice the child's war pension or state pension allowance, though in Mrs B's case the balance of the fees were waived by the Fund as her entire income consisted of a weekly pension.

With her elder son at Vanbrugh and her second son 'down for Vanbrugh', Mrs B moved into a small house, bought and furnished by the Fund. 'Please note any change of address,' she wrote cheerfully, and continued:

> I would like to try to tell you how grateful I am for all that has been done for us. I could never have given my children such a lovely home without your help. Thank you also for the financial assistance granted to me towards the cost of furniture.
>
> My eldest boy is very happy at Vanbrugh Castle School. He is a strong-willed boy who needs a lot of discipline and I feel that this can only be carried out by a man. My husband and I had always wanted him to attend a boarding school.

I feel that if any other woman in similar circumstances could be reassured that she would receive real help the way I have, it would save her a lot of distress and worry at a time when she is full of sorrow. I also feel that if the general public knew more about the marvellous help that the Fund has given to so many families, more people would donate more freely to the Fund.

Each widow in these cases, it will have been noted, stood to benefit from small insurance policies on her husband's life. In an increasing number of instances the deceased's life insurance cover is sufficient to complete the purchase of a house. The Fund does not desire to penalise the provident but distress must always be the ruling factor.

There was the case, for instance, of a flight lieutenant who had been buying a house on a mortgage covered by insurance policies. The widow was extremely reluctant to seek help but the Fund discovered that, although she owned the house, it was sparsely furnished. So they assisted with the purchase of essential furniture, the legal expenses in connection with the settlement of her late husband's estate, and the education of her eldest son, whose ambition was to be a pilot.

In another of the Hastings cases, a flight sergeant left a widow with four sons aged fourteen, twelve, nine and eight. In order to settle the family quickly in a home of their own, the Fund loaned money for house purchase, expecting the widow's capital not to exceed a moderate sum. When it was learned later that the flight sergeant had taken out four insurance policies, the widow promptly agreed to contribute towards the purchase of the house.

Throughout the 1960s there was an increasing interest among all ranks of the Royal Air Force in life assurance. Even so, of the ten officers and twenty airmen who died in the Hastings accident only five officers and fourteen airmen had taken out policies on their lives, thus helping to reduce the burden on the Fund. In the loss of three Shackleton aircraft of Coastal Command in 1967 not one member of the crews of ten men each was insured.

For every serviceman, such as the Hastings flight sergeant with adequate life assurance, there were many other officers and men who were not insured in this respect.

Until the introduction in 1962 of the Fund's Insurance Advisory Service, then under Air Commodore C. V. Mears, knowledge of life insurance within the Royal Air Force, notwithstanding Air Ministry publicity and in certain cases assistance with premiums, was in practice largely confined to talks from itinerant salesmen or the

Marshal of the Royal Air Force Lord Trenchard's statue, appropriately situated in Whitehall Gardens between the Ministry of Defence and the RAF Memorial on the Embankment, is another venue of commemoration, as when Lord Catto, Chairman of the Council, laid a pilot's brevet wreath there in the Fund's Diamond Jubilee year.

Services of Commemoration are held at St Clement Danes, the RAF Church in London's Strand, as on the occasion of the Fund's 60th Anniversary in 1979. The Pelican in Piety, the basis for the Fund's crest surmounts the altar.

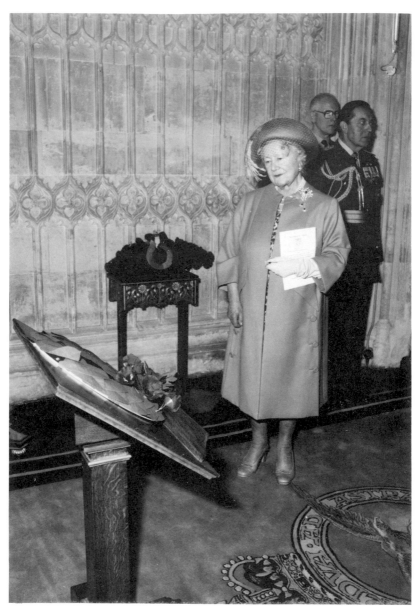

An annual memorial service for Marshal of the Royal Air Force The Viscount Trenchard is held in the RAF Chapel at Westminster Abbey. In February 1989, the occasion also marked the dedication of the memorial to six wartime leaders of the RAF. The Queen Mother attended and kept a short silence after she had placed a wreath on a table placed on the tablet marking the tomb of the Founder of the Royal Air Force Benevolent Fund.

RAF personnel do not restrict their financial contributions to the Fund to the half-a-day's-pay-a-year scheme. In 1982, the Mountain Rescue Team, Bob Foreman, Jim Morning and Pete Ross, crossed the Scottish Highlands from east to west, together with rescue dog, Teallach, to raise £85.

Air Marshal Sir Denis Crowley-Milling and David Shepherd with Sir Barnes Wallis, the airship and aircraft designer, famous for his invention of the dambusting bouncing bombs, and benefactor of the Fund, as he signs copies of the limited edition of Shepherd's celebrated Lancaster bomber scene, *Winter of '43, Somewhere in England*, sold in aid of the Fund.

Responding to an appeal to furnish extensions at the Fund's residential homes, RAF Catterick engaged in a major fund raising project for Princess Marina House. The station's effort enabled Group Captain Hawkins, Commandant of the RAF Regiment's depot, to lead station personnel to Rustington where LAC Holmes, youngest member of the party, presented the cheque. It was received by Miss Toni Turton, the oldest resident, a former Flight Officer who had served in the first and second world wars.

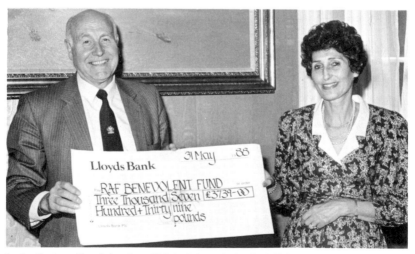

Lady Craig, wife of the then Chief of the Air Staff, delights Air Chief Marshal Sir Alasdair Steedman with a cheque for £3,739. The money was raised by the International Club for Air Force Officer's Wives, which has donated almost £50,000 since its inception twenty-six years ago.

The Aircrew Association is another supporter of the Fund. In 1985 Flight Lieutenant Pat Tuhill of the London branch presented a cheque for £1,000 to Air Chief Marshal Sir Alasdair Steedman, the Controller, in the Council chamber.

Air Commodore Freddie West, the 1914-18 War Royal Flying Corps VC, and Air Chief Marshal Sir Alasdair Steedman, Controller, watch Marshal of the Royal Air Force Sir William Dickson cutting a cake at the Royal Air Force Club in 1983 to mark the publication of the book, *A Lifetime of Service*, in aid of the Fund.

Donations are received from many service associated quarters. In 1981 Lord Scarman, chairman of the Malcolm Clubs, presented a cheque for £10,000, the Club's trading profits for the previous year, to Air Chief Marshal Sir Alasdair Steedman, the Controller.

Numerous fund raising occasions have been associated with the Battle of Britain. Air Chief Marshal Sir David Lee, a long serving chairman of the Grants Committee, was presented to the Queen at a gala performance of the feature film *The Battle of Britain* in 1969.

Princess Alexandra presents the 1984 Wilkinson Sword to Group Captain A. C. Tolhurst of RAF Finningley in recognition of the station's efforts on behalf of the Fund.

Princess Margaret, Guest of Honour at the fifth concert by massed bands of the Royal Air Force in the Royal Albert Hall in October 1988, presented, on behalf of the Fund, a *poignard* to Wing Commander Eric Banks, the RAF's Principal Director of Music, in recognition of his contribution to the success of so many fund raising concerts.

A scene familiar to the audience at the Fund's annual concert at the Royal Festival Hall as a symphony orchestra unites with the Central Band of the Royal Air Force 'to bring the roof down'.

activities of the hut corporal, who happened to be making something on the side as a sub-agent.

The Advisory Service will help any member of the Air Force to select the policy best suited to his individual needs. Glad to assist with the taking out of policies, Group Captain S. L. Swain and his successors have acted as intermediaries between service people and the insurance market. Every case is examined minutely and expert advice is sought from Lloyds Bank Insurance Services Ltd, with whom a close liaison developed when the bank acted as the Royal Air Force Pay Agent. When the Fund recommends an insurance policy the decision represents the joint advice of the Fund and the insurance department of the Bank concerned.

This service is free of charge and is of particular value to those wishing to buy their own home and requiring advice on assurance policies in connection with house purchase.

Since commission is such an integral part of the sale of life assurance, the question will be asked, 'Does the Fund receive commission?' The Fund derives no commission from the business transacted but the Bank makes an annual donation.

The Insurance Advisory Service does not preclude individual officers and airmen from making their own arrangements, but it does offer individuals the opportunity of a very sharp scrutiny of any polices that may be offered and advice upon their suitability or otherwise. Moreover, special arrangements have been made with insurance companies to meet particular service needs.

It is noteworthy that in numerous instances the Advisory Service has been able to counter an airfield salesman's contract with considerable improvement.

One of the more frequent calls for the relief of distress is caused by the financial vacuum in which many widows find themselves within hours of the death of their husbands. There is the need for sufficient cash to live on and there are often continuing hire purchase commitments, household expenses and the extra cost of the funeral. There may also be debts which the husband had intended to pay shortly.

Potentially, the widow may possess ample funds to meet all commitments and to leave a fair balance after settlement, but her husband's bank account has been frozen at death and his life policy, if there is one, cannot be realised until the completion of formalities, which may include an inquest.

In 1967 a new and separate organisation, the Royal Air Force Dependants Fund, was established at 67 Portland Place on the recommendation of the Air Force Board to ease this particular burden. The Trustees of the Dependants Fund, in the main, are serving officers with the Air Member for Personnel as President and the Controller of the Benevolent Fund as Chairman of the Executive Committee. The Secretary, on inception, was Wing Commander Innes Westmacott, another Battle of Britain pilot. Started with a donation of £50,000 from the Royal Air Force Central Fund, the Dependants Fund is self-supporting. At its inception members of the Royal Air Force and the Princess Mary's Royal Air Force Nursing Service were encouraged to subscribe sixpence a week from their pay at source.

When a subscriber dies the Dependants Fund sends a grant — in the late 1960s it was £500 and it is now more than £1,200 — to the nominated dependant within forty-eight hours of death being reported. Eligibility remains so long as a subscriber remains in the service and maintains the subscription.

The operation of the Dependants Fund in no way affects the normal activities or concern of the Royal Air Force Benevolent Fund, whose prompt help is available both to serving and past members of the Royal Air Force and their families and can be of a much longer-term and more permanent nature.

Chapter 14
The 1970s

*'There is no doubt that so long as the Royal Air Force exists and trains,
as well as fights in the air, there will be a need for the Royal Air Force
Benevolent Fund, which in memory of those who died or were
disabled whilst serving, must not lower its standard of relief to their
dependants.'*

Air Vice-Marshal Sir John Cordingley, 1962

Sadly, the setting of the seal on the establishment and accommodation
of the RAF Dependants Fund was one of the last actions of Lord
Knollys before his death at the age of seventy-one in 1966. Inheriting
the responsibilities of great charitable wealth which had been
collected in war by his predecessors, Wakefield and Riverdale,
Knollys had dedicated himself to the more difficult task of persuading
the public that a Benevolent Fund for the Royal Air Force was every
bit as necessary in a long and, it is to be hoped, permanent peace.

Greatly concerned by the mounting expenditure on relief, Lord
Knollys had taken a strong interest in the Insurance Advisory Service
established in 1962 and the new Royal Air Force Dependants Fund.
His enthusiasm for the encouragement of self-help was as evident as
the enthusiasm with which he had broadened the Fund's investment
portfolio at the outset of office. But, of all Lord Knollys's service to
the Royal Air Force Benevolent Fund, perhaps the most important
was the sang-froid with which he accepted the Fund's time-honoured
principle that over the years capital would be used if income was
insufficient to enable the Fund to meet its objects; and these included
the traditional but expensive principle of contributing heavily to
kindred organisations providing facilities for the benefit of Royal Air
Force personnel and their dependants. In his last year, for example,
£10,000 was given to the recently opened Royal Air Forces
Association home at Sussexdown to endow one bed in perpetuity for
a chronically sick or elderly Royal Air Force patient. As it happened
the first beneficiary was an elderly ex-member of the Women's

Auxiliary Air Force who, after serving as a corporal cook in the war, had fed the Vanbrugh boys for fifteen years.

That there is no question of budgeting by the Grants Committees, that awards are made in all cases on their merits, that outside organisations continue to be generously supported — this big-hearted, open-handed approach was Knollys's prime legacy to the Fund. But it is in the hearts of men and not in accountants' ledgers that actions and the names attached to them live on. So long as former Vanbrugh boys make their way in the world and new generations of children attend Duke of Kent School, Lord Knollys's leadership of the Royal Air Force Benevolent Fund will be recalled by those who passed through the Knollys Wing, and especially each year by the six or seven boys who benefit from the Knollys Holiday Fund, created by donations received in his memory.

On 3 May 1967 Mr Harald Peake, Chairman of Lloyds Bank, and a Director of Rolls-Royce among other appointments, was appointed Chairman of the Royal Air Force Benevolent Fund in succession to Lord Knollys.

In accordance with custom, the Fund had turned to the City and to business for a leader. Nevertheless, as with Lord Knollys, Mr Peake had been in the armed forces. In 1918 he served for a year in the Coldstream Guards, at first in the ranks and later as an officer. Three years before the outbreak of the Second World War he raised and commanded No. 609 (West Riding) Squadron of the Royal Auxiliary Air Force.

In November 1938 Mr Peake was appointed Director of the Auxiliary Air Force at the Air Ministry with the rank of Air Commodore. Following the outbreak of war he occupied the posts of Assistant to the Air Member for Personnel, Director of Public Relations, and Director of Air Force Welfare, before being transferred to the Foreign Office for special duties from November 1943 to 1945. He married Air Commodore Dame Felicity Hanbury, a former Director of the Women's Royal Air Force. Altogether a formidable and highly practical background from which to take the chair at 67 Portland Place, and, incidentally, to join Dame Felicity, already a member of the Council since 1956, and now a Vice-President and a member of its Finance and General Purposes Committee.

To the uninformed, the chairmanship of a service charity twenty-two years after the 1939-45 war might seem a sinecure but Harald Peake's election by the Council coincided with the publication of the 1966 Annual Report, which revealed a record relief expenditure of £890,272 that year.

Throughout the 1960s relief spending rose progressively, climbing from £527,979 in 1960 to £803,885 in 1967 and in 1969, the fiftieth anniversary year, an expenditure of £905,199 for 9,552 awards was more than ever before.

Now, why should this be? As the Fund saw in 1969, some of the financial burden might have been lifted as the life insurance advice and the Royal Air Force Dependants Fund gained impetus. But, outside this hope, experience suggested that the Fund could expect little or no lightening of the load.

House purchase loans which then accounted for forty-three per cent of the Fund's annual relief expenditure were, of course, technically recoverable — one day.

The value of today's money in 2019 is also questionable, if comparison between the values of 1919 and say, 1979 is anything to go by. Much depends on international stability and world peace, a cause in which even a much reduced Royal Air Force is still not without influence.

Meanwhile, it is particularly reassuring that currently it has been necessary to write off or convert to grant less than one per cent of loans sanctioned.

Although each house, for which such substantial purchase loans were made in the 1960s, was put in the widow's name, the Fund took a first mortgage on the house so that if the widow remarries or dies the house cannot be sold without the Fund recovering its money. It was said in criticism of house purchase loans that they were unnecessarily generous and that the Fund ought not to spend so much a year on making them. But the Royal Air Force Benevolent Fund is constituted to relieve distress and if the provision of a home for a widow and her children is necessary to meet this object then a house, and one that is within reason of the widow's choice, will be bought, subject to professional survey. It is the Fund's experience that houses and flats for letting to families with young children at reasonable or even unreasonable rents are almost non-existent.

Looking to the future the Fund correctly anticipated greatly increased demands upon its resources in the 1980s and onwards from aged widows and from officers and airmen whose earning power and whose savings had expired.

Some elderly widows from the First World War must have looked with wonderment at the lot of Royal Air Force widows as they reflected upon the long and hard road they themselves had travelled since 1919.

Indeed, the world has moved on at twice the pace since Princess

Marina accepted the Presidency in the moment of her own service widowhood in the Second World War. Sadly, the Princess did not live to lead the commemoration of the Fiftieth Anniversary. Princess Marina died in August 1968, only sixteen weeks after receiving in Council the congratulations of the Fund on the occasion of the Silver Jubilee of her Presidency. In twenty-five years Princess Marina had not missed a Council meeting. It was an annual duty which the Princess characteristically enriched with her deep and understanding sense of humanity, while at the same time being always ready to relieve a necesssarily businesslike occasion with a ready sense of humour, attributes which are clearly reflected among Princess Marina's remarks to the Council in May 1968.

Replying to the Chairman's congratulations on her Silver Jubilee, Princess Marina said:

You say, Mr Peake, that you can hardly believe I have been President for so many years. Nor can I! I assure you that I too find it very difficult to believe — and that it makes me feel like a sort of Methuselah! All the same I think I must remind you that Lord Portal and Mr de Rougemont, who both joined the Council immediately after the war, are almost as prehistoric as I am!

And here I must mention the remarkable good fortune that the Fund has enjoyed in the wonderfully long and loyal service given to it by successive Chairmen and Controllers, and members of Council as well. In the whole of my time here, we have had only three Chairmen: Lord Riverdale, Lord Knollys, and now Mr Harald Peake; during the same period, there have been only three Controllers, two of whom are with us today. I am so pleased to see Sir John Cordingley once again, but it is about Sir John Whitley that I should now like to say a few words.

Like every member of the Council, I have been extremely sorry to learn that Sir John will be resigning his appointment which he has held for the past six years. You have only to look at the details of the Fund's finances and other developments which are shown in the Report before you, to appreciate the progress the Fund has made during Sir John's term of office.

His enthusiasm, tact, courtesy and great abilities have been of outstanding service to the Fund, and on behalf of the entire Council I want to express our thanks and congratulations to him, and to wish him and Lady Whitley every happiness in retirement.

I want also to mention the retirement of Sir George Erskine who has been the Fund's Investment Consultant for the past eleven years. His immense contributions to the Fund throughout that time are known to all of you, and I can only say — in thanking him for his great services — how delighted we are that he, like Sir John Whitley, has agreed to remain a Member of the Council.

It remains for me to thank you all, once again, for the great kindness — and honour — that you have done me today and to express my best wishes to you and to everyone who works for the Fund during the coming year.

To mark the occasion of Princess Marina's Silver Jubilee as President on 11 March 1968, those who had been members of the Council at any time in the twenty-five years personally subscribed to a gift of garden furniture chosen by the Princess.

In a letter to the Chairman, Princess Marina expressed her great pleasure at this gift and suggested that next year's Council Meeting might take place at her home at Kensington Palace to enable the Council to see 'my lovely present displayed in my garden'. It was not to be.

With the President's death, Mr Harald Peake's first full year in the chair, Sir John Whitley's decision to follow Sir John Cordingley into retirement, and Sir George Erskine's retirement as Honorary Investment Consultant, 1968 was a year of great change among the Royal Air Force Benevolent Fund's officers.

However, there was no gap in the executive control of the Fund's day-to-day business. In accordance with long established policy the post of Controller was offered to a retiring senior Royal Air Force Officer and Air Marshal Sir John Whitley handed over to Air Marshal Sir William Coles in August 1968. Sir William Coles, a former Director General of Personal Services, came to the Fund almost directly from his former headquarters as Commander-in-Chief of Royal Air Force Technical Training Command and entered 67 Portland Place with what can be described, perhaps, as a very useful 'entrance fee'. As a result of Sir William's great personal enthusiasm his Command, in his last year of service, raised the record sum of £17,216 for the Fund.

Sir William had not been long in office when, to the Council's delight, The Duke of Kent, whose father had been killed flying on active service in August 1942 while Chairman of the Fund, agreed in the fiftieth anniversary year to accept the Presidency in succession to his mother.

Chapter 15
Bill Coles and
Duke of Kent School

While Cordingley had been a paragon of all the virtues which had been required to consolidate the Fund and its organisation after the Second World War, and Whitley, his successor, had kept it very much on course, Coles, who now took the controls, was the innovator and opportunist the Fund needed to work with the Chairman and Council towards the creation of investments and facilities more suitable to the demands of the 1970s.

Each step in Coles's career had helped to prepare him for his task, accumulating the mixture of opportunism, dash, social concern, compassion and understanding of human nature which was to stamp itself on his seven-year tenure as Controller.

At first he was a youthful Metropolitan Police bobby, who learnt about life on the beat, and who encountered the Royal Air Force while playing rugby so impressively for his native Oxfordshire that his opponents, coveting such a useful player, suggested he ought to apply for a commission as a pilot.

But there was the problem that in 1938, after four years in the police and at the age of twenty-five, Bill Coles had no exams to his name. He had failed to qualify for entrance to the Police College which Trenchard had founded at Hendon and acceptance as an officer in the RAF seemed an impossible dream.

Fortunately, however, the pilots whom Coles had met on the rugby field were determined to recruit him for the Service's XV and an enterprising flying officer invited him to the airfield at Hendon for an unofficial flying aptitude test. After the joy-ride the policeman was declared a natural pilot and, on the strength of this, submitted an application for a short-service commission and was accepted as an Acting Pilot Officer in October 1938. The DSO, DFC and bar, and AFC decorations, together with the United States DFC, which were to come his way were in time to justify the confidence of Coles's rugby friends. In all appointments of command Sir William was decorated. Much later they were astonished to find that they had also discovered the leader of the nation's first post-war Olympics bobsleigh team, which was provided by the RAF in 1948.

As Coles arrived at the Fund there could have been no more appropriate moment for planning for the future, because Peake's first year in the chair had convinced him of the need for gusts of change — a conviction which was strengthened, as it happened, by preparations for the commemoration in October 1969 of the Fund's fiftieth anniversary.

In its way the observance of the Fund's half-century served to underscore the need to move forward. As Peake laid a wreath at Trenchard's statue on Victoria Embankment on 23 October, the very day of the first meeting in 1919 of the Executive Committee of the Royal Air Force Memorial Fund, he and Coles knew that in some respect the Fund's attitudes and actions were almost as outmoded as conditions prevailing after the First World War. Even the Queen's attendance at a royal gala performance of the film *The Battle of Britain* served as a reminder that much of the Fund's financial strength was based upon the rewards of Trenchard's appeal in 1940 and on legacies and donations inspired by memories of the exploits of the Few.

Within four months of attending the gala showing of the film, Lord Dowding, Leader of the Few, was dead, a loss which further alerted those responsible for the Fund's future that before very long the Battle of Britain might become as much a part of history as Nelson's victory at Trafalgar — a battle which could no longer be said to provide an income for seagoing charities.

Certainly, the fiftieth anniversary commemoration of the battle in 1990 seems likely to be the last opportunity for a major appeal.

During Coles's service career in the twenty years which had elapsed between 1948 and his arrival at Portland Place social conditions in civilian life had altered so radically that the new Controller, in consultation with Peake, decided that the Fund should realign its finance, welfare, educational and appeal policies with the needs of the new society which an absence of war, the introduction of socialism and the Macmillan never-had-it-so-good years had combined to create.

Among the advantages to the Royal Air Force Benevolent Fund of Coles's recent appointments as Director General of Personal Services at the Ministry of Defence and Air Officer Commanding-in-Chief, Technical Training Command, and his proven career as a leader, was his knowledge of a fundamental change of attitude towards education at the Ministry of Defence. Broadly, the educational allowance had been extended to include all personnel serving at home as well as overseas. Taken together with educational problems arising from overseas service and postings, this suggested that the Royal Air Force would welcome a boarding school to assure continuity of education for children of families on the move.

Well, there was Vanbrugh Castle at Blackheath, the Alexander Duckham Memorial School, but it could accommodate only sixty boys and at this maximum had become uneconomic. Investigation by an architect of the possibility of expansion revealed that the idea was not tenable. Of its many disadvantages, one was particularly plain to Coles. As a former member of the Blackheath XV, among his rugby caps, Coles was well aware that Vanbrugh Castle School had no playing fields and was obliged to borrow them from the Blackheath Rugby and Cricket Club. Nor were there any recreational facilities, swimming-pool, or even a house for the headmaster — although until John Corner, a bachelor, retired in the autumn of 1973 and was succeeded by Mr W. P. Jones, a married man, this was not a major consideration.

Bill Jones was selected out of sixty applicants for the post and had served was a wartime flying instructor at the Central Flying School, Upavon, and later in India. He was as right for Vanbrugh and the transfer that lay ahead as had been Corner for the school in the years since its reopening after the Second World War, a headmastership which was recognised with an OBE shortly after his retirement.

After six years as headmaster of St Michael's School, at RAF Nicosia in Cyprus, preceded by fifteen years as head of the junior school at Kimbolton in Huntingdonshire, Jones understood the RAF's educational problems, particularly that of parents serving overseas. He was, therefore, wholeheartedly in favour of change in accordance with Coles's vision of the future for Vanbrugh.

'Vanbrugh', Coles said, 'ought to look more like a preparatory school and less like a fortress.' And in early 1971, as the school celebrated its Golden Jubilee, the Alexander Duckham Memorial School Committee, chaired by Air Chief Marshal Sir Walter Merton, took a step in this direction. After consulting the Fund's solicitors and the Duckham family it decided to offer admission from September 1972 to the sons of deceased and severely disabled officers in addition to those of NCOs and airmen. It was the first break in a long tradition and the beginning of a series of events which was to result, seven years afterwards, in the Fund's Diamond Jubilee year, in the already well-established Duke of Kent School with an ever-broadening field of admission, including the boarding of girls.

But now, as the School Committee recognised, the service educational allowance would result in an ever-increasing demand for places and, in any event, the economic advantages of a larger school must take precedence over a very human reluctance to accept change. There were also the considerations that cramped conditions and a necessarily restricted range of educational facilities and extra-curricular and sporting facilities were inhibiting opportunities for Vanbrugh pupils to compete for scholarships and bursaries available to the Fund at many public schools.

Eventually, resolution of the conflict over the removal from Blackheath proved easier than the search for an alternative property, the burden of which fell on Bill Coles with the professional help of Martyn 'Sandy' Sanders of Debenham, Tewson and Chinnocks, Chartered Surveyors, and the practical help of Paul Cutting, Secretary (Administration), who had dealt with the Fund's property investments since 1951. Briefed, as Coles recalled, 'to search the south of England for a place that looked more like a prep school with its own playing fields and capable of boarding between 120 and 140 pupils', they had spent two abortive years viewing fourteen unsuitable properties.

Then, in late 1973, when hopes were at their lowest ebb after investigating yet another unsuitable property near Ewhurst in Surrey, Coles, Paul Cutting, Bill Jones, Vanbrugh's headmaster, and Sandy stopped off at a village pub to refresh and console themselves.

It so happened that on the way to the rejected estate they had noticed an imposing Victorian building in extensive grounds which housed a school called Woolpit. As the party lifted its glasses Coles, the opportunist, observed: 'If only we could find a place like that, somewhere we could build on to if necessary. Let's ring up and ask if we can just come and have a look.' Within half an hour they were being shown round by the headmaster. Just as they were leaving Coles asked point-blank: 'I suppose you wouldn't want to sell this place?'

At last Coles's luck had turned. He had put his blunt question at the very moment when Woolpit faced problems. After twenty-eight years in the ownership of The St Thomas's Church Schools Company, it lacked the financial resources to pay for the expansion which would enable it to almost double the total of its eighty-five boarders and twenty-five day boys to an economic number. Mr John Hall, the headmaster, advised Coles that an approach to the Board of Governors might be welcomed, especially as Mr Trevor Jones, then Deputy Chairman, had served in the RAF.

Thereafter, events moved swiftly and shortly after the visit Coles received a letter from the headmaster offering amalgamation. On 10 January 1974 the Controller returned to Woolpit for a further reconnaissance and a week later Peake, Coles, Trevor Jones, together with Alan McLintock and other colleagues of the school board, put their heads together to examine the prospects for a merger.

From the start the Woolpit governors could not have been more helpful and co-operative. They had the will and the room to expand the school to an economic size but were without the wherewithal; whereas the Fund, facing an almost identical expansion problem so far as numbers were concerned, could find the money but was unable to enlarge Vanbrugh in the claustrophobic urban environment of Blackheath, in south-east London.

Before the end of February John Hall and Bill Jones, the headmasters of Woolpit and Vanbrugh, had exchanged visits and each side had accepted in principle that the Fund should take Woolpit over in return for discharging its liabilities. On 4 April 1974, Peake headed a joint meeting of the Fund's Finance and General Purposes and Alexander Duckham School Committees at Woolpit and members were overwhelmingly in favour of going ahead.

However, such a large undertaking could not be entered into without the observation and completion of certain formalities. Thus, Peake, after obtaining the Council's approval of the merger in principle on 8 May 1974, informed the President and Council Members by letter that, subject to the approval of the Charity Commissioners, the Woolpit governors would convey the school, playing fields and about fifteen acres of freehold land to the Fund as a gift. In return the Fund would continue the fee-paying education of children already at the school or previously accepted for places.

Delightedly, the Chairman wrote that the Fund's surveyors estimated the value of the gift as at least £225,000 and that it had been arranged to buy a further ten acres, with buildings, known as Woolpit End — hitherto leased to the school — for £25,000. An additional fourteen-and-a-half acres of woodland had been offered to the Fund and this land would be purchased for £7,250.

He explained that work on the Woolpit buildings would probably cost £35,000, while a new block of classrooms and dormitories had been estimated at £150,000.

Formal negotiations were opened and, after their completion during the year, the Fund, thanks to the generosity of the Woolpit governors, took possession of the fine Victorian mansion and the freehold of some forty acres in the Surrey countryside. Peake wrote to tell his colleagues on the Council that the Fund planned to transfer its Vanbrugh pupils for the start of the September term in 1975. However, the amalgamation depended at least upon the completion of the new dormitory-classroom block to provide the additional accommodation required. Subsequently, as plans were prepared, it was decided, on Peake's insistence, to provide a general-purpose gymnasium-assembly hall and six houses or flats for the staff. Air Commodore Peter Vicary, the Fund Branch Secretary, Education, was given the task of overseeing and co-ordinating the whole development project.

Then came delay because of alarm in the Waverley Planning Authority about the immensity of the development proposed for Woolpit. Quite reasonably, it explained that Woolpit lay within the Metropolitan Green Belt and enjoyed the particular advantage of being situated in the Surrey hills in an area of outstanding natural beauty. Conferring with Peake and Coles at Woolpit, Sir Michael Creswell, Chairman of the Authority's Planning Committee and a member of Surrey County Council, explained sympathetically that the area was about to become part of a national park.

These and other detailed difficulties overcome, the contract for the whole development was finally let and the construction of the dormitory-classoom block and the modification of the main house, particularly of its kitchens, went ahead as rapidly as possible.

Meanwhile, with the encouraging approval of Professor A. N. Duckham and his sister Mary, Lady of Cults, the freehold of the Vanbrugh Castle School buildings was sold to the Blackheath Preservation Trust Limited in March 1977 for £177,500, which the Duckham family most generously agreed should be devoted to Duke of Kent School.

The Variety Club of Great Britain decided to finance four scholarships for Foundationers at the school for six years. They also presented a school bus, bringing the Club's ultimate contribution to the school to £35,000.

Since the playing fields were to become a central feature of the school a most generous and helpful offer was received from the MacRobert Trusts, through its Administrator, Air Vice-Marshal Frank Dodd, to provide a grant of £20,000 (subsequently increased to £22,000) to increase the playing field area, which would thereafter be known as the MacRobert Playing Fields.

The source of the MacRobert fortune was Sir Alexander Mac-Robert, an industrious Scot of humble origins who had worked hard at night school in Aberdeen before sailing for India in 1884. He was vastly successful, managing Cawnpore Woollen Mills and becoming Chairman of the British India Corporation and receiving a baronetcy. When he died in 1922 he left a fortune.

MacRobert's first wife, Georgina, had died in 1905 and he married Rachel Workman, an American who inherited a considerable estate. He had three sons by his second wife and this is where the link with aviation and the RAF begins. Alasdair, who inherited the baronetcy, was Chairman of the British India Corporation when he was killed while piloting his own aeroplane near Luton. Succeeding his brother, Sir Roderick MacRobert joined the RAF before the outbreak of the Second World War with a short-service commission. Among his appointments before being killed in May 1941, in a Hurricane attack on Mosul airfield, was that of ADC in Palestine to Air Vice-Marshal Arthur Harris, who was later to become Marshal of the Royal Air Force Sir Arthur Harris, or, more popularly, Bomber Harris. Within weeks the third MacRobert brother, Sir Iain, had also died when his Coastal Command Blenheim failed to return from a North Sea air search for the crew of a missing bomber.

Shortly after the loss of her third son, Lady MacRobert bought a Stirling bomber and four Hurricane fighter aircraft for the RAF. The bomber went to war with the name 'MacRobert's Reply' painted on its nose and three of the Hurricanes were named after Alasdair, Roderick and Iain, while the fourth was simply called The Lady. All four Hurricanes fought in the desert war with No. 94 Squadron, in which Iain MacRobert was serving on the day he died in the Middle East. Lady MacRobert took a strong personal interest in all her benefactions to the R AF and the MacRobert Trusts have carried on her good work since her death in 1954.

After such a generous gift from the MacRobert Trusts the Fund went ahead to make a showpiece of Duke of Kent School's playing fields. The headmaster was authorised to buy a powered roller and to arrange for the drainage of the cricket and rugby fields.

Another generous gift was received from the Hayward Foundation. Sandy, the Fund's surveyor, knew Sir Charles Hayward and mentioned the Duke of Kent School development to him. When Coles wrote to the Hayward Foundation, giving them details of the impending expansion of this RAF school and sending a copy of *The Debt We Owe*, a cheque for £10,000 was received by return.

During 1975-76 John Hall and the Woolpit School continued to function amid the contractor's rubble and the combined school started work on the first term of the 1976-77 academic year. A Board of Governors appropriately chaired by Sir Walter Merton was appointed to include the former Chairman of the Woolpit School Governors, Mr Trevor W. Jones, and two other Woolpit Governors together with Mrs Ruth Croome, Mr Alexander Duckham's youngest daughter; the wife of the Commandant, RAF Staff College (Lady Williamson, succeeded by Mrs Peggy Curtiss); Mr Tim White; the Director of Training (Education); and Air Commodore Peter Vicary. All the Fund Governors are former members of the Vanbrugh Castle Management Committee.

Within the first year of operation the new school, with the permission of the Queen and the agreement of the Fund President, was renamed Duke of Kent School and was honoured by an informal visit by the Duke on 3 March 1977. It was also decided to open the school to the children of all serving personnel as full fee payers to fill available vacancies, priority having been given to children who had lost their fathers in the service.

It was further decided to make twenty places available to girls thus making Duke of Kent School one of the first co-educational boarding preparatory schools in the country.

Chapter 16
Princess Marina House

Throughout the period of the negotiations which were to result in the removal from Vanbrugh to Woolpit, the Controller and his staff, enthusiastically encouraged by Peake, were also heavily engaged in preparing the way for Princess Marina House, an equally ambitious and expensive development, which was not to reach full fruition as a residential and convalescent complex at Rustington on the Sussex coast until the Diamond Jubilee year. But this is to look ahead from the Golden Jubilee, when an outstandingly generous action was to provide the Fund with a landmark at the close of its first fifty years.

The origins of Princess Marina House — whose existence owes everything to the moment on 30 September 1969 when Mrs H. Newton Driver handed a cheque for £100,000 to Lord Ward, a former Air Minister and the Fund's Honorary Treasurer, to endow the Newton Driver Memorial Fund in memory of her husband—are to be found in the Second World War when Mrs Newton Driver ran an officers' club in the West End of London.

As Mrs Newton Driver explained at Portland Place when she presented the cheque,

> During the Second World War we had a very strenuous time at the English-speaking Officers' Club in Park Lane. None of my staff would live in because of the bombing. I was alone there with just one young girl who said she would like to die with me.
>
> Night after night I just went to bed with slacks and jumper on. The telephone would often ring and it would be the Railway Transport Officer asking for accommodation for servicemen who had nowhere to go. They would never take no for an answer. Very often I had to put a mattress on the floor and to make up those and our chesterfields into beds. When they arrived out of the blackout I would always ask 'Are you hungry? Have you had a meal?' and invariably they would reply, 'We are famished'. So we would all go to the kitchen and they would sit on the kitchen table, on the dresser, sinks, everywhere, and have cocoa and sandwiches. Throughout the war that went on.
>
> The one big topic of conversation was: what were they going

to do after the war — these brave, eager boys, especially the Royal Air Force? They had marvellous plans. Then a few weeks later I would hear that they had crashed. It did something to me and I always said that if I could help the Royal Air Force in any way I would do so.

Therefore, now that I am semi-retiring, I would like to give the proceeds of my work from all these years to the Royal Air Force Benevolent Fund and it will be a most wonderful thought to me that when I have passed on I shall be still helping the Royal Air Force.

Twenty-one years earlier in 1948, three years after the end of the Second World War, recognising that her London club had served its purpose and that the post-war period of resettlement and rehabilitation had created new needs, Mrs Newton Driver transferred the club to a beachside property at Rustington, where it was opened by Prince Philip.

In those days, conforming with its wartime status as an officers' club, it received British Commonwealth and United States Army, Navy and Air Force officers and ex-officers, including those of the women's and nursing services, and their relatives and friends.

Thus, as the Royal Air Force Benevolent Fund took over The Newton Driver Services Club it seemed appropriate to continue the tradition of convalescence and very soon up to sixty men and women were guests at any one time. There was the difference, however, that rank was irrelevant as a qualification and admission was at first restricted to elderly or partially disabled serving or ex-members of the RAF and WRAF, Princess Mary's Royal Air Force Nursing Service, and their adult dependants. Within a year, though, this exclusivity was reconsidered and admission of Army and Navy personnel was approved, when vacancies existed, as being in accordance with the spirit of Mrs Newton Driver's wishes.

In permitting the Fund to acquire her club under the endowment arrangement of 1969 Mrs Newton Driver received deep personal satisfaction and was further heartened by its immediate success under the Fund's management. After her death on 19 June 1970, from injuries received in a motoring accident, the Fund learnt that Mrs Newton Driver, who was well into her eighties, had bequeathed her adjacent land and property of considerable value and potential use to the Fund.

Shortly after its acquisition of the club the Fund's first guests were enjoying the restful and comfortable centre for which its management committee, chaired by Air Chief Marshal Sir Wallace 'Digger' Kyle, with Wing Commander Ted Holloway as the first Secretary, and its manager, Group Captain G. F. Corden, now held responsibility.

Very soon the eligibility of all ranks for accommodation was emphasised by the presence of Air Marshal Sir Richard Atcherley, a former Council member of the Fund, who spent most of the last few weeks of his life there. The Air Marshal subsequently was taken ill *en route* to Cape Canaveral, where he had been invited to watch the launching of a moon mission and was rushed to Aldershot Hospital where he died.

Among the earliest guests at Princess Marina House were some who had stayed there when it was the Newton Driver Services Club and naturally one of the first questions they asked was why it had been renamed Princess Marina House. The explanation was that, since Princess Marina's death in August 1968, the Fund had sought a suitable memorial to its long-serving President and had been delighted when the Duke of Kent approved the use of his mother's name for the centre at Rustington. Nor was the wartime effort and peacetime generosity of Mrs Newton Driver to be overlooked, because Banner Cross, one of the adjoining houses she bequeathed to the Fund, was renamed Newton Driver House and has been converted into a nurses' residence.

From the outset Princess Marina House was not self-supporting, those with RAF connections being charged about £16 a week or according to their means, while Army and Navy guests had to pay a full economic rate.

In 1971, its second full year, Princess Marina House accommodated 279 RAF guests for a total of 593 weeks and fifteen former members of the Army or Navy for twenty-four weeks at a cost, after contributions, of £30,149. Days out by the sea were organised by other service charities, including the Not Forgotten Association, one of the Fund's oldest associates, which maintains an ambulance coach and provides outings, entertainments and personal gifts for disabled and wounded service or ex-service people.

It was at this stage that the Fund, taking note that of the fifty places at the centre nineteen were occupied by long-term residents, began to consider the problem of caring for those who needed periods of nursing. Until now it had relied considerably on the Royal Air Forces Association's acceptance of some such cases at its nearby Sussexdown home, but, as the demand for such treatment grew, it became clear that Sussexdown, for all RAFA's good will, could not be expected to meet all the Fund's needs indefinitely.

While this all-important matter of expansion was being considered, certain problems arising out of Mrs Newton Driver's will were resolved and Coles was relieved to hear from her executors that the Fund could take possession of Banner Cross and St Bega, another adjacent house, thus facilitating a first enlargement of Princess Marina House. Consequently, in 1972 as many as 331 RAF guests and nineteen long-term residents benefited from the peaceful seaside surroundings, as did also ten Army or Navy guests, at a total cost of £52,127, reduced to £35,629 from income. Thereafter the occupation rate rose progressively, a record being set in 1973, with 383 RAF guests spending a total of 772 weeks, twenty long-termers in residence and eight ex-Army visitors. The cost was £65,350, offset by an income of £47,030.

Satisfactory though this occupation rate was, particularly in view of the closure of the main building for rewiring in December, the management committee felt that Princess Marina House was not being used sufficiently for convalescence by RAF servicemen and women or their wives and husbands. Ex-service people were every bit as welcome, but the Fund wished to encourage younger men and women from RAF stations to make use of the centre. Certainly, there could be no finer place to relax and regain strength after an illness or operation than at the RAF's very own seaside resort, which now comprised five buildings, including a clubhouse, a putting green and tennis courts with changing-rooms and showers. But good reports spread throughout the service and as a result the Committee decided to enlarge the lounge, dining room and sun lounge.

Throughout the gradual development at Rustington the Duke of Kent, while following every aspect of the Fund's advances since succeeding his mother as President, understandably had retained an especial interest in Princess Marina House. Knowing that expansion was planned for the new year he dropped in by helicopter on 29 May 1974, to see what the Committee had planned to further improve the centre and to find out for himself why it had proved so popular and established such an excellent reputation for convalescence.

It seemed to the President, as he remarked to the Management Committee during his visit, 'marvellous value', a plaudit which expressed in figures for that year reflected net expenditure of £61,852 for 418 RAF guests, twenty long-term residents and seven guests from the other services.

Thus, in the following summer of 1975, as Coles cleared the Controller's desk in the Council chamber at Portland Place he knew that to the groundwork for the removal from Vanbrugh to Woolpit he could add the achievement of helping to transform Mrs Newton

Driver's club into a convalescent centre comparable with the best elsewhere in Britain.

The Duke of Kent had observed that there seemed little scope for improvement, but Peake, Air Marshal Sir Denis Crowley-Milling, Coles's successor, Air Marshal Sir Harry Burton, who had succeeded Kyle as Chairman of the Princess Marina House Committee, Wing Commander Allan Scott, who was now the Secretary having recently retired from the Royal Air Force where his last appointment had been Air Attaché in Madrid, and Wing Commander A. F. Carvosso, the centre's new Manager, were already looking further ahead.

Chapter 17
The Royal Air Force Benevolent Fund Housing Trust Ltd and Welfare Work

Ranking high among the radical changes of course during Coles's controllership was the Fund's policy on housing widows and their families. In the early 1970s the property boom obliged the Fund to spend ever-increasing sums on homes. Characteristically, it was the Scottish Branch which set the alarm bells ringing at Portland Place.

Attending an Annual Meeting of the branch in Edinburgh, Coles was warned by Sir Ian Johnson-Gilbert that the Scots felt the Fund was being too prodigal in the manner in which it provided houses for widows.

It was true that although the houses were put in the names of their widow owners, in the event of remarriage a widow was expected to return to the Fund as much money as it had provided at the time of her bereavement. But the Scots regarded this as a bonus for the new husband who in all probability had not served in the RAF. It was wrong that such men with no call on the Fund should benefit from it, however indirectly.

Coles returned from Scotland with the clear message that a means should be devised through which the Fund could retain an interest in all such homes and thus gain from any rising values. The outcome was the introduction of the Royal Air Force Benevolent Fund Housing Trust Limited.

At the time of the incorporation of the Housing Trust in 1972 it was still the Fund's general policy to resort to house purchase where a widow or a severely disabled ex-member of the RAF with young children had been unable to find a suitable home to rent. Applications from fit ex-service people with dependant children and, exceptionally, from serving personnel, were also considered when rented accommodation was out of the question.

However, over the years, the reduction of suitable rented property on the market and ever-rising rents were to turn the Fund almost exclusively towards a policy of house purchase and also towards broader qualifications. Consequently, applications from ex-members of the RAF with dependent children were no longer exceptional. Further, serving members, with long or pensionable service, were to be eligible for interest-free loans as they prepared to leave the RAF, to help them put down a deposit on a house, such loans being subject to repayment from gratuities or terminal benefits.

In its operation of the Housing Trust the Fund observes two ground rules. Where it has to contribute more than half of the purchase price it buys and owns the property under the Trust so that after its sale the Fund benefits from any appreciation and can use the money to help another family. On the other hand, if an applicant can provide more than half the purchase price then the Fund will ease the burden of buying the property by awarding an interest-free mortgage loan.

Yet, as in all its welfare activities, the Royal Air Force Benevolent Fund is always ready to take a view of particular circumstances and the Housing Trust enjoys considerable elasticity. For instance a young corporal, who was happily married with two children had completed a twelve-year engagement in 1973 and had bought a house with some assistance from the Fund, intending to start a business as a photographer from home. But before they could move into the house the couple were involved in a serious motor accident and each received severe facial, hand and body burns. The injuries were so bad that the husband was unlikely to be able to go ahead with his plan to launch out as a photographer. In these distressing circumstances the Housing Trust bought a house for the family outright and put in a washing machine, washing-up machine and special door handles to enable the corporal and his wife to live as normal life as possible with the children.

The corporal wrote:

> I am finding it hard to put onto paper the words I use daily to describe your organisation to social workers, friends and family. Apart from the considerable financial help, which not only allowed us to survive, but put both our minds at ease, there have been the social visits to the hospital and our home which have been invaluable for the encouragement they have given us. I'll never be able to repay your personal help and your organisation will always have our gratitude.

Lest spending on the scale required for such large developments as the Duke of Kent School and Princess Marina House and the purchase of houses — 145 families costing £318,193 in 1969 — should seem to distort the picture of the Fund's welfare activities, the Grants

Committees, the Controller and staff were as much exercised by day-to-day calls for assistance as had been their predecessors during the first fifty years. There was the difference, however that in spite of inflation the Fund's income and capital additions from investments, the pay deduction scheme, other RAF self-help schemes, and legacies and donations enabled the Grants Committees to make individual awards without drawing on the Fund's capital, which, however, they are always prepared to do if necessary.

Examples selected at random from beneath the heading 'Kinds of Assistance' in the annual report for 1969, the Golden Jubilee year, reflect the variety of the Fund's welfare actions. For instance, help with prams in two cases, £56. Tools and working equipment were bought for sixteen people at a cost of £702. Travel and removals ran to £10,742 for 292 families. Clothing, bedding and footwear are itemised at 1,033 awards totalling £17,253; debts due to sickness and other reasons, 2,048 awards amounting to £100,318; and all aspects of the Fund's educational help cost £123,792 for 808 cases.

Thus, while hundreds of thousands of pounds were spent or appropriated for the two major developments, thousands of comparatively small individual awards were made after investigation in the field and discussion in committee, contributing to a grand total in Golden Jubilee year of £905,199 for 9,552 awards.

In Diamond Jubilee year, when welfare expenditure is running at a rate of £2 million a year, it may be asked how much could be achieved for less than £1 million. The answer, as in previous years, is to be found not so much in statistics as in the human stories presented to the Grants Committees. If the following examples from 1969 can only give a general impression of the Fund's welfare assistance in that year, they bring out two emerging factors. These are the complicated nature of many cases and in consequence a growing demand on the knowledge and expertise of the staff at Portland Place, in the branch offices and among the Fund's regular helpers and associated members of such bodies as the Royal Air Forces Association. Paying funeral or pram expenses where necessary was a stroke-of-the-pen decision, but, as the following examples illustrate, many cases called for tact, discretion, patience and understanding. In other words, more than mere money.

An Aircraftman Second Class, young and single, had served five years before being discharged because he was schizoid, a condition which prevented him from retaining a job. Nevertheless, he was a brilliant mathematician and keen to take a two-year electronics course. The Fund helped him complete the course. He passed five examinations, three with distinction. Then he suffered another breakdown in health, but recovered sufficiently to take the City and Guilds Certificate with a view to settling into a job for which he had qualified.

Many years after a young pilot officer had been killed in a bomber brought down over Germany, his elderly and partially blind mother, unable to find suitable accommodation, was much distressed because she had been obliged to put her faithful dog into kennels. It was urgent, her doctor said, that she should have a home with a ground floor. The Fund assisted with the purchase of a maisonette and some extra money to put it in good repair. The elderly lady and her dog were reunited. The pilot officer's sister who lived with her mother wrote:

> It is very difficult to word the gratitude I feel towards the Royal Air Force Benevolent Fund. I thank you for helping my mother and I, when no one else could or would: for giving us a new start when we both thought we had reached the end.

In the 1960s and the 1970s survivors or their dependants of the First World War were a dwindling responsibility, but in Golden Jubilee year the following letter from the widow of a Private in the Royal Flying Corps typified their needs:

> I feel I must write and say thank you for the grant you made me. You cannot know all this has meant to me. I am not a woman who gets into debt needlessly, but what I had to get was a real necessity. Now, thanks to you, I have settled my debts. You see I am seventy-four and I was afraid I might have died with the debt unpaid.

Among the criteria taken into account by the Grants Committees is the extent to which families where able, have made provisions for themselves. The Committees warm to the provident who despite their own best efforts are subjected to worry and distress in the moment of crisis.

During Coles' controllership the Insurance Advisory Service continued to go from strength to strength, considerably broadening its scope beyond impartial advice or a second opinion on life assurance matters to advising on all aspects of family protection, savings, house purchase, education, financial planning and commutation of retired pay. At the end of 1974, following the retirement in September of that year of Group Captain Swain, his successor as senior executive of the Insurance Advisory Service, Group Captain R. J. Gosnell, could report savings-type policies of more than £1,125,000 in sums assured with a further £970,000 of temporary life assurance comprising convertible-term assurance or family-income policies.

At this rate the Insurance Advisory Service had become the source of a considerable flow of business in collaboration with the insurance department of Lloyds Bank, Cox's and King's branch, the RAF agents, who, if required, help applicants to negotiate such policies as are recommended.

By the end of 1974 the RAF Dependants Fund had nearly 90,000 members, subscribing 10p a month, and the basic death grant was £800, subject to the Trustees' discretion.

Visiting RAF units, Coles found that the prudence of subscribing such a small sum voluntarily was brought home convincingly on the occasions when an accident resulted in the deaths of several men on the same station and their comrades heard of the immediate cash payments received by widows.

Indeed, such was the reputation of the Royal Air Force Dependants Fund that many subscribers wrote to the Trustees asking if they could increase their weekly subscription in order that their beneficiaries could receive a greater cash sum. This was investigated by the Managing Trustees, who included Coles as Controller. He, in conjunction with Sidney Swain, looked into this possibility but, as this would change the basis of making the Dependants Fund a separate charity, it was not possible.

Faced with the ever-increasing number of servicemen who wished to protect their families beyond the single cash grant made by the Dependants Fund, Sidney Swain, in conjunction with the Air Member for Personnel's department, did some more homework. As a result of this, on 1 July 1971 the Air Force Board, in conjunction with the Finance and General Purposes Committee of the Benevolent Fund, launched the Royal Air Force Dependants (Income) Trust, underwritten by the Provident Mutual Life Assurance Association, under the Secretaryship of Wing Commander F. W. Tame. This enabled members of the Dependants Fund, if they so wished, to subscribe more to make their beneficiaries eligible to receive a monthly income, or alternatively, a lump-sum payment. This enabled the Trustees to follow up the single lump-sum payment from the Dependants Fund by a tax-free monthly income from the first day of the month following the death of the subscriber. Such an income is payable until the subscriber would have reached the age of fifty-five, or sixty in some instances. A bonus increase from the date of joining is added each year to the income and this bonus growth, currently six per cent compound, also continues to be added if it becomes payable.

Altrenatively, the beneficiary of the deceased subscriber can, at the Trustees' discretion, commute the income for a tax-free cash payment. At the end of each accounting year, on 30 June, any net income from the Trust is covenanted to the RAF Benevolent Fund.

Well, those are the bald terms, but what makes the effort so very worthwhile to the staff of the Insurance Advisory Service and the RAF Dependants Fund and Income Trust are the letters of appreciation which arrive in every post. Group Captain Swain made the point to the Finance and General Purposes Committee shortly before he retired, bringing to its notice a letter from a flying officer of the Air Movement Squadron in Hong Kong. Not only did this young officer express surprise at the existence of 'D Income', as the service short-hands the Trust, but the accounts staff in the colony were 'perplexed at the remarkable protection for such a small premium'. Stating that he intended to make use of its Mortgage Saving Scheme, the flying officer wrote to Swain: 'I feel considerably more at ease than before I received your advice. The letter was logical to a layman and all the enclosures were explicit and of value . . . My fear of being caught by a pushing salesman has been slightly relieved and my understanding of jargon has been improved. Many thanks for the care you have taken.'

Early in his tenancy of the controllership Coles had become concerned at the rapidly increasing burden that the casework mountain was imposing on his staff. For this and other reasons he felt that a reappraisal and possible overhaul of some of the administrative and staff recruitment machinery at headquarters was required. There were those on the staff, among them his secretary Elizabeth Ticehurst, whom he promoted to private secretary after Squadron Leader Stansfield's retirement — she is now at Sir 'Jock' Kennedy's side as Personal Assistant — who were not receiving the responsibilities and rewards for which they were experienced and equipped. There was also the problem of replacing retiring or resigning staff with people of sufficient ability, because salaries at the Royal Air Force Benevolent Fund were no longer competitive in the open market.

Naturally, Coles was as concerned as had been any of his predecessors to conform with the Fund's long-standing policy of keeping administrative expenditure to a minimum. In 1969, the Golden Jubilee year in which £905,199 was spent on relief, this was £141,953 of which £103,563 covered salaries, wages and staff pensions. Yet he also feared for the Fund's future administrative efficiency if pay at Portland Place was not brought more into line with commercial standards and promotion prospects made more attractive.

Peake, with his banking and business background, wholeheartedly supported the Controller's opinion and the Finance and General Purposes Committee authorised a survey of the administration. This was undertaken in 1971 by the Management Services Department of Barton, Mayhew and Company, the Fund's auditors, and as a result certain customary business practices were introduced, including a modification to the establishment of typists to concentrate the work of shorthand and audio typists who had been working individually for the various departmental Secretaries. Possibly the most helpful change to emerge from this review was the removal to Portland Place of the all-important Appeals Branch from its outpost in two rooms on the top floor of the Oxford Circus branch of Barclays Bank, a move which enabled the Controller to have immediate personal contact with Group Captain Arbuthnot, the Appeals Secretary. Accommodation above the bank had been obtained with the help of Lord Portal, a Barclays director, and as Appeals moved out the Insurance Advisory Service whose presence at headquarters was not so essential, moved in.

At the time of the survey the possibility of wholesale removal from Portland Place and out of central London, which had been considered and rejected in an earlier review, was reconsidered. As hitherto it was decided that such an upheaval would not be in the overall interest of the Fund's welfare objectives, particularly because of its extremely favourable lease of the building. Other arguments which helped to end the proposal were the headquarters' accessibility in the West End of London to the majority of members of the Grants and other Committees and the importance of the Fund's general and personal relationships with the Ministry of Defence, other government offices, associated charitable organisations and also with its professional advisers.

The latter consideration is excellently illustrated by the proposal for another fundamental departure which was considered during Coles's controllershp. This was the possibility of applying for a Royal Charter. While the pros and cons were being investigated, the benefit of close consultative contact with Charles Russell and Co., the Fund's solicitors, was much appreciated. In the event, the Fund was advised not to make application because such a status would enable the Privy Council to insist upon certain restrictions on its powers of investment. The Fund was not prepared to surrender its investment freedom. It also rejected incorporation under the Companies Act and has since carried on its business under the High Court scheme which has served it admirably for more than thirty years.

Chapter 18
Finance and Fund Raising:
Into the 1970s

It was in this realm of investment and City of London expertise that Lord Portal's persuasion of Peake to accept the chairmanship was to prove exceptionally fruitful. Portal's death on 21 April 1971 was a sad and serious loss to the Fund. During the preceding quarter of a century he had served as Deputy Chairman to Riverdale, Knollys and Peake, in whose favour he had declined the opportunity to succeed to the chair. This was a characteristically selfless action considering that the chairmanship would have crowned a connection stretching back to 8 March 1939 when, as an Air Vice-Marshal and Air Member for Personnel, he was appointed to the Council, as indeed also on that day was a certain Group Captain Cordingley.

After the new Deed of Trust had freed the Fund from its low-yield investment fetters — effectively from 1 January 1949 — Portal, for all his other banking and business commitments, had not spared himself in assisting the Fund to mix its gilt-edged portfolio with a blend of equity and property investments.

In their four years as Chairman and Deputy Chairman, Peake and Portal, notwithstanding an expenditure on welfare of nearly £3½ million, had seen the Fund's net assets increase from £6,027,086 in 1967 to £6,941,742 in 1971.

Throughout the inflation-scourged 1970s Peake's performance as Chairman of the Council and the Finance and General Purposes and Appeals Committees repeatedly reinforced Portal's inspired recruitment of Peake, who built a formidable financial team as Lord Ward of Witley, Air Minister from 1957 to 1960 and a Vice-President of the Fund since 1958, accepted the office of Honorary Treasurer in 1969 following the resignation of Lord Thurso. In 1968 Lord Catto of Cairncatto joined his fellow Morgan Grenfell director, Sir George Erskine, on the Council, and succeeded him on the Finance and General Purposes Committee, becoming its Deputy Chairman in 1974.

At the time of the Golden Jubilee in 1969 the team's money management was already proving remarkably effective despite prevailing economic conditions. A decision taken in September 1968 to increase the equity investment target to £2.5 million at cost had been implemented. Advantage was also seized of the high interest rates available from local authorities and by the end of 1969 the Fund had placed about £250,000 in this sector. Although the London Stock Exchange index was down on the year the Fund had managed to mark the close of Golden Jubilee year with the market value of its stocks and shares exceeding book value by more than £1 million.

Financially the picture in 1970 was not so sanguine, with securities dropping to more-than-book value of some £650,000. Yet such were the Fund's liquid assets that there was no need to sell securities at depressed prices.

In 1971 Lord Ward was able to report a big improvement. Taking advantage of favourable opportunities and the City expertise provided by Peake and Catto, the Fund's stock market holdings at £7,603,567 exceeded book value by £2,322,711.

In 1972 Peake's prudence in getting the Fund out of fixed-interest stocks and into equities and convertibles — stocks and shares to the net value of about £300,000 were bought during the year — was manifest. For in this year equities and convertibles continued to appreciate eighty-five per cent above cost as against a fall to nine per cent below cost in the market value of the Fund's fixed-interest stocks. Between 1968, Peake's first full year as Chairman, and 1972, the proportion of equities and convertibles in the portfolio had risen from thirty-one per cent to fifty-two per cent — with a target of sixty per cent book value in view — and the annual rate of income from all investments had improved from seven per cent to eight per cent. It was a satisfactory end to an investment year at the start of which Peake had been honoured with a knighthood in the New Year Honours list — although the council in congratulating him acknowledged that the honour also recognised Sir Harald's services to the Royal Air Force before and during the Second World War as well as to banking and the community.

Before passing forward from 1972, the retirement of Flight Lieutenant J. A. B. Cairns, the Finance Secretary, who had been responsible for so much of the day-to-day detail of the Fund's money business for twenty-six years, should be recorded. He handed over to Wing Commander E. J. Holloway, who had joined the Army shortly after the outbreak of War, transferred to the Royal Air Force in March 1941 for pilot training and seen operational service in Bomber Command and North Africa. In later service he commanded No. 58 Canberra Photographic Reconnaissance Squadron for three years and after Flying College, where he was on the same course as the then Controller, Denis Crowley-Milling, completed an Air Ministry tour in the Assistant Chief of the Air Staff's Intelligence Department. His last appointment was Senior Personnel Staff Officer of Coastal Command. He joined the Fund Welfare Branch in 1967, and was Secretary of Princess Marina House before taking over from Cairns.

Such is the contrariness of the City that a setback might have been expected in the following year. The *Financial Times* index fell by thirty-two per cent and the Fund was highly selective and restrictive in its stock market dealings. Cash available for new investment was placed for preference at high interest on short-term deposit. The Finance and General Purposes Committee noted gravely that the fall in market values had reduced the real value of all the Fund's investments to £6,892,251, a reduction of £1,740,300 on the previous year.

With continuing inflation and with a record annual outgoings of more than £1.6 million on the relief of distress, 1974 was another difficult year. Investment was all but at a standstill, the Fund being kept liquid while any surplus money was placed on short-term deposit with local authorities to take advantage of high interest rates.

Nevertheless, although the Fund, together with most investors, suffered from the effects of the home and overseas recession, Peake and his colleagues could fairly report that it had held its own in a year which had been the worst ever in the London stock markets. In contrast with a 46.8 per cent drop in the *Financial Times* index, the Fund's portfolio had declined by thirty-eight per cent, a net reduction of about £2.5 million in market values. Nevertheless, accumulated funds had risen from £8,355,974 to £9,037,342, but the annual report on the accounts warned that a testing time lay ahead.

Before moving into 1975, as a matter of record it merits note that amid all the problems of 1974 the Fund overhauled its form of accounts to give effect to the Statement of Standard Accounting Practices with regard to the treatment of reserves, laid down by the Accounting Standards Steering Committee. The effect was to necessitate the Fund taking all exceptional profits and losses and income such as legacies, hitherto regarded as capital, into the income and expenditure account and then into the accumulated funds in the balance sheet. The opportunity was also taken to simplify the form of the income and expenditure account and the balance sheet by transferring much of the detail to separate notes.

In the event, in 1975 the Royal Air Force Benevolent Fund stood up rather better than the gloomy forecast of an expected 'testing time' and Peake confidently informed the Council that investment income had increased and that the portfolio's market value was substantially higher than in the previous year. In fact, this could be described reasonably as an understatement, because market values of stocks and shares had risen in the year from £3,841,746 to £6,704,552, a feat for which Peake in his annual Chairman's statement gave generous credit to Lord Catto, Deputy Chairman of the Finance and General Purposes Committee and Chairman of merchant bankers Morgan Grenfell, which company's advice had been so largely responsible for the improvement in a year of such perplexity for investors.

Stocks and shares were not alone among investments calling for careful monitoring in the years of Coles's controllership. In the Golden Jubilee year of 1969 the Fund's property portfolio remained at a book value of little more than £1 million. It was a time of much competition in the property market and even the Royal Air Force Benevolent Fund, expertly advised by its surveyors, Debenham, Tewson and Chinnocks, found it difficult to buy properties with good covenants and producing its expected average return of fifteen per cent. With boom conditions running into 1970, the Fund's holdings remained much the same and a target of £1.5 million was not achieved.

Then, gradually the picture changed and, while a continuing shortage of suitable buys prevailed in early 1971 — with the consequent investment of £100,000 in Charity Property Trusts — Debenham's efforts were more fruitful and Peake's Finance Committee raised its sights, setting £1.75 million as its property sector investment target. By the end of the year properties totalled £1,156,724 at book value.

This improvement, however, was short-lived and in 1973 no leasehold properties were bought because yields were less than could be obtained from gilts and other fixed interest stocks.

There was a similar standstill in 1974. No leasehold property was bought and book values, further reduced by amortisation, continued to fall and were £657,821 in 1975.

Among the challenges facing Coles as he succeeded Whitley in the summer of 1968 was the problem of creating income other than from capital investment. The Fund, as he knew, was currently finding about thirty per cent of the £900,000 it was spending on the relief of distress from its annual income. Coles had joined the Fund, as it will be recalled, from Technical Training Command after raising £17,216 within the Command and, therefore, he was already an acknowledged fund raiser.

Early in his controllership Coles was concerned as to the extent to which the Fund's appeal to the public for money was linked to the past achievements of the Royal Air Force. It was a question which greatly exercised Peake, not only as Chairman of the Fund but particularly as Chairman of the Appeals Committee, and also, of course, Group Captain Arbuthnot, the Appeals Secretary. The difficulties were that the service was contracting and that such routine operations as NATO reconnaissance flights, exercises in West Germany, even helicopter rescue flights and famine relief mercy missions did not stir hearts and minds and tended to be taken for granted.

The diminution of the Royal Air Force and its activities was reflected in the membership of the Council itself, its numbers dropping from thirty-five to thirty-two chiefly because of the amalgamation of Bomber, Fighter, Signals and Coastal Commands into Strike Command, demonstrating that even Air Officers Commanding-in-Chief are not exempted from the perils of redundancy.

Consequently, while the Fund, with the continuing advice of Peter Taylor, its public relations consultant, strove forcefully to publicise needs arising from the reducing commitments of the Royal Air Force, the Council conceded that large unsolicited donations and legacies must still depend on past exploits and people's memories of them.

Therefore, while it has been explained that after the Golden Jubilee commemoration the Fund would have to look forward in the realm of appeal, it remained inevitable that it still had to look back.

At the time, this policy paid the Fund handsomely, especially as 1969 was the year in which the feature film, *The Battle of Britain*, received a Royal charity première on 20 October at London's Dominion Cinema. It was a glittering occasion attended by the Queen, Prince Charles, Princess Anne, the Duke and Duchess of Kent, the Duchess of Gloucester, Prince Michael of Kent and Princess Alexandra. After the performance the Chairman presented the Queen with a leatherbound copy of the Golden Jubilee edition of *The Debt We Owe*, an edition which, incidentally, has contributed over the years to the Fund's income. It is impossible to attach a figure to the book's influence on donations and legacies, but at least one sum of £10,000 can be attributed to it, in that the donor's cheque arrived by return of post after receiving a copy. This windfall was part of the year's total of £245,526 from legacies and capital donations.

As well as providing the Appeals Department with such a splendid opportunity to bring in money (in all the Fund and the Royal Air

Forces Association shared £12,520 from London and provincial premières), that gala night, attended by so many aces and survivors of the Battle of Britain, was the scene of numerous reunions and nostalgic conversations.

For the Chairman's wife, Dame Felicity Peake, the sequence in the film where the airfield at Biggin Hill is bombed in daylight, and the actress Susannah York playing an officer counts her WAAF dead, was particularly poignant. In August 1940 the then Section Officer Felicity Hanbury, who was later to command the Women's Royal Air Force in the rank of Air Commandant, had been that officer and the part had been written round her experiences.

Other than its direct financial assistance to the Fund, the *Battle of Britain* film contributed to Golden Jubilee year's total of £276,565 received from all appeal sources, other than legacies and capital donations, at home and abroad by stimulating a flow of free-will offerings, which included £7,531 from church collections, £2,675 raised by the Jersey branch of the Royal Air Forces Association in Battle of Britain Week, and ten shillings from an eleven-year-old boy who staged a model aircraft display.

The fiftieth anniversary year had provided an opportunity to remind the public of the Fund's existence and work but the Royal Air Force and related sources remained the chief fount of the Fund's income. In that year servicemen's and servicewomen's voluntary subscriptions through the half-a-day's-pay-a-year scheme had reached £131,754 which, together with £12,500 from the RAF Central Fund — the Royal Air Force Benevolent Fund Second Development Trust also received £12,500 from this source — £6,818 from retired personnel, £25,581 from RAF units and numerous contributions from wives' clubs and other service sources, provided £203,268 of the £276,565 total. That old stand-by the Royal Tournament contributed £8,219 and Battle of Britain Week collections, excluding the RAFA's Wings Appeal, enabled that organisation to pay £17,636 into the Fund's exchequer. At £46,385 ordinary subscriptions and donations from the public were more than £16,000 up on the previous year.

All in all a good year, but, like the Council, the Finance Committee counted the cost of relief and members were not satisfied that it was good enough. Ordinary income at £1,033,123 had fallen short of expenditure by about £14,000.

The Appeals Committee was open to ideas, however modest, the results of which might supplement such hardy annuals as the RAF Anniversary Concert and the Souvenir Book. One such idea in this year was the Used Stamp Scheme, through which service people and the public were asked to collect stamps of all sorts and send them to the Fund in packets of not less than 1,000 stamps at a time. Arrangements were made with the stamp trade to bulk sell to collectors for the Fund's benefit. Another enterprise was to stimulate the parks and gardens department of country and seaside resorts to plant floral displays featuring the RAF and the Fund. These flower-beds offered the dual benefits of reminding the public about the Fund and raising money. In 1969 a Folkestone floral display brought in £720, despite the vandalising of a concrete collection box.

In the following year Peake, reporting as Chairman of the Finance and General Purposes Committee, noted with a hint of surprise that the deficit between ordinary income and record welfare awards of £935,000 was again £14,000, despite a drop in support from the public; legacies and donations having fallen to about £200,000.

But the RAF had managed to prevent the gap widening and to enable the Council to record with gratitude that a total just short of £334,000 had provided thirty-five per cent of the amount paid to relieve distress. As Peake observed in his financial report, had it not been for the decision of servicemen and women to allow their annual subscriptions to remain at half-a-day's-pay-a-year after the April 1970 introduction of new pay scales, the deficit would have risen to more than £60,000.

Such was the appreciation of the importance of the service subscriptions that Coles was at great pains during his visits to RAF units to emphasise that the Fund was looking for a 100 per cent of voluntary subscribers and to explain the desirability of entering into seven-year covenants, whereby for every £1 a year given the Fund could recover 63p from the Inland Revenue, thus receiving a total of £1.63. It was also publicised that, whereas covenant facilities had so far been restricted to officers, warrant officers and senior non-commissioned officers, they were available henceforth to corporals and airmen who paid standard-rate income tax. As in previous years every new penny counted and the Fund was indebted to the most modest of donors, not least among whom was the schoolboy — he was not a Vanbrugh pupil — who sent 75p at the suggestion of his headmaster after being caught running a book on the Grand National.

After the excitement of its Golden Jubilee the Fund had returned to a more workaday existence, yet 1970 was not without its brighter interludes, particularly a belated fiftieth anniversary reception, arranged at Lancaster House in London on 21 April by the Air Force Board of the Defence Council and which was attended by the Duke of Kent and the Rt Hon. Denis Healey, Minister of Defence. There was also the annual concert on 3 April, provided this year by the Birmingham Symphony Orchestra and, as ever, the Central Band of the Royal Air Force. The soloist was Jeffrey Siegel, the international pianist.

In October 1971 Group Captain Arbuthnot retired after running the Appeals Department for eight years, handing over to Air Commodore John McKelvey. Arbuthnot's last year was his best, the Fund receiving £410,913, which represented nearly forty-one per cent of the cash paid out to relieve distress. Service contributions of £337,748 had never been higher. If legacies and donations were a dismaying twenty-seven per cent lower at £151,691, Arbuthnot had still set his successor a stiff challenge. The concert at the Royal Festival Hall on 2 April, the last Arbuthnot was to organise, had, as Peake told the Council, produced 'a very happy result' for the Group Captain, all seats being sold within three days of the box office opening in early March. But then it was not every year that Princess Anne was guest of honour, that the Royal Philharmonic Orchestra was available to join the Central Band, and that Moura Lympany was soloist. It was the sixteenth anniversary concert to celebrate the founding of the Royal Air Force on 1 April 1918, and it brought the total concert revenue to £15,442.

Arbuthnot could also take pleasure in the fact that in his last year Prince Philip offered to make an annual donation; and that a growing awareness of the aims and achievements of the Fund, obtained through Peter Taylor's regular news releases to RAF station publications, resulted in two remarkable donations — £12,394.50 from Little Rissington and £8,736.27 from Akrotiri in Cyprus.

One of the Fund's strong points is that its permanent staff represent a cross-section of service experience. While the Controllers, since Cordingley's retirement, have been former pilots who achieved Air Rank, others — among them Paul Cutting, for so long the Administration Secretary, a war-time navigation officer of a Lancaster bomber squadron, and Air Commodore Peter Vicary, whose last appointment was Air Office Commanding, the RAF Record and Pay Office, Gloucester — entered the ranks under the raw discipline of the pre-war service. Such an officer was Air Commodore McKelvey, an engineer who had joined as a fifteen-year-old aircraft apprentice in 1929 and retired in 1969 as Air Officer, Wales, and Commandant of RAF St Athan.

Taking over from Arbuthnot in the autumn of 1971, McKelvey had little time to influence the year's results, but Christmas provided him with two modest opportunities to show his mettle. Finding that in 1970 the bustling Air Marshal Ivor Broom, commanding No. 11 Group and to be knighted in 1975 — a Baptist minister's son of whom, as a wartime Mosquito pilot, it had been said he could drop a bomb on a postage stamp — had raised £630 by the sale of Christmas cards, the Fund enlarged the idea.

Although the production and sale of greetings cards had been ruled out previously as unrewarding, experience proved that Broom and his wife had organised a valuable pathfinding scheme. The Brooms were delighted to hear from the Fund that of a range of eleven designs 218,890 cards were sold. In addition 26,050 issues of very special cards had also been sold, and while not quite so profitable had produced useful publicity for the Fund.

McKelvey's second opportunity was to organise the Annual Festival of Nine Lessons and Carols at the Royal Air Force Church of St Clement Danes, at which the Venerable L. J. Ashton, Chaplain-in-Chief, Royal Air Force, received on behalf of the church a casket containing gold, frankincense and myrrh from Group Captain E. G. P. Jeffery, the last commander of the RAF's closed Muharraq base in the Persian Gulf. If the collection of £137.26 that December Sunday contributed marginally to the Appeals Department's total, the occasion was of much significance to the future promotion of the Department's work.

From his seat in the congregation, McKelvey's attention was caught by a wood carving above the altar, the 'Pelican in Piety', which appears on the jacket of this book and which was to become the badge of the Royal Air Force Benevolent Fund. At Christmas 1971, McKelvey knew that the Fund, which had hitherto adopted the RAF badge, needed an emblem of its own — and here above the altar of St Clement Danes stood the answer.

One of Trenchard's many services to the Fund had been his swift gaining of permission for it to use the RAF badge as its emblem. Thus any potential benefactor receiving an appeal on notepaper bearing the familiar circle broken by eagle's wings and inscribed with the motto 'Per Ardua ad Astra' would recognise its authority. The motto had been approved for the Royal Flying Corps under an Army Order of 1913, but it was not until 1922 that Trenchard had obtained approval of the RAF badge — by approaching King George V personally for an immediate signature. Thereafter the paperwork had been minimal. The King had signed that the design was registered with the Royal College of Arms.

The RAF badge had served the Royal Air Force Benevolent Fund for half a century but, when Air Commodore McKelvey was appointed Appeals Secretary and fund-raising attitudes became more aggressive, even commercial and entrepreneurial, it seemed appropriate for the Fund to match its RAF badge with a distinctive emblem of its own. It was an aim which McKelvey thought would present few problems but which, without a Trenchard to march into the monarch, took five years to achieve.

The concept began to take off when Portal, attending his last Council meeting before his death in April 1971, said that he thought the Fund ought to have a tie, but that this would not be possible until it had a suitable badge.

Portal was spared the agonies of the five years in which the Fund, spearheaded by McKelvey, clashed in the most gentlemanly fashion with the Royal College of Arms until agreement was reached on a design for the badge. Indeed, it was not until January 1976 that McKelvey was able to inform the Controller: 'The receipt of a recommended design for a Fund badge from Garter marks the end of a battle with the College of Arms which started early in 1971. I was particularly pleased to see that the recommended design is almost identical to the original proposal.'

The design, the 'Pelican in Piety', was chosen because the Fund felt that the pelican, shown with its babies in the carving above the altar at St Clement Danes, symbolised the humanity which guides its decisions. At the outset, the suggestion had been approved by the Venerable L. J. Ashton, the then Chaplain-in-Chief of the RAF, who wrote: 'I cannot think there would be any ecclesiological or theological reasons why this emblem should not be used and indeed it would be a happy association between the Royal Air Force Benevolent Fund and the Church of St Clement Danes.'

The significance of the Fund's selection of and insistence upon the 'Pelican in Piety' can be found in an old belief that the pelican has the greatest love of all creatures for its young and pierces its breast to feed them with its own blood. It is on this basis that the pelican came to symbolise Christ's sacrifice on the Cross because of His love for all mankind, an interpretation which is supported by Psalm 102:6 — 'I am like a pelican of the wilderness', an accepted allusion to Christ.

In practice, the long beak of the white pelican includes a sac which retains the little fish with which it feeds its young. While feeding them it presses the sac against its neck, thus appearing to pierce its breast with its bill. The belief that the pelican drew blood from its breast was given credence in folklore by the reddish tint of its breast feathers and the red tip of its beak.

Although McKelvey's memorandum to the Controller had referred to 'the battle' with the Royal College of Arms, in fairness to Garter Principal King of Arms it should be explained that the College's procrastination involved no dispute over the use of the pelican. The chief difficulty was over the inclusion and style of the crown, for which Home Office permission was required. The Home Office was sympathetic in general but appeared to disapprove of the use of a crown badge on ties.

The Home Office viewed the Fund as a civilian organisation and, therefore, held reservations about the grant and use of the ensigned St Edward's crown in the interest of maintaining the value and significance of royal emblems.

The long delay was further compounded by the unfortunate circumstance that before a painted design could be sent to the Queen for her approval the Herald Painter was, as York Herald of Arms informed the Fund, 'mugged on the underground railway on his way home from work'.

It will ever remain a matter of regret to McKelvey that he had no Trenchard to bypass the middlemen, gatecrash the Palace and get the design approved on the spot.

Gradually, as McKelvey settled in as Appeals Secretary, the more contemporary fund-raising image which had seemed so desirable once the Fund had passed its half century began to emerge. The Appeals Committee, headed by Peake, was delighted in 1972 that activities to keep the Fund in the news and raise money were extended. Such events as Group Captain Douglas Bader, the legless Battle of Britain fighter ace, presenting the sports cups and prizes at Vanbrugh Castle School speech day in July, the Vanbrugh boys visiting the RAF base at Akrotiri in Cyprus in August, and a Whirlwind helicopter from the RAF station at Thorney Island giving an air-sea rescue display off the beach at Princess Marina House, played their part in helping the Fund to accumulate a total of £431,013, or about forty per cent of 1972's expenditure on the relief of distress. Among other efforts to keep the Benevolent Fund in the minds of both the public and the service were pictures of Corporal Michael Buxton of RAF, Colerne, handing a cheque of $500 to the Controller, money his team had received for winning a mock Battle of Waterloo at Houston in Texas, and also of the Controller visiting the Thrift Shop at RAF Stanmore, after it had presented £250 to the fund from its profits. Further, Air Vice-Marshal Broom had been in action again. At the annual carol service at St Clement Danes he presented the church with a goblet dating from the Napoleonic Wars 'as a late payment of a debt owed since 1940'. The goblet had been engraved by Miss Honoria Marsh, that rare artist, a diamond-point engraver, after being bought with money, donated to the Fund, raised in Broom's No. 11 Group, which in 1940 under the leadership of Air Vice-Marshal Keith Park — later Air Chief Marshal Sir Keith — had scrambled its squadrons from the forward airfields of south-east England between London and the sea.

In another gesture to help the Fund Miss Honoria Marsh also created a larger Royal Air Force goblet. On it the artist engraved the Churchill Statue in Parliament Square and Big Ben with the hands at 19.40. Around the base of the glass are symbolic smoke and flames with the inscription: 'This Was Their Finest Hour'. Nine aircraft, including the Hurricane, Spitfire, Lancaster and Mosquito, fly around the great goblet, which also includes the badges of the Royal Air Force and the Society of British Aerospace Companies. Miss Marsh signed an inscription on the base of the bowl: 'For All Those Who Did Not Fly Home — Lest We Forget'. The goblet was purchased by the SBAC with a donation of £5,000 to the Fund and is on permanent display at the Royal Air Force Museum, Hendon.

The effectiveness of keeping the Fund to the fore with the service can be appreciated from the fact that of the 1972 contributions total of £431,013 almost £351,000 had been contributed by servicemen and women, representing more than £3.25 each. However, satisfactory though this was, the Fund was concerned that those who had served were not making a comparable contribution and it was thought desirable to reach out to them and seek to supplement their share of the Royal Air Forces Association's contribution which, in 1972, was £22,065.

Possibly the most heartening part of McKelvey's first full year as Appeals Secretary was a big leap forward in legacies and capital donations, which at £252,003 were sixty-six per cent up on the previous year. This achievement was greatly assisted by the final payment from the Hattersley Bequest through which Mr R. E. Hattersley, an Ormskirk engineer and industrialist, who had died in 1949, left his fortune to the Fund. In a Council chamber ceremony on 20 April 1972, Mr Hubert Nicholson, a former chairman of Peglers (Holdings) Limited with which Hattersley (Ormskirk) Limited had merged, handed Peake a cheque for £25,000, bringing the total bequest to more than £700,000.

Very early spring had been propitious for the Fund in this year because, six days before Mr Nicholson's visit to Portland Place, the Duke and Duchess of Kent had attended the annual concert at the

Royal Festival Hall, the Duke attending as guest of honour for the first time since succeeding his mother as President. It was a happy augury because more than ninety per cent of the house was sold before the box office opened in March and within thirty minutes of its opening bookings were closed, creating a record £1,780 profit for a single RAF anniversary concert and bringing the total received from seventeen concerts to £17,222.

Spring is a time of reawakening and each year the early spring flowers in Regent's Park, where Fund staff take a lunch-hour stroll, confirm that yet another Appeals campaigning season is about to begin. Preparations for the summer's regular Battle of Britain and other outdoor activities must be well advanced, including those for the money-spinning *Royal Air Force Souvenir Book*, which in 1972 and 1973 made profits of £18,553 and £21,968, shared with the Royal Air Forces Association.

However, the problem, as ever, was to create or develop new sources of income and publicity. In the spring of 1973 Coles and McKelvey, with the help of Peter Taylor, whom Peake had now invited to join the Appeals Committee, began to take a more intimate interest in the Mosquito Memorial Museum at Salisbury Hall, the birthplace of the prototype de Havilland Mosquito, near St Albans in Hertfordshire. Since its opening in 1959 and its modest gate money contributions to the Fund, the Musuem had been enlarged sufficiently to attract increasing numbers of visitors until it had been acknowledged at Portland Place as a regular source of money and publicity for the Fund. By now McKelvey had joined the Salisbury Hall Committee as the Fund's representative and on 23 July 1973, at a Salisbury Hall ceremony, Group Captain John Cunningham, Chairman of the Mosquito Memorial Museum Committee, later to become the de Havilland Museum Trust Limited, presented Coles with a cheque for £1,000 with which to establish the Mosquito Memorial Fund as a subsidiary fund, to perpetuate the memory of the de Havilland Mosquito and of those who fought and died in the wooden aircraft whose exploits earned it the affectionate nickname of 'The Wooden Wonder'.

In 1973 the Fund's total income of £454,506, representing thirty-five per cent of the year's outgoings on the relief of distress, together with a record £394,472 in legacies and donations — fifty-seven per cent up on 1972 — owed much to the drive of McKelvey and his staff and Peter Taylor's public relations activities. Among these was the unveiling by Coles at the Royal Air Force Museum, Hendon, of the Fund's own exhibit. The display includes the log of Winston

Churchill's flight to Moscow in 1942 and a victory bell, one of many cast from the metal of destroyed Luftwaffe aircraft and sold during the Second World War on behalf of the Fund. It was also a year in which the flower-bed scheme, hitherto adopted at Folkestone, Blackpool, Southport and Scarborough, blossomed, enabling Taylor to report to the Appeals Committee that a particularly colourful floral rendering of RAF badge and wings had been planted in Calverley Grounds at Tunbridge Wells. Further flower-beds were to be planted at Torquay and Hastings in 1974 and 1975.

Here it should be added that, although the flower-beds have brought much pleasure to Taylor, he takes more pride in being a founder member, indeed the sole survivor, of the committee which launched the anniversary concerts, having produced twenty-five programmes.

The annual anniversary concerts cannot but produce some of the more moving moments of each Appeals year, the rousing music and the RAF march evoking so many personal memories among a predominantly service and ex-service audience. But in 1974 even the thunder of the stirring RAF march was stolen as the Dambusters March was played. For, centred in the Chairman's box as guest of honour, sat Sir Barnes Wallis, creator of the dambusting, bouncing bomb with which in 1943 Wing Commander Guy Gibson and his Lancaster crews breached the Mohne and Eder dams. As the music filled the Royal Festival Hall the entire audience rose to its feet in honour of Wallis, an audience which undoubtedly included men who owed their survival to Wallis's sturdy geodetic construction of the Wellington bomber, and men serving in the RAF whose education had been paid for at Christ's Hospital through the foundation created by the silver-haired inventor.

Presenting Sir Barnes that evening with the Fund's Battle of Britain poignard for outstanding services to the Royal Air Force Benevolent Fund, Sir Harald Peake reminded the gathering that in 1951, despite personal needs and a large family, the inventor had given his £10,000 bouncing-bomb award to launch the educational foundation at Christ's Hospital.

In terms of publicity it was difficult to compete with the pull of the name and reputation of Sir Barnes Wallis, but throughout 1974 the Fund fostered a round of activities to keep its work before the public and help to bring in £456,792, while legacies and capital donations for the year rose a further 26.5 per cent to just under £500,000.

Christmas card sales, so tentatively developed from the Brooms' do-it-yourself pilot scheme, had grown to the extent that the Fund was now selling eighteen different designs and, thanks to two designs, featuring the Red Arrows and St Clement Danes Church, donated by Chris Wren, *Flight International's* renowned cartoonist, was planning a further sales drive for the following year.

For all this, the emphasis of appeals still lay emphatically, if understandably, on the past exploits of the RAF. This did not, however, make the Fund any the less delighted with its share of the proceeds of Battle of Britain Week, for which the RAF's maintenance of the Flight of vintage aircraft is the essential element. In this respect annual surgery and convalescence is as imperative for the Flight Hurricane, Spitfire and Lancaster as for some of the former aircrew of those historic aircraft at Princess Marina House or Sussexdown. Consequently, in 1974 the Fund was indebted to the Silentbloc Holdings Group for making it possible to run the Merlin and Griffon engines in the Spitfire and Lancaster for a further ten years. At RAF Coltishall, the home of the Flight, Group Captain L. Swart, the Commanding Officer, received on behalf of the Fund a cheque for £250 from Mr R. A. Muir, Chairman of Silentbloc, the company's nominal charge to the Ministry of Defence for 100 essential onion couplings.

The following year's concert opening of the campaigning season, when Air Commodore F. M. F. West, the last surviving RAF holder of a First World War VC — he died in 1988 — was guest of honour, saw the beginning of Bill Coles's round of farewells, before his retirement in August 1975 closed the happy and fruitful partnership in the fund-raising business with Peake, Holloway, McKelvey and the staff at Portland Place.

Sadly Sir William was only able to enjoy four years of retirement. He died suddenly on 7 June 1979. A Thanksgiving Service was held in St Clement Danes Church on 31 July 1979, when the Church was crowded with serving and ex-serving members of the Royal Air Force, including those on the Staff of the Fund, and representatives of the Royal Air Forces Association, the 'Not Forgotten' Association, 194 Squadron Association and the Metropolitan Police.

Chapter 19
Four Eventful Years

Any reader of this account cannot but have been impressed by the good fortune which has attended the Royal Air Force Benevolent Fund in its choice of Controller. Throughout the Fund's seventy years the Council has appointed the man for the moment. There had been Uncle Mac, later of *Children's Hour*, who had received King Alfonso's fiver; Squadron Leader Erskine-Lindop, who had been the Secretary of the Fund during the Second World War, when it expanded tremendously, before the Fund had a Controller; Air Vice-Marshal Sir Hazelton Nicholl, who found and equipped 67 Portland Place; Cordingley, with his Victorian attention to detail and attitudes to hard work and thrift; Whitley, who visited most RAF stations; Coles the extrovert sportsman who led the Fund into the 1970s, inspiring the forward moves towards two of the Fund's greatest goals; and now in mid-August 1975, just four years short of the Diamond Jubilee, entered Crowley-Milling.

If, as the former Battle of Britain fighter pilot arrived at Portland Place at the age of fifty-six, it was premature to describe Air Marshal Sir Denis Crowley-Milling as yet another man for the moment, the rapid developments and the new directions leading up to the celebration of the Diamond Jubilee were to demonstrate that Peake, who had urged the appointment of Coles, had picked another winner.

It is not easy to equate the quiet, compact Air Marshal in half-moon spectacles with the fighter pilot of 1940. Even Dowding, for all his immense regard for the very young pilots he called his 'chicks', was as surprised as he was delighted in his declining years how well some of them had done in the higher ranks of the service or in business.

To name but two survivors of the Few, Group Captain Sir Hugh Dundas, who has since enjoyed a distiguished business career, and was a member of the Fund's Council and Finance and General Purposes Committee until May 1989; and Mr H. M. Stephen became managing director of the *Daily Telegraph*.

Denis Crowley-Milling, unlike so many of his fellow survivors of the Battle of Britain and of the Second World War, had stayed on in the RAF and joined the Fund after representing Britain at the

Central Treaty Organisation — an appointment reflecting his flair for diplomacy which had marked three years in the late 1960s as Commander RAF and Principal Air Attaché in Washington. These appointments had been preceded by periods commanding the RAF in Hong Kong, directing air operational requirements at the Ministry of Defence, and commanding the RAF's Nos 38 and 46 Groups.

Thirty-four years after the Rolls-Royce engineering apprentice received an attractive offer from industry as retirement in the rank of Air Marshal appeared on his horizon. In the event Crowley-Milling side-stepped industry and, encouraged by Marshal of the RAF Sir Andrew Humphrey, then Chief of the Air Staff, who had been his Commander-in-Chief when Crowley-Milling commanded Nos 38 and 46 Groups, he accepted Peake's invitation to succeed Coles.

Taking over from Coles, the new Controller knew that he had inherited a smooth-running organisation and it was not long before the salesman in him — in Washington Crowley-Milling had played an important part in selling the Harrier jump-jet to the US Marines — asserted itself. His chief role, he decided, should be to commit his talents to the complementary interests of publicising the Fund's work and bringing the money in. It was a policy of which Peake wholly approved. At a time of relentless inflation and ever-increasing demands on the Fund's resources Crowley-Milling's drive was precisely what was required.

The new Controller looked at the figures. Expenditure at the end of 1975 after his five months in office would be running at the rate of £1,818,484 a year against ordinary income of £1,833,599. Moreover, two of the most expensive and cash-consuming developments ever undertaken by the Fund were in the pipeline: the conversion of Woolpit into Duke of Kent School and the large-scale development of Princess Marina House. The costs of each project, with furniture and furnishings, were eventually to rise to nearly £1 million at the school and over £1 million at Princess Marina House.

As the new Controller, guided by the Council and Finance and General Purposes Committee, saw it, the Fund had spent bounteously on the post-war resettlement and housing of servicemen and women and on the education of their children, but now, with the 1980s in view, the needs of veterans of the Second World War as they reached old age had to be paramount.

Statistics do not disclose the plight of the bedridden fitter who had serviced Lancaster bombers on frozen airfields in wartime winters, the arthritic air-gunners, the varicosed, overweight former WAAF or WRAF cook, but the Fund had to face a situation in which many such people would be numbered among its beneficiaries, with disabilities ranging between ten per cent and 100 per cent. In discussions with Sir David Lee, Crowley-Milling was especially alerted by him to the numbers in which twenty per cent disability cases of more than thirty years ago developed into disability of eighty per cent or more as ex-servicemen and women advanced from middle to old age.

Most of the war-time leaders had already departed: Dowding in 1970 and in the same year Thurso, who as Sir Archibald Sinclair had been a wartime Air Minister; Portal in 1971. In the Fund's Diamond Jubilee year, Dowding's 'chicks' were in their sixties. Thus, far from the needs of ageing veterans receding, survivors of the Second World War would require ever more costly care and succour as their war began to feature in the history lessons at Duke of Kent School.

Duke of Kent School differs in so many respects from Vanbrugh that in Diamond Jubilee year, three years after Vanbrugh's merger with Woolpit, it seemed almost invidious to make comparisons. Yet such were the heart-searchings from the smallest Vanbrugh boy to the most senior members of the Fund's Council that preceded the break and the move, that respect for them demanded a hearing.

Boys and grown-ups cross such chasms with differing perspectives and yet it was Arthur Rodgers, a former Vanbrugh pupil and later a master at Duke of Kent, Bill Jones, headmaster, and Michael Morton, the Fund's longest-serving schoolmaster, who produced a common outlook. It was this: they had exchanged one remarkable view for another; they missed the quaint passages and dungeons of the castle and the school had gained much from the admission of girls.

Each of these points serves to exemplify an essential difference between Vanbrugh Castle and Duke of Kent. If Vanbrugh might have been custom-built to appeal to the romanticism of an eight-year-old boy writing in his first week of term from the heights of Blackheath, 'Dear Mummy, I live in a castle and can hear the ships on the river at night', Vanbrugh's stout main gates, broad grey walls and crenellation presented a stark, ancient appearance.

In contrast, Duke of Kent School set in forty glorious acres in the Surrey Hills and with a view which stretches to Chanctonbury Ring — and on a clear day a blue pinpoint glimpse of the sea — is everything a fee-paying preparatory school can aspire to be. The country mansion built in the 1880s by Sir Henry Doulton, the ceramic tile pioneer, together with the modern annexe and hall built by the Royal Air Force Benevolent Fund, combine to remind the school's boys and girls of the stolid values of Victorian Britain, while providing them with a kitchen, dining-hall, science laboratory and dormitories as remote from that period as the moon might have seemed to Doulton.

Cementing the merger, the Fund respected Doulton's fabric and interior decoration — the headmaster's tiled ornamental bathroom is a museum piece — as it also respected the memory of Woolpit School, amalgamating its traditions with those of Vanbrugh. A quiet place of worship and altar to the left of the front hall remains in use, recalling that Woolpit was founded in 1949 by Dr Francis Brown, the Rector of nearby East Clandon. Dr Brown's wish was to educate the sons of clergy and the St Thomas's Church Schools Company was formed to manage the school as it moved to Woolpit House from its one-room start in the Rectory. Dr Brown gave up his living at East Clandon and was headmaster from September 1950 until leaving five years afterwards for Milton Abbey School.

From the moment of Coles's first inquiry, Dr Brown's successor, Mr John Hall and his wife, who had come to Woolpit from the Cathedral School at Wells, put their all into smoothing the merger, retiring only after Bill and Peggy Jones were as thoroughly at home at Woolpit as they had been at Vanbrugh Castle. However, even the Halls' departure did not break the link with Woolpit's excellent record. Mr Ingram Blenkarn, who had joined Dr Brown as a master at the school's inception, stayed on and took over among other duties, the burden of collecting the fees as bursar. His colleagues also elected to carry on. Nor were any of the eighty-five Woolpit boys removed by their parents. The Fund was also delighted that several of Woolpit's Governors, headed by Mr Trevor Jones, joined the new Board under the chairmanship of Air Chief Marshal Sir Walter Merton.

At the outset, Duke of Kent's pupil population of 135, of whom forty were Vanbrugh pupils, or Foundationers as those assisted by the Fund are known, and ten other service-connected new boys, was imbalanced in favour of Woolpit. The Fund's policy was to increase the RAF presence gradually as Woolpit boys moved on to public schools. By Diamond Jubilee year, of a total of 157 pupils there were forty-three Foundationers, seventy-seven were fee-paying service children, twenty-one were fee-paying boarders and sixteen were fee-paying private day pupils. Of the total some twenty pupils were girls of RAF parentage.

In its second term the merged school had settled down sufficiently for the Governors to welcome the Duke of Kent's offer to visit it on 3 March 1977. He lunched with the boys, talked with many of them in the classrooms and toured the grounds and MacRobert Playing Fields.

The school, as the Duke found it, was divided into four houses named Churchill, Whittle, Armstrong and Hillary. Much consideration had been given to the selection of these names. Those of RAF leaders and heroes were avoided deliberately because Duke of Kent School included non-service children (Whittle's name was used because of his jet engine, not because he was an Air Commodore). Nevertheless, the RAF has received its due recognition throughout the school buildings. Just as the name of the Duke of Kent's Air Commodore father, who was killed on active service in 1942, is honoured in the title of the school, classrooms and dormitories are named after Trenchard, father of the RAF and founder of the Fund, Tedder, Deputy Supreme Commander in Europe to Eisenhower, Guy Gibson VC, leader of the Dambusters, and many others.

The memory of Sir Harald Peake, who before his death in May 1978 had done so much in Council and Committee to ensure removal from Vanbrugh Castle and promote the wisdom of spending generously on new buildings, is fittingly perpetuated in a hangar-size all-purpose chapel, hall, theatre and gymnasium which bears his name; as it is also at the swimming-pool which he made available in all seasons by paying for a convertible roof as a personal gift to the school.

Yet such excellent facilities and heavy investment do not of themselves constitute a successful school without one essential ingredient — the right spirit. Here the Duke of Kent was impressed by the happy, well-ordered routine, the simple rules based on common sense, and an overall insistence that courtesy, kindness and consideration for others is expected at all times.

Towards the end of the 1980s when it can be argued that such standards have shown a national decline, Duke of Kent School sets a meritorious example. In economic service phraseology, the Royal Air Force Benevolent Fund defines the school's objectives thus: 'To provide for the optimum development of character and intellectual ability of all pupils whilst fostering the qualities of integrity, unselfishness, leadership, self-discipline and self-confidence'.

It was fitting at a time of so much change in the Fund's leadership and outlook that Marshal of the Royal Air Force Lord Elworthy, a Vice-President since 1964, who was shortly to return to his native New Zealand, should address the school as principal guest at the July 1978 Speech Day and describe it as 'one of the most imaginative creations of the RAF Benevolent Fund'. The departure of the Elworthys saddened all at Portland Place, where Lady Elworthy was to be much missed in Council, as a member of the Finance and

General Purposes Committee and Deputy Chairman of the Grants Committee since 1974.

In March 1979 Air Chief Marshal Sir Walter Merton, who had been primarily responsible for the 'imaginative creation' of Duke of Kent School, retired as Chairman of its Board and handed over to Air Chief Marshal Sir Lewis Hodges. After previously chairing the Vanbrugh Board since 1967 and the Fund's Education Committee and serving on the Council and Finance and General Purposes Committee, Sir Walter could leave Duke of Kent in the knowledge that it was flourishing, paying its way and full to capacity.

Determination by the Royal Air Force Benevolent Fund to extend the facilities at Princess Marina House dovetailed happily with the philosophy which had diverted Crowley-Milling from industry after retiring from the service. If the Controller and ex-RAF colleagues at Portland Place, in the Fund's branches and among its hundreds of voluntary helpers could find pleasure and satisfaction from working and associating in a familiar, well-ordered atmosphere, then it was a duty to attempt to provide similarly congenial surroundings among the convalescent, sick and disabled, and also their dependants.

Wherever possible, present and former members of the RAF and, accommodation permitting, the Army and Navy should be rescued from the wards of a much-stretched National Health Service and cared for among people whose shared memories, experiences and standards would accelerate a convalescent's restoration to health and comfort the long-term residents.

Crowley-Milling, ably assisted by Allan Scott, threw himself wholeheartedly into the excutive task of creating the development at Princess Marina House — once not unreasonably described in the RAF *News* as 'the Savoy of the South Coast' enabling fifty long-term residents, some in need of light nursing, to be cared for while buildings going back to Mrs Newton Driver's days continue to provide convalescent accommodation for a further fifty men and women.

Late in 1976 the groundwork resulted in the Council's approval in principle of the construction of a building to accommodate about fifty partially disabled and aged people in the grounds of Princess Marina House at an estimated cost of £800,000 and, as Peake reported to the Council, £650,000 had been appropriated from the 1976 accounts to meet part of this expenditure.

In the following year the total of guests established a new record of 569, illustrating that the Rustington complex was already bursting at the seams. However, a new house for the Manager was almost ready, making his former house, Adref — part of the original arrangement with Mrs Newton Driver — available for use as a club within the large development for which planning permission had now been received.

The specification for this building work had been put out to tender and Mr Donald Ensom of Debenham, Tewson and Chinnocks had been appointed Project Manager. In consultation with Allan Scott he co-ordinated the professional team and Scott acted as the 'link man' with the Committee. Supporting its desire to press forward speedily with the work the Fund appropriated an additional £700,000 in the accounts for 1977 towards its cost.

Any novelist, playwright, short-story or documentary writer short of inspiration would be rewarded by a visit to Princess Marina House. Cocooned temporarily or permanently in its comfort are to be found people with as interesting and extraordinary reminiscences as are likely to be found in any such centre in Britain.

The stories are as varied as the ages and experiences of their narrators. Nursing his beer in the club one could find Ron, who, looking back from his late eighties, could remember helping de Havilland with experimental work in 1913. He served in the Royal Flying Corps in the First World War and, after a civilian interval as a toolmaker, returned to the RAF as a flight sergeant, retaining his RFC service number of 981, such a low number that wherever Ron was stationed it was difficult to convince the squadron that it was correct. He was one of the early birds of the service and one of the first long-term residents in 1969.

Toni Turton flew — yes, flew — at Netheravon in 1918 and, at the age of forty-six, rejoined in 1941. She would have jumped back into uniform at the outbreak of the Second World War had she not been in a reserved occupation as a schoolteacher. Then, at forty-six, she was allowed to resign — in consideration of her age — and rejoin.

No less absorbing are the stories of the convalescents. Obviously these will depend upon who happens to be staying as a temporary guest. On a particular morning two men and two women are exchanging reminiscences over coffee in the sun lounge. The men are widowers and the women are widows, but it is their association with the RAF, Army or Navy rather than their bereavements that has brought them together in Sussex-by-the-Sea.

There is the Chinese lady from Lymington in Hampshire. When the Second World War broke out in 1939 she was the wife of a British businessman in Singapore with two small children. Her husband packed his bags and returned home to join up. When Singapore fell and the Japanese marched in she slipped quietly out of town and into her family village as a bird might seek the protective colouring of its environment. Her husband trained to parachute into Malaya to join the anti-Japanese guerrillas and in the hope of making contact with his family. Becoming unfit while training, he was unable to carry out his plan and returned with the British Military Administration when Singapore and Malaya were reoccupied in September 1945.

Now he was dead, but his widow was eligible for the care and comforts of Princess Marina House; as was the former WRAF balloon operator whose husband, who had served in the wartime Air Force, had died recently of a heart attack. Unnerved by the stress and strains of losing her husband and contending with the problems of his business, she needed a change and a rest and here she was. And here, too, were the two widowers.

Each of the men had served in the Second World War yet their lives had run dissimilar courses until a common need of convalescence had brought them together in this sunny lounge within a hundred yards of the sea. Here was Bill, who had joined the RAF as an apprentice in 1930 and had helped to plan the invasion — eventually the peaceful reoccupation — of Singapore and Malaya as a staff officer in India. He had not retired from the service until 1968 at the age of fifty-five, when he started a civilian career as an executive working with the British Aircraft Corporation on the air support system for Concorde. After six years with the company he had started a second civilian career as a works manager in the manufacture of exhaust systems. At sixty-six, after heart surgery and the loss of his wife, he was convalescing, improving his French and planning a third civilian career in the Common Market.

Andy, the second widower, rolls up the trouser leg of his recently amputated right leg and tells his story. He is sixty-four and wears a neat white beard, but his dark, deep sunk eyes are as quick and sharp as in the days before the Second World War when he learnt to fly as a Civil Air Reserve pilot in his native New Zealand. He flew Fairey Battles with No. 103 Squadron in 1940 and his subsequent exploits as a Wellington bomber pilot with No. 108 Squadron in the Middle East are recorded in the official history of the Royal New Zealand Air Force. But the historians do not narrate how Andy converted to Liberators and fell asleep in the Liberator ferrying his crew from the Middle East to pick up a Liberator of their own. Andy was picked out of the wreckage of the ferry Liberator in the mountains of Mourne. His legs were badly damaged and burnt but he escaped to Northern Ireland from the Irish Republic and was sufficiently repaired to return to flying and to drop paratroops from a converted Whitley bomber after the invasion of Normandy.

Now, all these years afterwards, the old leg wounds had played him up — and they had lopped a leg off at the Queen Victoria Hospital in East Grinstead, the Sty of the Guinea Pig Club, it will be recalled. There he had encountered Lady McIndoe, widow of Sir Archibald McIndoe, and she had diverted Andy in the direction of Princess Marina House whence, after a rest, he returned to his self-employed business of making and selling sails for racing yachts.

The coffee trolley is wheeled away and Sister Christine Hall reminds Bill that it is time for his heat treatment; and as it is now midday, Wing Commander Arthur Carvossso, who had managed Princess Marina House since November 1973, suggests a visit to the club. Can it be more than a coincidence that, as with Bill Jones, Headmaster at Duke of Kent School, Carvosso is a former Second World War flying instructor, that Bill Coles as an instructor had examined Crowley-Milling in the Canal Zone of the Middle East for his routine pilot's instrument re-rating?

It must be a certainty that the patience and encouragement with which pupil pilots from such varied educational and social backgrounds were taught to fly to operational standards during and after the war had equipped Bill Jones and Arthur Carvosso for their respective responsibilities in their fifties. Carvosso flew with the RAF for twenty-eight years and had all but accepted a senior post with the Red Cross when Bill Coles invited him to manage Princess Marina House. The gravitational pull of the RAF way of life, as with Crowley-Milling and almost all who serve the Fund, had proved decisive and it was only when he was interviewed for the appointment that Carvosso discovered that the Chairman of the Princess Marina House Committee was Air Chief Marshal Sir Wallace 'Digger' Kyle, the the Australian whom he had served recently as personal staff officer.

Flight Lieutenant Frank Smith, Carvosso's deputy manager, came to Rustington with similar sentiments and, although no ex-officer could be more suitable for the post, his recruitment owed everything to the chance that Coles was playing golf with a Ministry of Defence friend when he dropped the hint that he was looking for a retiring officer with a Princess Mary's nursing sister wife. Could he find somebody who would fit the bill? Coles's opponent had produced Frank and Berwyn Smith and it was only after the couple had joined the staff of the Royal Air Force Benevolent Fund that Frank encountered Paul Cutting, the Secretary (Administration) and a member of the Princess Marina House Committee. Smith and Cutting had joined the RAF on the same day in the 1930s at Ruislip, where a certain Group Captain Cordingley was their Commanding Officer.

Such coincidences and service relationships cannot but fuel the great warmth and friendliness which contributes to the convalescence and well-being of the guests and residents at Princess Marina House.

Throughout the Fund's offices and branches the spirit of the RAF in war and peace pervades its welfare work, but no more so than in the Princess Marina House club where, from behind the bar in this period, the silver handlebar moustache of Squadron Leader Gower Peachment and the steady hand at the optics of his wife Peggy recall that he fought in the Battle of Britain and she survived the bombing of Biggin Hill, where she had been one of Dame Felicity Peake's WAAFs.

Perhaps the best feature of the whole Princess Marina House complex is the care that has been taken to facilitate the self-propulsion, either on foot, crutches or in chairs, of disabled people. Lifts do not take off like rockets, nor do they open and shut at speed as if to suit their own convenience. They await the whim of the user with admirable patience in these times of high-speed technology. Passages, such as the link-way to the club in its separate house, have been designed to make wheelchair travel possible and comfortable. This is a consideration which was especially appreciated by Lady Burton, the wife of Air Marshal Sir Harry Burton, Kyle's successor as Chairman of the Princess Marina House Management Committee, and Crowley-Milling's former Commander-in-Chief. Lady Burton, who was a polio victim and in a wheelchair, was to be a source of much practical advice.

The club was opened on 24 July 1978 by Lord Catto, shortly after his succession to the late Sir Harald Peake as Chairman of the Royal Air Force Benevolent Fund. In the course of the ceremony Catto unveiled a portrait of Marshal of the Royal Air Force Sir Andrew Humphrey, who was Chief of the Defence Staff at the time of his death at the age of fifty-six. Henceforth, the bar has been known a The Andrew Humphrey Room. It is furnished from donations received by Lady Humphrey, who is a member of the Fund's Council and Finance and General Purposes Committee, and advised on the furnishing of the development.

'There is a cosy, well-stocked and friendly little bar,' wrote Mrs Newton Driver in the post-war brochure for her Services' Club at Rustington. Although Mrs Newton Driver would not recognise the much larger Andrew Humphrey Room as it is today she would be as much at home with its users as in her wartime London club or indeed its 'cosy' predecessor. Nor would she fail to find the occasional familiar face. Rose Jackson, looking after the linen, was at Rustington from the start; as also was Topsy, Mrs Newton Driver's black cat. Topsy, until her death in 1979, was fed and cared for by the RAF Benevolent Fund under the terms of its acquisition of the property and Mrs Newton Driver's bequest.

Among the Fund's reasons for launching its large-scale development at Princess Marina House was a desire to overcome the problem of burdening its Storrington neighbour, the Royal Air Forces Association's home at Sussexdown, with patients suffering from extreme disability and requiring constant nursing. There will, no doubt, continue to be people for whom the Fund will seek and pay for places at Sussexdown while, reciprocally, the Royal Air Forces Association will recommend convalescents for Princess Marina House as one of the many two-way arrangements between the organisations.

Here it should be emphasised that never in their long relationship has the rapport between the Fund and RAFA been so harmonious and it helped in recent years that Coles, Crowley-Milling's predecessor, had been the Fund's representative on RAFA's Council and that Crowley-Milling was a close personal friend of long standing with RAFA's President, Air Chief Marshal Sir Augustus 'Gus' Walker. It was particularly helpful that the one-armed Air Chief Marshal served as RAFA's representative on the Fund's Council and was a Vice-President of the Fund.

With its network of clubs and representatives throughout the country, the Royal Air Forces Association gives enormous assistance by investigating cases on behalf of the Welfare Secretary of the Fund and his staff.

While RAFA has Sussexdown and its own convalescent home, Richard Peck House at St Annes-on-Sea in Lancashire, the interdependence of the organisations was never so evident as in Diamond Jubilee year. In the simplest terms, the apparent contradiction of there being two such organisations, with what would appear to be many similar objects, can be explained thus: their efforts are complementary. The Royal Air Forces Association normally turns to the Royal Air Force Benevolent Fund for grants and loans when it wishes to relieve the distress of its members. Through its clubs and its Battle of Britain fund-raising activities it contributes generously to the Fund. It also helps where cases are outside the Fund's scope, for example by assisting pilgrimages to war memorials and providing an advice service on pensions, disability awards and job-seeking.

The Fund, for its part, is so indebted for the assistance it receives

from the Royal Air Forces Association that it will listen sympathetically to any request for special expenditure involving a large sum of
money. As an example, in 1974 the Fund, after being approached by
Air Vice-Marshal Sir Ben Ball of RAFA for a loan of £60,000
towards building a new wing at Sussexdown, offered an interest-free
loan for the total with repayment spread over five years. In the event
the RAFA repaid £30,000 and the Fund converted the balance of
£30,000 to a donation, which was used to name three beds at
Sussexdown in memory of Peake, Bandon and Cordingley, making a
total of six beds endowed by the Fund.

Towards the end of his first six months as Controller, Crowley-
Milling was as impressed as Coles had been by the sheer volume of
welfare work processed at Portland Place. In his Chairman's report
for 1975, Peake, making the point that the new Controller had taken
over 'a highly efficient and dedicated staff of eighty-five men and
women', said that 'at first sight this might appear to be on the large
side'. However, it had not taken Crowley-Milling very long to
appreciate that, quite apart from the Fund's many other activities,
servicing the Grants Committees required painstaking hours of work,
often involving lengthy and detailed negotations to provide housing,
education, transport or domestic help. In 1975, not only had 7,368
awards been made at a cost of £1,494,033, but 902 applications had
been declined mainly due to the absence of any degree of distress.
Refusals were as time-consuming as acceptances and, because it is
less easy to say no, often more testing of the staff's emotional
resources. It is not difficult to imagine, for example, the work
involved before the following case was presented to a Committee
chaired by Lady Elworthy, who in 1970 had become the first lady
member of the Finance and General Purposes Committee and who
was then Deputy Chairman to Air Chief Marshal Sir David Lee,
Chairman of the Grants Committee.

The wife of a sergeant with seventeen years' service had died from
cancer. She had been in considerable pain for some time and could
not cope with their four young children. The Fund found boarding
schools for the children, bought their uniforms and paid the fees after
taking into account the service educational grant. But this was only
part of the Fund's involvement. The sergeant was buying a house on
mortgage and with only a short time left to serve a move into quarters
would be unsettling. The sergeant's case was strongly recommended
by his station commander and the Committee sanctioned assistance
which went far beyond the school fees and uniforms, taking in funeral
costs and debts.

Among the year's awards there were many such considerable undertakings, but the spending of smaller sums can often involve more investigation, care and discretion. A sergeant observer had been killed in 1941 on flying operations and his mother had died soon afterwards. Now his father, aged seventy-eight, lived alone. The Fund would not have heard of this elderly man's distress and lack of interest in life had it not received an anonymous letter from a sympathiser. Because the old man's son had served and died in the RAF, the Fund made a grant to buy a new radio and other necessities.

A flying officer of the Second World War had died of cancer in December 1974, leaving a severely disabled widow suffering from osteo-arthritis. She had an invalid car, but could move in her cottage only with the aid of sticks or a frame. She had lived there for some years and it was considered best that she should remain among friends. But there was the problem of meeting mortgage repayments from a very limited income. The Fund took over her mortgage with repayments delayed indefinitely.

It merits note, incidentally, that despite inflation 1975 witnessed a small reduction in cases and the cost of relief, reductions which Sir David Lee attributed to a drop in requests for house purchase loans and to increased war pensions, supplementary benefits and other pensions and allowances. It seemed also that the benefits of the Insurance Advisory Service and RAF Dependants Fund and Income Trust were beginning to reduce the demands on the Benevolent Fund.

In 1976 the upward trend in relief expenditure resumed, 7,859 people receiving assistance totalling £1,759,626. The Fund's surplus of ordinary income over expenditure was £32,761 compared with £15,115 in 1975.

But 1977 was a very much better year. While relief of distress was as ever the first priority in spending income, the Council was much encouraged that welfare spending had dropped from 7,859 cases to 6,916 and the overall cost, including administration, was down to £1,689,141. Moreover, the surplus of ordinary income over expenditure had soared to £579,494. Possibly with some of the Fund's less provident beneficiaries in mind, Peake told the Council: 'It is always prudent to live within one's income and this we have again succeeded in doing.' He warned, however, that it seemed unlikely that the lower trend in the cost of relief would continue in 1978.

It fell to Lord Catto to bear out Peake's warning. Reporting to the Council on the Fund's activities in 1978, the new Chairman disclosed that expenditure of £2,023,322 on the relief of distress had exceeded £2 million for the first time, bringing total annual expenditure to almost £2.5 million. Fortunately, however, increased income at £532,069 from the RAF and from investments — up from £1,033,239 to £1,099,637 — and a marked increase in legacies had enabled total income at £2,493,793 to exceed total expenditure ot £2,488,261, if only just. At the end of the year investments at book value stood at £9,030,796 compared with the 1977 figure of £8,617,964. In all the circumstances the Chairman regarded the results as 'highly satisfactory', a further £500,000 having been appropriated to the Development Fund which had now financed the expansion at Duke of Kent School and was financing the Princess Marina House development. Such results, Catto told the Council, were 'a great credit to his predecessor, Sir Harald Peake, who in the last few years of his life had devoted himself wholeheartedly to the Fund's interests'.

Such results, as Catto, a merchant banker, was only too well aware, could not be achieved without much painstaking work before the balance sheets could be prepared for the Finance and General Purposes Committee and the Council. Since succeeding Jack Cairns as Finance Secretary six years earlier, Ted Holloway had expanded the scope of the Finance Department considerably so that the Secretary and his staff had become much more closely involved with investment decisions and procedure. Ted Holloway accompanied the Controller at the routine meetings with Morgan Grenfell and took a leading role in the preparation of proposals for the purchase and sale of stock.

Another important aspect of the Finance Department's role in maintaining the Fund's income and capital is the persistence — and compassion — with which it recovers loans. Here the Finance Secretary is much assisted by a number of ladies, each of whose length of service as Portland Place is such that their knowledge of cases stretching back for many years helps them to interpret in human terms figures spewed out by the Fund's computer. It would be ungallant to the ladies who staff the department to total their combined years of service, but suffice it to say that the aggregate provides invaluable continuity, especially where loans and their repayment are concerned.

Notwithstanding the fact that in 1975 reduction in welfare cases and the cost of relief had proved short-lived, Sir David Lee, in suggesting that the Insurance Advisory Service, Royal Air Force Dependants Fund and Income Trust may have contributed to this bonus, had put his finger on a vital element as the Fund approached the 1980s, with all the threat to its financial defences an ageing ex-service population implied.

Crowley-Milling followed Coles's example of driving home the benefits of these three additional arms to the Benevolent Fund. He was ably assisted by Ginger Murray, another Battle of Britain pilot, who had now become the senior executive of the Insurance Advisory Service, and by Wing Commander Freddy Tame who, in addition to running the Dependants (Income) Trust, had taken over the secretaryship of the Dependants Fund from Innes Westmacott, who had to leave due to the effects of injuries sustained in an aircraft crash many years previously. By the end of 1978 the Royal Air Force Dependants Fund had only to reap the remaining five per cent of servicemen and women to produce a 100 per cent membership — a prime target for the Diamond Jubilee year. It was highly telling that up to October 1978 the Trustees had made 1,271 grants totalling £807,905 with each grant since the beginning of March 1977 being £900. Membership of the Royal Air Force Dependants (Income) Trust had reached some twenty per cent of Dependants Fund subscribers by 1978 as a result of an increase of 2,000 in the first six months of the year. Many of the subscribers to the Income Trust have taken additional units of benefit which would have provided their beneficiaries with a greater income than the £440 per year cover by the basic membership benefit. On leaving the service, subscribers may without any evidence of health continue the cover provided under the Trust into civilian life as a direct policy with the underwriters. This can be in the form of an endowment or whole life cover or as similar benefits as provided under the Trust while in the service.

Meanwhile, life and other policies resulting from the counsel of the Insurance Advisory Service continued to multiply and by the end of 1978 impartial advice had — with much help from Mr R. L. Jones, the Fund's insurance consultant, and in retirement its honorary consultant — been given to 13,470 members of the RAF, the sums assured amounting to almost £21 million.

An extremely satisfactory aspect of the increasing use of the Insurance Advisory Service, RAF Dependants Fund and Income Trust was that in the 1970s service people were so ready to take advantage of them in addition to giving half a day's pay a year to the Royal Air Force Benevolent Fund and contributing through a range of activities at RAF stations. As did his predecessors since Dowding's insistence on the scheme shortly before he fought the Battle of Britain, Crowley-Milling, from the beginning of his controllership, kept a weather eye on income from the service, an income which rose to £466,733 in 1976 but dropped back slightly to £465,744 in 1977. Despite the setback Peake felt it was still a creditable achievement, taking into account a diminishing RAF and the effects of inflation. He told the Council: 'A service which helps itself to this extent need not feel ashamed of appealing for public supprt.'

The Controller's instinct, however, was that the service could do better and he launched a drive to secure more covenanted subscriptions, introducing the simple expedient of making it necessary to opt out of a covenant rather than into one when undertaking to subscribe to the half-a-day's-pay scheme. In 1978 of some eighty-three per cent of serving subscribers thirty-three per cent had signed covenants, contributing towards a total income from all RAF sources of £532,069.

In his early weeks at Portland Place there were moments when Crowley-Milling, the *Financial Times* at his elbow as he settled down behind the desk in the corner of the Council chamber, must have wondered whether after all he had not opted for a career in business. He relished his share of the responsibility for the Fund's investments and power to sanction market deals within certain limits. He was most ably assisted by Ted Holloway. Indeed, he was working and living much in the style of the managing director of a fair-sized company — his 'company' had accumulated funds at the end of 1975 of about £10 million — and it helped that he was fortunate in being the first Controller to make his London home, at Peake's request, at 8 Clarendon Close in West London, a mews house which had formed part of Mrs Newton Driver's bequest. The availability of Mrs Newton Driver's London home greatly assisted Crowley-Milling's energetic pursuit of all aspects of the Fund's welfare, investment and fund-raising activities. It was a place where he could entertain Fund supporters. It was almost as if he were living 'over the shop'. His successors at Portland Place, Steedman and Kennedy, were also to make a London home there.

Peake, the banker, Catto, the merchant banker investment consultant, and Crowley-Milling, supported by an array of expertise in Council, Committee, and among the staff, presented a formidable money team behind, as Peake told the Council in 1976, his 'determination to maintain the present strong financial position of the Fund'.

In 1976 income from investment was up from £814,863 to £887,131 and ordinary income was £2,156,122 compared with £1,833,599 in 1975. One particularly satisfying aspect was the rate at which loan repayments were rising, amounting to £630,271 in 1976 against

£449,259 in the previous year. Peake noted that this was partly due to the fairly recent policy of making short-term loans to members of the RAF within the last two years of their service to help them to adjust to civilian life and thereby diminish a potential source of distress. As an example, a WRAF corporal, leaving the service after twenty-two years and wishing to buy a caravan for her retirement, received a loan against her terminal gratuity so that she could have the caravan ready to move into from service quarters.

Working closely with Morgan Grenfell, the Fund kept investments under close and constant review in the years leading to the Diamond Jubilee and, while Peake's death in June 1978 was an irreplaceable loss, the election of Lord Catto, the investment consultant, to the chairmanship — he was now also chairman of Morgan Grenfell — was a considerable compensation. By 1977 accumulated funds had risen from £10,651,587 to £11,714,954. In 1978 they were £12,710,102. Investments in 1978 at book value were £9,030,225 compared with £8,617,964 in 1977 and a gratifying increase was achieved in Diamond Jubilee year.

Legacies and capital donations were sources of addition to capital which also closely engaged the Controller's attention. The occasional windfall, such as the Hattersley bequest or a legacy of £242,000 received in 1975 from Mrs M. E. M. Lousada, whose only son Ormond had been killed as an air-gunner in November 1944, make legacies something of a lottery in the annual accumulation of capital. Donations and their sources are just unpredictable. Over the years Mr Ian Smith, the Rhodesian politician who served in the RAF as a fighter pilot during the Second World War, has remembered the Fund and its needs by passing on fees for his articles published in British newspapers. It will be recalled that when McKelvey took over from Arbuthnot in 1971 legacies had nose-dived by twenty-seven per cent to £151,691, making them nearly £100,000 down on Golden Jubilee year. Subsequently, in McKelvey's early years as Appeals Secretary, they had recovered substantially, rising from £474,357 at the end of 1975 to £493,305 at the end of 1976, Crowley-Milling's first full year. A drop to £279,786 in 1977, the year of McKelvey's retirement from full-time employment, impressed the Fund with the urgency for a special effort in this direction. Crowley-Milling therefore sought to regularise the likelihood of legacies so far as might be possible by inviting McKelvey to carry on part-time as Legacies and Trust Officer. After his experience as Appeals Secretary no one was more conscious of the needs of contact-keeping with potential benefactors and their legal and accountancy advisers, of chasing bequests in the pipeline and hunting for new legacies. McKelvey glady accepted the new appointment.

There was the difficulty, however, with the Portland Place offices bursting at the seams, of finding suitable accommodation there. But legacy hunters are not easily daunted and McKelvey, displaying the enterprise which had brought him from boy apprentice to Air Commodore, took possession of what used to be a tiny attic bathroom and very soon the results of his labours in this specialist field were apparent.

It is fitting to close this chapter with what proved to be a particularly profitable money-raising operation.

The Controller had long admired the wildlife and aircraft paintings of David Shepherd when the artist, grateful to the service for flying him to Aden and Nairobi, asked, 'Can I do something for the Royal Air Force?' The question, first put to Air Marshal Sir Maurice Heath, who had arranged the Aden visit, was referred to the Fund where Crowley-Milling said: 'Why not paint the last Lancaster for us?' Bascially, the proposal was for a portrait of the RAF's most illustrious Second World War four-engined heavy bomber. No more than 850 signed and numbered prints were to be sold at £150 each on behalf of the Fund. Donation of a further £100 would secure one of a limited number of 176 prints signed by Marshal of the Royal Air Force Sir Arthur Harris — Bomber Harris — and by Sir Barnes Wallis, whose bouncing bomb had been carried by Wing Commander Guy Gibson's Lancaster force in the breaching of the Mohne and Eder dams.

But David Shepherd's great enthusiasm considerably broadened the project. He explains:

> I owe a very great debt of gratitude to the Royal Air Force, for it was through their flying me to Kenya in 1960 that I became a wildlife artist and it seemed only reasonable, therefore, to accept their invitation to paint a picture to raise funds for the Royal Air Force Benevolent Fund. Moreover, it was a marvellous opportunity to return to one of my first loves which I had almost totally neglected for several years, aviation art, and paint a Lancaster bomber, my favourite aircraft.

> I hope I have been able to evoke, in my painting, the memories and feelings which must still be fresh in the minds of thousands of ground and aircrew, now dispersed all over the world, who flew 'Lancs' with the Royal Air Force during those momentous days of the Second World War. How many must

still remember 'their' Lanc at far-flung dispersals; a watery sun casting long shadows on a chill autumn evening; the leafless elms of a countryside 'somewhere in England'; the wet runway and the mud; and all the untidy clutter of last-minute preparations before take-off; final adjustments to an engine — 'the revs were a bit low on the port inner last night over Essen, Fred — it's Cologne tonight, so get 'em right' — and the inevitable bicycles. I hope it is all there, the feeling of those historic times.

As the illustration of the painting shows, it was — but not before a painstaking search for period vehicles and other bomber airfield paraphernalia had authenticated the setting. On the last day the last Lanc sat for its portrait it refused to rain and water was sprayed around the dispersal point to catch the reflection of the sky.

Once the painting was ready the Fund adopted the limited-edition formula Shepherd had followed with his paintings 'Tiger Fire' and 'African Afternoon', which raised more than £200,000 between them for the World Wildlife Fund.

A reception was held in the RAF Museum, Hendon, in the spring of 1978 for the buyers of the numbered prints of 'Winter of '43, Somewhere in England'. The winner of the draw for the lucky number was offered the opportunity of commissioning the artist to paint free of charge a canvas measuring up to thirty inches by twenty inches, framed, of any aircraft in flight or any wildlife subject.

The net proceeds of £91,000 were devoted to Princess Marina House, the development of which and the care of its residents owes so much to the generosity of David Shepherd.

Chapter 20
The International Air Tattoo is Introduced

For some while before Crowley-Milling's appointment as Controller, his predecessor, Air Marshal Sir William Coles, and Air Commodore McKelvey, the Appeals Secretary, had been nurturing an idea. It has been seen how in Coles's time the Appeals Committee had started to seek ways of bringing in money and publicising the Fund which would free it of excessive reliance upon the RAF's glories and in particular the events of 1940. In mid-summer 1975 McKelvey, recognising the salesman in the new Controller and confident of an enthusiastic response, said: 'Why don't we go back into the business of air shows?' After all, if flying was what the RAF was all about and peacetime conditions had reduced the operational opportunities of a much-contracted service, then — as the Society of British Aerospace Companies spectacular exhibition and flying displays, mostly of civilian aircraft, at Farnborough had shown — the Fund's own air shows of service aircraft ought to be capable of providing the complementary benefits of bringing in money and generating useful publicity.

Making his submission, McKelvey played the trump card that a fund already existed within the Royal Air Force Benevolent Fund for the specific purpose of organising air displays. This was the Royal Air Force Benevolent Fund Development Trust, which had been formed twenty-five years earlier with a grant of £30,000 from the Air Council and which, when the Appeals Secretary approached the Controller, had reached almost £100,000.

Crowley-Milling was immediately attracted by the proposal. Having joined the Fund within a month of retiring from the service he was only too well aware that RAF cutbacks had reduced the fund-raising 'At Home' days at its stations. Thus, when the Royal Air Forces Association, which for the past five years had run a series of volunteer-organised Embassy Air Tattoos supported by W. D. and H. O. Wills, abandoned its plan for a 1975 air tattoo after withdrawal of the tobacco company's overall support — the financial risk was unacceptable — the Royal Air Force Benevolent Fund decided to step in.

Confronted by the risk element Peake brushed it aside: 'Find the man to run it and go ahead.' McKelvey already had his man and he returned to Paul Bowen, the acknowledged expert in the air tattoo business, who had just seeded the idea with the Appeals Secretary for a two-day International Air Tattoo at RAF Greenham Common near Newbury in Berkshire.

When it happened on the weekend of 31 July and 1 August 1976, fifty-six years after the Fund's first tentative Aerial Pageant at Hendon in 1920, the International Air Tattoo was a vast success.

Organised on a scale beyond the wildest dreams of Air Vice-Marshal Sir John Salmond — who, having been over-modest about possible takings in 1920, had sent six officers' wives home with £1,000 each to put under their pillows for the night — it yet retained at least one link with Hendon's glorious past: presiding over the organising committee was the legless Battle of Britain air ace, Group Captain Sir Douglas Bader, who, as a very junior officer, had flown in some of the pre-war air displays.

When Crowley-Milling, as Chairman of the Tattoo, McKelvey, Bowen, Tim Prince and Frank Windle, the directors of flying and administration respectively, and their committee colleagues immersed themselves in preparations there must have been moments when they were appalled at the magnitude of what they had set out to achieve. Never before in Western Europe had such an ambitious air display been attempted. Detailed planning was required to accommodate and fly more than 200 aircraft from twenty air forces.

Naturally, the RAF provided the centrepiece of the tattoo. Led by the Red Arrows aerobatic team it thrilled crowds of an estimated 120,000 people over two days with the Gazelles helicopter team, its Falcon free-fall parachutists, and Harrier, Phantom, Lightning and Vulcan displays. Since no such show would be complete without the Battle of Britain Flight, the Lancaster, Hurricane and Spitfire received an ovation which owed as much to their presence as to the knowledge that presiding over the proceedings was the legless ace who in September 1940 had led the wing of sixty Hurricanes and Spitfires from five of No. 12 Group's squadrons stationed behind London to give Luftwaffe aircrews a 'pasting' over the capital. Not until this surprise deployment of Air Vice-Marshal Leigh-Mallory's Big Wing tactic had the Luftwaffe encountered so many RAF fighter aircraft at one time over London and south-east England in daylight.

But this was history, better left perhaps to Bill Jones and his staff at Duke of Kent School, because also here at Greenham Common were NATO aircraft and crews, possibly including the sons or grandsons of the German pilots who had jousted with Bader's wing of British, Canadian, Czech and Polish squadrons in the summer of 1940.

Here, too, was the United States Air Force, sympathetic but neutral in 1940, but with a Flying Fortress at Greenham to remind spectators of its part in destroying Nazi Germany's industrial war machine and a fly-past of its swing-wing F-111s to emphasise its predominant role in the West's NATO shield. As Paul Bowen was to note, without the enthusiasm and unstinting support of General Ellis, Commander, United States Air Force, Europe, Major-General Evan W. Rosencrans, Commander 3rd Air Force, USAF, his staff at RAF Mildenhall and the commanding officer, officers and men of the USAF based at Greenham Common, the tattoo would not have been possible.

Much financial assistance and practical help in kind was received also from the great commercial enterprises which in the past had built Britain's air power, often with private venture aircraft such as the Spitfire, Wellington and Mosquito. For instance, Hawker Siddeley, apart from making a donation of £5,000 through an advertisement for the programme, had helped to create an International Hunter Meet, a gathering of twenty-five Hawker Hunters. Sponsors were many and generous and especially welcome was W. D. and H. O. Wills whose withdrawal of support had ignited the Fund's determination to go it alone, yet who nevertheless participated, supplying a £1,000 silver Embassy Jet Aerobatic Trophy for award to Europe's best aerobatic pilot; while Shell provided a trophy for the best individual effort.

After the weekend, when the money had been counted, Crowley-Milling was tempted, in honour of Salmond, to put £43,292 under his wife's pillow for the night. But the Fund had moved on since 1920 and Wing Commander Holloway, the Finance Secretary, might have been appalled. In the event, the Royal Air Force Benevolent Fund kept £35,622 after making payments to local charities and the funds of the other services in recognition of their contribution to the success of International Air Tattoo '76.

Despite the success, it would have been understandable if, upon reflection, the Fund had refrained from organising further tattoos. Behind the achievement lay a mountain of administrative detail during which many lessons had been learnt, not least that where aerobatics are concerned local farmers appreciate more than two weeks' notice.

No such undertaking is likely to be without its crisis. There was very real alarm in the week before the Tattoo when contractors

The Duke of Kent School in the Surrey hills succeeded the Fund's original school at Vanbrugh Castle, Blackheath, in 1976.

This splendid library at Duke of Kent School was provided by the generosity of RAF personnel serving at Bruggen in West Germany.

After opening the extension to Alastrean House, the Fund's residential home in Scotland on 27 July 1988, the President, the Duke of Kent, planted a Chinese Rowan tree in the grounds. He is accompanied by Air Marshal Sir Peter Bairsto, Chairman of the Alastrean Board of Management and Mr Geoffrey Jarvis, Factor of the MacRobert Trusts, which after making the house available to the Fund, contributed £300,000 towards the costs of the extension.

Alastrean House residents enjoy a round on the putting course.

Members of the Alastrean House Board of Management and the Fund's Finance and General Purposes Committee assembled in Aberdeenshire for the opening of the Care Wing by the Duke of Kent on 27 July 1988. (Left to right) Air Marshal Sir Peter Bairsto; Group Captain D. A. J. Starkey; Group Captain A. M. Mackintosh; Air Chief Marshal Sir Alasdair Steedman; Air Marshal Sir Richard Wakeford; Mrs I. Scott-Sutherland; Lord Catto; Lady Humphrey; Air Chief Marshal Sir John Aiken; Air Commodore Dame Felicity Peake; Air Vice-Marshal D. T. Bryant and Air Chief Marshal Sir Thomas Kennedy.

Princess Marina House, the Fund's convalescent and residential home at Rustington in West Sussex.

Special events create links between the Fund's establishments as when Duke of Kent School pupils sang carols with Princess Marina House residents at Christmas in 1982.

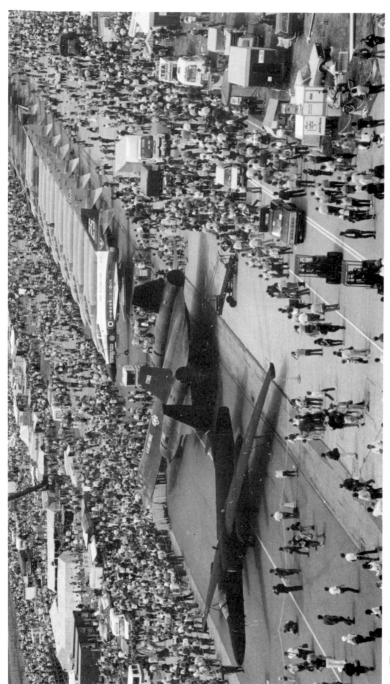

The International Air Tattoo, staged first at RAF Greenham Common and more recently at RAF Fairford, has proved a magnificent fund raising attraction.

Prince Michael of Kent was on hand to congratulate five winners of Sir Douglas Bader Flying Scholarships at the 1983 Tattoo. (Left to right) Mr A. Barratt; Miss T. J. Mattinsley; Mr T. R. Leonard; Mr G. J. Rann and Mr P. J. Lowe.

Sir Douglas Bader, the then President of the International Air Tattoo, greets the Duke of Kent at RAF Greenham Common on the occasion of the 1981 event.

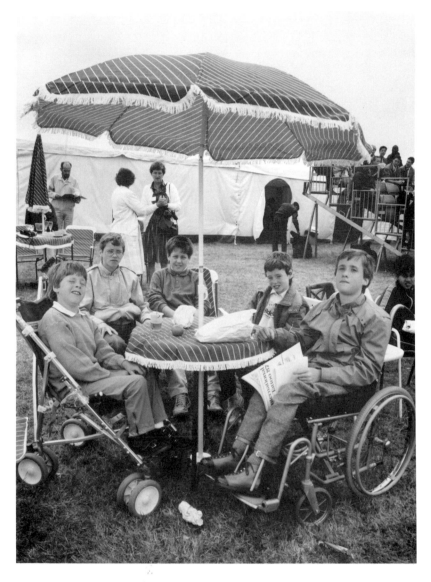

Disabled and disadvantaged children receive VIP treatment as guests in the Fund's enclosure at the International Air Tattoo.

As Patron of the International Air Tattoo, King Hussein flies in from Jordan to attend. The occasion also provides a useful opportunity to present certificates to holders of Sir Douglas Bader Flying Scholarships for the Disabled.

Pictured here at the June 1988 Tattoo, four Flying Scholarship winners (left to right): Wendy Morrell; Noel McConkey; Simon Weston; Geoffrey Schwalbe.

warned that they could not lay cables to the exhibition site and catering tents because cable supplied by the Army was unsuitable. Yet such is the Fund's rapport with industry that McKelvey telephoned the manging director of Sterling Cables, who had the correct cable delivered the same day — and with the compliments of the company.

The International Air Tattoo was here to stay, a new concept in aviation celebration pioneered by the Royal Air Force Benevolent Fund in partnership with Paul Bowen, its Tattoo Director, Bowen's small permanent staff and many volunteer helpers.

After the experience of 1976 the 1977 International Air Tattoo was even more successful, 120,000 visitors and impressive donations and assistance from industries and individuals contributing towards a profit of £80,000, every pound of which was earmarked for the Princess Marina House development.

The entertainment provided by the 1976 and 1977 Tattoos and their financial success had more than justified the more aggressive fund-raising posture which Crowley-Milling, jet-propelled by Peake's ready-to-have-a-go philosophy, had introduced.

Such was now the recognition of the Royal Air Force Benevolent Fund's Tattoo as the international meeting place of so many air forces and as an exhibition centre for companies in the aerospace sector of industry that, after its further success in 1977, the Fund decided to make the event biennial. The chief reason for this was an earnest desire not to compete with its generous supporter, the SBAC's biennial Farnborough Air Show.

Therefore, air shows have since been organised in the fallow years, like the Anglo-American Air Festival which Paul Bowen's team fielded at Bassingbourn on 27 and 28 May 1978 at the invitation of Lt. Col. H. M. du V. Lohan, Commanding Officer, Depot, The Queen's Division. Although attendance at 50,000 was less than half that at RAF Greenham Common, the effort was rewarded by profits of about £32,000, half of which came to the Fund, the other half being shared between the Army Benevolent Fund and the Ex-Services Mental Welfare Society. Moreover, it combined the merits of enabling the Tattoo team to sharpen its edge for Diamond Jubilee year and providing a baptism for Air Commodore Rooney who, after McKelvey's retirement in July 1977, was now the Appeals Secretary and would very soon be involved with the arrangements for the Tattoo of Tattoos on the weekend of 23 and 24 June 1979. Sadly Rooney died on 17 March 1979, after a short illness.

To visit RAF Greenham Common in March ten years ago was to

gain an insight into the build up of successive June Tattoos. Dark rain clouds shrouded the Berkshire Downs in the direction of Highclere, where the Queen's horses exercised for the approaching flat-racing season. The air base with its runway and taxiways — their wide acres gave away that they were built to accommodate the B-52 — was empty and silent and it was a relief to see a patrolling police car. Yellow petrol bowsers stood despondently at dispersal points as though forgotten after some long-past emergency. It was eerie, but in the stillness of this vast air base in deep freeze search for life ended at two tall flagstaffs which flew the RAF and United States colours outside an office building. Inside a coloured US Air Force sergeant, scarred and decorated, a man who had known Saigon, answered: 'The International Air Tattoo? Sure, Hut 91.' He belonged to the 7273rd Air Base Group, USAF, which maintained this ghost air base as a stand-by for NATO reinforcement. Thanks to the Americans this Second World War glider base was in mint condition and its runway had been resurfaced recently. Two miles south of Newbury and midway between London and Bristol on the M4, it was the ideal venue for the biennial International Air Tattoo, presented in aid of The Royal Air Force Benevolent Fund in association with Nationwide Building Society. There was the extra advantage that rail and light civil aircraft visitors could arrive at the adjacent racecourse's railway station or landing strip. The racecourse also provided a camp-site. Fees received by the racecourse were devoted to the Injured Jockeys' Fund.

Hut 91 was more reassuring than its avenues of deserted neighbours. There was the tap of typewriters, the ringing of telephone bells, a clinking of coffee cups. Paul Bowen, the Tattoo Director, was speaking to Amman: 'Yes, we'd love to have the Royal Jordanian Air Force. Will the King be attending himself? Well, we have to ask such questions.' Tim Prince, the Flying Director, called Switzerland. He understood the Swiss Air Force never left home, but hoped to send a team in June. Excellent, but what back-up aircraft were available? There was a silence and some embarrassment. It seemed that the only support aircraft available were two Ju 52s received as a gift from Adolf Hitler before the Second World War and the Swiss did not wish to offend any susceptibilities. It was difficult to explain to them that, a Ju 52, a flying Ju 52, would of itself make a star attraction for the Tattoo.

While Bowen and Prince were processing inquiries from some twenty air forces and several companies offering teams for the Fund's Diamond Jubilee year Tattoo, permanent and volunteer staff acknowledged the daily receipt of cheques in payment of advance bookings which provided an all-important cash flow. Bowen picked a cheque from the pile. It was drawn on a bank in Melbourne and it was from an Australian who had booked through the Melbourne Tourist Office and was bringing his family. Sensibly, the Australian had applied for club memberships of Friends of International Air Tattoo '79. It was open to adults aged seventeen or over at £10 and at £5 for children from the age of twelve. It provided a family season ticket for the two-day event and included such additional services as mailed news sheets and a ten per cent discount on all official souvenir items.

Hut 91 was deceptive. Its bright decor, fitted carpets, busy typewriters were out of dimension with the arena within which it organised an International Air Tattoo for two days every two years and possibly an intervening but smaller air show elsewhere.

Paul Bowen thus builds up a picture of International Air Tattoo '79, but it could as readily be that of '76 or '77 — before the decision was taken to go biennial — or of '81, and even '89.

As spring moves into summer 100 soldiers will arrive from Army barracks at Bassingbourn in Hertfordshire to move stored bedding into the village of empty barrack blocks. Civilian contractors will transform the bleak grass verges of the runway with instant chalets, enclosures, tents and gardens for the banks, aerospace and other business enterprises which invite guests and parties to this Derby week event of the world of international aviation. The President's enclosure, sponsored by Nationwide Building Society and the pilots' enclosure, sponsored by Wilkinson Match Safety Division will be prepared and the ground exhibition contractors will move in.

The loss of tranquillity on this giant air base is a gradual thing from the first spasmodic hammering until all is built, all is ready, and there is a momentary return to silence.

By now Bowen, Prince and their small permanent staff are being reinforced by an army of dedicated volunteers, dogsbodies as they self-deprecatingly call themselves, who take service leave or civilian holiday to help the Fund. Frank Windle, a Captain in the 28th Amphibious Engineer Regiment, arrives from West Germany as director of administration; Kit Townend, an aviation scientist who has arranged publicity throughout the run-up, arrives from Bournemouth; and among many others with specialist volunteer posts Annette Hill, who as a wartime Air Transport Auxiliary pilot logged 1,200 hours in Spitfires and similar types, is information officer.

More than 200 flying aircraft and some 140 static exhibition aircraft require considerable turn-round expertise in support of air force or company ground crews. To supply such technical services, including refuelling, twenty-five ground staff come in from the Aircraft and Armament Experimental Establishment at Boscombe Down, where the RAF's celebrated Empire Test Pilots' School retains its honoured pre-Commonwealth title.

The prerequisite of any flying display is safety. In the run-up Duncan Simpson, former chief test pilot for Hawker Siddeley, later deputy director of the Society of British Aerospace Companies, selects and chairs his team of test pilots and others with experience of Farnborough, Paris and previous International Air Shows. Painstakingly Simpson and his Flight Safety Committee vet every visiting pilot, team and 'act', and where necessary reject performers even if their aircraft and crews have arrived.

By now a ghost air base has been transformed into a ghost air show until in the silence the first approaching aircraft is heard. From this moment the International Air Tattoo is truly in business to bring money into the Royal Air Force Benevolent Fund. For a year the control tower has been a shell. Now five volunteer Civil Aviation Authority air traffic controllers who have given up holiday time begin to work to the tight schedule which Bowen and Prince — themselves former air traffic controllers who resigned from secure civil service posts to become International Air Tattoo and Aviation Consultants — have prepared in the past months.

Perhaps the first aircraft to touch down is *City of Ardmore* the first production C-130 still in service with the United States Air Force, the first of some twenty-five Hercules transport aircraft flying in for the Hercules Meet, the feature of the 1979 Tattoo. For not only is it the Royal Air Force Benevolent Fund's Diamond Jubilee year but it is also the twenty-fifth anniversary of the introduction of the western world's air force and civil air freight Hercules fleets. Twenty-five years after the second Lockheed prototype C-130 flew in California, and with more than 1,500 Hercules aircraft in use, the Hercules Industry Team, comprising twelve companies involved in the aircraft's production and components, has made the Fund's Tattoo the venue of its own celebration.

Although the Hercules Meet was the feature of the 1979 Tattoo, anniversaries can sometimes accumulate in embarrassing numbers, as happened in the Fund's Diamond Jubilee year. The Tattoo staff were stretched to accommodate them. However, it was not overlooked that on 15 June 1919 Captain Alcock and Lieutenant Brown, flying a Vickers Vimy, completed the first non-stop trans-Atlantic flight from Newfoundland. Consequently, as it also happened to be the twenty-first birthday year of the McDonnell-Douglas F-4 Phantom, a trans-Atlantic west-east flight was arranged for Press day. Appropriately the Phantom was crewed by Squadron Leader Alcock, a nephew of Captain Alcock, sponsored by Rolls-Royce, whose engines powered the Vimy and the Phantom, and a fellow officer named Browne.

Other anniversaries commemorated at the International Air Tattoo '79 were the maiden flight twenty-five years earlier of the English Electric (BAC) Lightning and the thirtieth birthday of the English Electric Canberra, each aircraft was still in RAF service. Finally on 5 April 1979, it was also the thirtieth anniversary of the fifteen member countries of the North Atlantic Treaty Organisation, in the absence of which RAF Greenham Common would probably not be available for such a magnificent fund-raising opportunity.

Such is the variety of the types and nationalities of the aircraft and their crews as they arrive that the skilled Civil Aviation Authority volunteers in the control tower can expect surprises. The mix is almost unbelievable. Here comes a Hercules, now a torpedo-carrying Swordfish biplane, a Dakota, a Lancaster, the Red Arrows, a Spitfire, a Tornado, a Hurricane, a Tomcat, yes and here are the teams from the Royal Jordanian and Austrian Air Forces. Truly an aviation cocktail of high-octane ingredients.

As the aerobatic and display teams of at least twenty air forces and several civilian companies fly in in Marlboro and Rothmans Pitts Specials and the Goodyear airship arrives, the Flying Control Committee meets.

In the past months there will have been many meetings, of which the most important have been regular progress committees, but now the Flight Safety Committee's deliberations and recommendations transcend all other considerations. With so many air forces, so many teams and individual competitors of so many nationalities and languages exhibiting their pilot skills above many thousands of spectators in this international meeting-place of the air, the Royal Air Force Benevolent Fund takes the realistic view that safety is the critical factor. An Army field hospital has been staffed and casualty evacuation helicopters stand by, but every precaution is taken to see that they will not be required.

Never in the field of aviation, as Winston Churchill might have said, was so much tact and diplomacy called for. Pilots who do not measure up to the Committee's standards are forbidden to fly. Pilots who deliberately flout its rules are sent home. There are heartaches, but poor rehearsal does not preclude below-standard performers from practising and improving in time for reassessment before the Tattoo opens.

While the Lockheed-Georgia Company's award of the Hercules Concours d'Elegance Trophy for the best turned out Hercules attending the Meet presents no such problem, the Flying Control Committee is much exercised to preserve a balance between the brilliance required to win the flying trophies and its requirements.

The principal trophies at the Diamond Jubilee year Tattoo were the Embassy Trophy, presented by W. D. and H. O. Wills for the winner of the international jet aerobatic competition — the pilot who gives the best solo jet performance; the International Display Sword presented by Nationwide Building Society for the best flying display by an overseas competitor; and the Shell-UK Oil Trophy for the best overall flying display.

Each International Air Tattoo has its special features — the Hunter of 1976, the Tiger Meet of 1977 and the Hercules Meet of 1979 — but pervading the two-day event is its central theme, which as its late president, Sir Douglas Bader, stated, is to foster friendship among participating nations, to allow NATO and other armed forces to demonstrate their roles and above all to help the Royal Air Force Benevolent Fund keep pace with the continuing inflation which ever increases the cost of relieving distress.

All too soon the two days have passed and the last of the farewells have been said, but friendships have been forged which will be renewed in two years' time, possibly earlier at Farnborough or in Paris and in service or business exchanges. The last visiting aircraft departs, the instant gardens wither in the skips of their removal, the tents, chalets and enclosures disappear and local farmers breathe 'Thank God'.

As RAF Greenham Common resumes its bleak appearance there is a big smile on the face of Sheila Pinnegar, Deputy Secretary Finance to Wing Commander Holloway and finance manager of the International Air Tattoo. Yet again the takings are up and, after donations to other service and local charities in recognition of their help, the Fund has done well, with every penny earmarked for the Princess Marina House development.

After the event, Paul Bowen, Tim Prince, their staff and volunteer dogsbodies experience depressing withdrawal symptoms. After so many months of so much effort it would be surprising if in the emptiness of the air base and the stillness of Hut 91 there were not a sense of loss and deprivation, a feeling of 'that was the Tattoo that was'. The psychological factor is recognised by the current Controller and this is why the next Tattoo begins where the last one ends.

The Controller books a weekend away from it all for the Tattoo leaders and their wives, where, taking his wife too, he relaxes with them while they hold a wash-up meeting and launch plans for the next International Air Tattoo. That the venue has since moved to Fairford does not alter the nature of the tattoo or its organisation. The IAT has gone from strength to strength.

Chapter 21
The Steedman Years

Alastrean House —
'A place of honour by the hearth for the winged ones.'

Lady MacRobert

When Air Chief Marshal Sir Alasdair Steedman was appointed Controller in 1981 he was already well acquainted with Portland Place. The Commandant of the RAF Staff College served as an *ex-officio* member of the Fund's Finance and General Purposes Committee and, holding this appointment from 1972 to 1975, he had attended committees under Peake's chairmanship. Since the Commandant's wife is a member of the School committee, Dorothy Steedman also had a head start. Aged eighteen, and just finishing his education at Hampton Grammar School, in 1940 Steedman saw the condensation trails of the Battle of Britain, heard the rattle of gunfire and wished he was up there. He volunteered, learned to fly near Stoke-on-Trent and got his wings under the Empire Air Training Scheme at Swift Current in Canada. He was to have been a fighter pilot, but learning that there was a six month wait, he volunteered for an Army Co-operation squadron. He never regretted it.

Inevitably Controllers arrive at Portland Place conditioned by their service careers and, being human, not without a prejudice or two in their outlook. Steedman, privately a compassionate man, came in at a time when the crescendo of need for which his predecessors, 'the building Controllers', as he describes them, had prepared was beginning. Circumstances dictated his self-declared role as a spending Controller. The figures speak for themselves. In 1980 the Fund paid out £2.709 million on 8,128 awards. In his last full year (1987) 14,777 cases were assisted at a total of £8.56 million.

A natural evangelist and fluent speaker, Steedman was a tireless traveller, spreading the Fund's message at home and overseas. Wrapt gatherings at RAF stations were astonished. To many the Fund had been a mysterious treasure chest into which they dropped their annual donation of half a day's pay and which distributed it to the needy survivors of two wars. Now here was a forceful and compassionate man who probed the needs of serving men and women and their dependants; who explained that its most costly cases are very often those of men or women who die, suffer accident, disablement or disease while serving; that the Fund helps families rebuild their lives; that it buys more houses for widows than it sells.

Of all the Controllers, Steedman probably came closest to succumbing to the occupational hazard of letting his heart rule his head. To his inherently compassionate nature was added an imaginative tendency to identify with those the Fund was helping. The buff folders at Grants Committees were people not cases and never more so than when applicants were members of the Guinea Pig Club. Burned on the legs and arms in Italy as a No. 241 Squadron Spitfire fighter pilot, he felt a special affinity with 'McIndoe's Army', in the words of the Guinea Pig anthem in which he joins heartily as a guest at East Grinstead reunions.

Peake's death in 1978 was a paramount influence on the swift, almost abrupt imposition by Steedman of his style on the conduct of the Fund's affairs. While Peake, perhaps the Council's most energetic chairman, probed detail and liked to maintain a strong grasp through his chairmanship of the Finance and General Purposes Committee, his successor, Catto, while no less dedicated, preferred to keep Steedman on a very long rein. This suited each man's *modus operandi* perfectly and Steedman remains indebted to the chairman for his trust and confidence. As station commander at RAF Lyneham during Air Chief Marshal Sir Edmund Hudleston's period as leader of Transport Command, he had admired the Commander-in-Chief's talent for briefing subordinates and then letting them get on with it. It was a lesson Steedman applied as he himself climbed to Air Rank and which he carried with him to Portland Place.

Personal initiatives on the part of Controllers, as with Coles's seizure of the opportunity to move Vanbrugh to Woolpit and evolve the Duke of Kent School, have inspired some of the Fund's most fruitful decisions. Steedman, a Scot, was perhaps more aware than his predecessors of the disparity between north and south in the provision of convalescent and residential care. When he heard that Alastrean House, formerly house of Cromar, a seat of the Aberdeens, and more recently in the MacRobert family, might be available, he moved fast. MacRobert benevolence towards the RAF had not ceased with MacRobert's Reply, the Stirling bomber, and Sir Roderic, Sir Alasdair and Sir Iain, three of the four Hurricane fighters presented to the RAF by Lady MacRobert in memory of her baronet sons during the war.

The house had since been a convalescent home and then a leave centre for officers. Ending that role for Alastrean, the MacRobert Trusts was obliged by its deeds to offer Alastrean to the Fund. It must have helped though that Air Marshal Sir Richard Wakeford, chairman of the Trusts was also the Fund's director in Scotland. So Air Vice-Marshal Frank Dodd, the Trusts' administrator, called Steedman from Scotland: 'You don't want it do you?' Dodd was both surprised and pleased when Steedman, after a quick staff study, said enthusiastically, 'Yes please.' A £5 a year peppercorn rent was agreed. Additionally the Trust provided £120,000 for conversion to accommodate the disabled, and a further £360,000 towards the £500,000 cost of an extension. There could have been no more satisfying farewell in Steedman's last week as Controller than to attend the opening on 27 July 1988 of the Care Wing by the Duke of Kent, the occasion of the president's first visit to Alastrean.

Situated near the village of Tarland in the scenic rolling foothills of the Grampians, Alastrean, attractively fashioned in pink granite, is somewhat reminiscent of a small chateau. It has established itself with so much popularity as a retirement home since it opened in 1984 that there is always a waiting list for its forty residential beds. But Mrs Maureen Robertson, its bustling manager, accepts that this does not imply Alastrean is suitable for every applicant. Its peaceful seclusion, while attractive to many elderly people, is not universally so. Thus great care over selection of applicants is taken at Portland Place and the Fund's Scottish branch in Edinburgh, and every prospective resident lives in for a trial period of eight weeks. But once happily settled, a resident slips contentedly into a cosy, if cocooned routine of comfort. The standard of accommodation and meals is that of a good country hotel, with the assurance that in the event of illness or serious disability matron will cosset one in the care quarters. There are eight double and twenty-four single rooms, and most have an *en suite* bathroom. Inability to pay does not exclude, but those of sufficient means contribute £98 weekly towards the £180 a week cost, which is excellent value.

Tasteful conversion has created a retirement home, but the grounds are much the same as when the Aberdeens, the Wee Twas as they were affectionately known by their Balmoral neighbours, inhabited the House of Cromar. The Chinese Rowan tree planted by the Duke of Kent to commemorate his visit sustains a tradition, an avenue of royal trees dating back beyond Queen Mary and to the turn of the century when the house was built by the seventh Earl of Aberdeen. Created Marquis of Aberdeen and Temair in 1915 after being Viceroy of Ireland, he died in 1934 and the house passed to Lady MacRobert, widow of Sir Alexander who had made a fortune in India and who owned the neighbouring estate of Douneside. It is fascinating to reflect that had not MacRobert, who left school in Aberdeen at thirteen and risen from clerk in Cawnpore to founder of the giant British India Corporation, secretly paid some of Aberdeen's considerable debts, Alastrean's present residents would not be living there. MacRobert had eased Aberdeen's problems knowing that under a settlement agreed in 1919 the house would some day pass to his family.

Another chance circumstance also contributed to the Fund's eventual good fortune. MacRobert's wife, Georgina, had died in 1904, and in 1911 he married Rachel, daughter of the American-born Himalayan explorers, Dr and Mrs William Hunter Workman. Rachel's eldest son having been killed in a flying accident in 1938 and her husband's brothers having been killed in the war in 1943, as has been described earlier, she endowed the House of Cromar as an RAF aircrew leave centre and re-named it Alastrean. The name is a compound of *alar*, a wing or winged one, *astre*, a hearth or home, *astrean*, belonging to the stars. Though many have surmised that the name is an amalgamation of her sons' christian names, Lady MacRobert regarded it as representing 'a piece of honour by the hearth for the winged ones'.

She died in 1954, but Alastrean's management committee chairman, currently Air Marshal Sir Peter Bairsto, Dodd's successor as the Trusts' administrator, Lieutenant-General Sir Robert Richardson, Colonel of the Royal Scots, and their colleagues perpetuate her sentiment. Certainly her presence remains pervasive. She is buried at the foot of a massive piece of red granite in her Douneside garden and the ashes of her eldest son, Sir Alasdair, lie in a great Cairn in the grounds of Alastrean.

Alastrean exudes an atmosphere of quiet contentment. The eight-week trial period normally eliminates applicants who find it too reclusive. This is not to say that residents opt out totally, but for a man like James, an octogenarian former prisoner-of-war of the Japanese who escaped from Singapore in 1942 only to be recaptured in Rangoon, or his friend, an RAF widow in her eighties, it is a rest home second-to-none. As with Princess Marina House, any balance of Alastrean's £98 a week or £161 double fees, after private and DHSS deductions, is paid from Portland Place, where Group Captain

Don Starkey looks after the paperwork for both homes. Fortunately, the conversion of the Aberdeen family's House of Cromar has been so discreet that there is no suggestion of institutional life, a happy circumstance which is much assisted by the cheerful and totally unstarched manner of Maureen Robertson, the manager, Kathleen Diack, the matron, and the nursing and domestic staff who care for forty residents. Moreover, Mrs Robertson, always aware of the possibility of problems arising from Alastrean's remoteness — though Tarland village is but a step away — arranges shopping trips to Aberdeen, twenty-five miles distant. She also encourages hobby activities — there is a well-equipped workshop — and arranges games nights.

Stages in Alastrean's development, from the moment of that twinkle in Steedman's eye when Dodd offered the MacRobert Trusts' property to the Fund, reflect the alacrity with which it was gratefully accepted and converted from its previous role as a leave centre for RAF officers, dating as far back as 1943. In 1984, after the changeover, the central heating system was replaced and upgraded. To supervise the work, the Fund appointed a Board of Management under the chairmanship of Air Marshal Sir Peter Bairsto, a former fighter pilot and at the time only just retired as Deputy Commander-in-Chief at Strike Command. One of his first actions was to ask Maureen Robertson, manager of Alastrean for the MacRobert Trusts, to stay on. Such was Bairsto's expedition that on 20 May in the next year the Fund's residential home for the north of England and Scotland was functioning. Then, on 27 September the Queen Mother, recalling memories of visiting Lady Aberdeen there with Queen Mary and the future King George VI in 1924, was welcomed by Air Marshal Sir Richard Wakeford as Chairman of the MacRobert Trusts and Catto.

By 1986 Alastrean was well established as Princess Marina House's northern counterpart in most respects but one. It lacked a Care Wing, an omission which Steedman moved swiftly to make good. The Fund's Finance and General Purposes Committee gave its blessing and with the sanction and financial help of £360,000 from the MacRobert Trusts, an extension (which includes six single hospital rooms on the ground floor and nine first floor rooms adaptable as singles, or doubles for married couples, and also as nurses' accommodation) was operational that June. Opened formally by the Duke of Kent on 27 July 1988, its popularity has since produced a waiting list.

There is also a waiting list for Princess Marina House, a reversal of the situation at sunny Rustington early in Steedman's career as

Controller. Much had happened at the Sussex home since an active year in 1978 when Catto had opened the Andrew Humphrey Room and Crowley-Milling had signed the contract for its £1 million development. Building the new North Wing went ahead in the next year while Newton Driver House was converted into nurses' flats. Meanwhile, Lady Humphrey chaired a committee to furnish the new wing. Despite the inevitable disruption during construction, Princess Marina House accommodated 539 convalescent guests at a cost of £100 each, though no guest was asked to contribute more than £50 a week, nor was anybody unable to afford the sum turned away. On 9 July 1980, the North Wing, named after the President's mother, was opened by the Duke of Kent.

Assessing occupancy at Princess Marina House shortly after arriving at Portland Place in 1981, Steedman noted that it was building towards 100 per cent, but was concerned that the rank balance favoured officers and their widows. He urged an increase in its use by NCOs and airmen or their dependants. Next year the benefits of the major development were more evident and satisfying. The North, or Care Wing, contained forty-nine residents, each of whom was eligible to remain for life, while the numbers of guests, mostly fortnightly convalescents, accommodated in the South Wing, continued to rise. Elderly, frail, or just lonely people unable to afford a change were also welcomed.

As the Care Wing settled down, lessons were learned, one of which was that the incidence of infections and illness rendered its four-bedded wards unsuitable. Consequently, in 1983 one such ward was divided into three single rooms, facilitating private nursing care where necessary. By 1984 the number of convalescent holiday visitors had climbed to 1,000 and produced a waiting list. In the next year, need, always the decisive factor in accepting applications for both wings, was more than ever the imperative of a 'passport' to Princess Marina House. The South Wing received 1,010 guests and at the North Wing, full the year round, vacancies were filled immediately from the waiting list. Much the same situation pertained in 1986, and in order to achieve Steedman's desired rank balance a temporary embargo was placed on applications from former officers and their dependants.

Taking stock of Princess Marina House's physical inability to cope with an ever increasing demand, the Fund's Finance and General Purposes Committee sanctioned an extension to the South Wing to contain one single and seven double rooms capable of accommodating convalescent or long-stay guests. Similar 'house full' conditions prevailed throughout 1987, providing a high note of success to coincide with Wing Commander Arthur Carvosso's retirement after fourteen years as manager; and a challenge for his successor, Group Captain Eric Goodman. However, availability of the South Wing extension from 17 July 1988 helped Goodman to get off to an encouraging start and the extension was opened officially by the Duke of Kent on 26 September. This additional accommodation permitted Princess Marina House to raise its 1988 guest numbers to 1,041, and enabled Portland Place to lift the embargo on former officers and their dependants. This decision had not long been made when, yet again, the Care Wing had a considerable waiting list.

In the Fund's seventieth anniversary year, it was salutary to be conducted through the Duke of Kent School by Alison and Robert, each of whom had lost a pilot father. The corridors may display household names of the 1939-45 War, but their scurrying, book-laden denizens denote, as with Alison and Robert, losses of life and limb in the less desperate if equally sacrificial business of deterring war. No one can be more aware than Roger Wilson, the head, of the perils facing peacetime aircrew. His son is a helicopter pilot.

Some children have lost mothers. Others, of course, represent the school's dual role as the educator of families of service and civilian parents who are in no distress, but value its style and record. The group captain's son — his father is serving in Bangladesh — encountered whilst tucking into a pork chop in the dining hall, is an example of service children of fee-paying parents who are assisted by the Ministry of Defence boarding school allowance. That an NCO's son is at the same table demonstrates that rank is irrelevant.

Responsibility for selection of Foundationers and the making of grants rests with the Education Committee which meets at Portland Place, presently under the chairmanship of Air Marshal Sir Charles Ness. A member of the Fund's Council and Finance and General Purposes Committee, he chairs the Duke of Kent School's Board of Governors whose responsibilities cover an average total of 176 pupils, of whom forty-one are Foundationers — all paid for by the Fund — 101 service boarders, eleven civilian boarders and twenty-three local civilian day boys and girls.

Although he flew in Bomber Command towards the end of the war, Ness, Air Member for Personnel from 1980 to 1983, brings recent Air Rank experience to his voluntary posts. As he fashions the Fund's education policy for the 1990s he can move forward from the firm ground established by his predecessor, Air Chief Marshal Sir

Lewis Hodges, renowned as a wartime escaper and Special Operations Executive pilot, whom he succeeded in 1985.

Sadly, another change at the top was necessitated when Bill Jones, the head who had achieved the move from Vanbrugh so successfully in 1976, died unexpectedly towards the end of the 1980 Spring term. Michael Morton, the deputy head and an old Vanbrugh hand, breached the gap until Roger Wilson, the present head, took over. Morton stayed on until 1982 when he retired after seventeen years' dedicated service to the Fund, first at Vanbrugh and then at Duke of Kent. He was succeeded as deputy head by J. H. Day.

The new head's period of sixteen distinguished years at Christ's Hospital has been noted earlier. Educated at King Edward's School, Birmingham, and Corpus Christi College, Cambridge, he has maintained the Vanbrugh and Duke of Kent Schools' reputation for all-round excellence. That year there were also important board changes. Following the resignation of Trevor Jones who had done so much to effect the transfer of the former Woolpit school to the Fund, and F. M. White, another Vanbrugh veteran, the appointment of L. G. D. Baker, headmaster of Christ's Hospital, strengthened the Duke of Kent's association with that school.

The past decade at the Duke of Kent has seen a steady improvement in buildings and facilities. In 1979 further gifts from the Variety Club of Great Britain enabled a changing room for girls to be built at the swimming pool and also provided full fee bursaries for four Foundationers for five years. The Variety Club helped again in 1982 when a Music Centre, comprising a large room for orchestral rehearsal and ten practice rooms, was opened by the Club's chairman, Tom Nicholas. Among further changes on the education front, Air Commodore A. P. Vicary, who had masterminded the transition from Vanbrugh to Duke of Kent, retired as the Education Secretary at Portland Place, being replaced by the Welfare Secretary, Air Vice-Marshal Michael Robinson.

Next year, the name of Sir Harald Peake being so intimately associated with the school — Peake Hall speaks for itself — it was particularly appropriate that his widow, Air Commodore Dame Felicity Peake as principal guest, should have presented the prizes and trophies at Speech and Parents' Day. Examination results in 1984 reflected the school's annual success in obtaining scholarships and places in a range of senior schools. Scholarships were obtained at Oundle and Trent College while a girl Foundationer was awarded a bursary place, partly financed by the MacRobert Trusts, at Gordonstoun. Fittingly, Guy Dodd, the headmaster of Lord Wandsworth, a college with a long record of accepting Foundationers, and now as Duke of Kent governor replacing Baker, did the Speech Day honours as principal guest.

The Gordonstoun bursary for a girl Foundationer was evidence of the increasing demand for girls' boarding places and, taking note, the governors reaffirmed the board's opinion that an ideal balance should be 130 boys to fifty girls. This ought to retain the school's overall character and its sporting competitive edge. Therefore, steps were taken to accommodate up to fifty girls, and in 1985 two all-weather areas were provided for their netball and tennis. Here, again, the Variety Club gave generous help, providing £6,500 towards the £17,000 cost.

By 1987 it did not need the newly installed teaching computers to discover that popular demand for girls' places had over-run the ideal balance. Air Chief Marshal Sir David Craig, Chief of the Air Staff, and Lady Craig as principal guests at the summer Speech Day, noted that of 173 pupils fifty-nine were girls. Last year the total population had risen to 176 of whom sixty were girls. But the prime consideration, priority of admission for Foundationers, remained sacrosanct and forty-one Foundationers, twenty-six boys and fifteen girls, were assisted as necessary by the Fund. At Speech Day it was again the Christ's Hospital head's turn to present the prizes. In a particularly good year for sporting achievements, Richard Poulton, successor to Baker as head at Christ's Hospital, had what must surely be the unique experience of being confronted by a youthful captain of cricket — Alexander Earl — with a batting average of 113.

Chapter 22
A Sharp Focus on the 1980s

'Unthinkable not to help.'

Lord Catto

As will have become plainly apparent from the account of preceding years, the Fund's activities form an annual pattern of spending and receiving — spending always comes first in the Fund's philosophy — a consistency which, irrespective of individual Controllers' inclinations, is confirmed in the chairman's annual reports to the Council.

Since the exits, the entrances and the pats on the back are also there, selection from and comment on Catto's reports of the 1980s — other than news of developments at the International Air Tattoo, the Duke of Kent School and Princess Marina and Alastrean Houses which have been described separately hitherto — provides an overall view how the Fund fared in the period.

In 1980 total expenditure exceeded £3 million for the first time. Of this, spending on relief of distress of £2.5 million set another record. This was largely due to more homes being bought by the Housing Trust and the doubling of the cost of running Princess Marina House following its extension. The variety of appeal sources outside such routine events as the Royal Air Force Anniversary Concert and displays put on by the International Air Tattoo organisation was maintained by Air Commodore Mike Stanton, Appeals Secretary, and his staff. Advantage was taken of the fortieth anniversary of the Battle of Britain to hold a dinner in conjunction with the Variety Club of Great Britain at the Battle of Britain Museum, Hendon. The Duke of Kent attended and was received by Marshal of the Royal Air Force Sir John Grandy, successor to Marshal of the Royal Air Force Sir Dermot Boyle, as Deputy Chairman. Grandy had commanded No. 249 Hurricane Squadron, during the Battle. A handicrafts centre at the Duke of Kent School benefited from £5,314 of the money raised by the event. The enduring sense of national deliverance by the RAF in 1940 was reflected in numerous donations, not least £10 received anonymously 'with thanks for a free life since 1940'.

If total expenditure at £3 million had astonished in 1980, the next year's advance of nearly £41,000 on that figure on welfare alone indicated the likelihood of ever increasing annual distress benefits. But net International Air Tattoo Organisation proceeds of £170,000, surpassing those of all previous air shows, were an encouraging sign on the other side of the balance sheet, and particularly gratifying in his retirement year to Crowley-Milling who had nursed the Tattoo Organisation since establishing it in 1976. It was a flourishing legacy for Steedman, latterly United Kingdom Representative to the North Atlantic Treaty Organisation, who succeeded him shortly afterwards. Support from other sources was up, receipts from Ministry of Defence, commands, stations, and units topping £1 million, a tribute to the effectiveness of the half-a-day's pay a year and covenant scheme. Figures representing those other important arms of the Service's self help, the Royal Air Force Dependants Fund and (Income) Trust were also encouraging, grants made by the former since inception in 1967 now totalling £1,116,600.

Meanwhile, the Dependants Trust, to which members of the Dependants Fund had subscribed since 1971 to provide additional tax free income or lump sums for nominated dependants, now made annual awards to beneficiaries totalling more than £186,000 a year. That 960 cases — another increase — were advised by the Insurance Advisory Service was another indication of service people's readiness to provide for themselves.

Yet there will always be those who, however provident, will face unexpected calls on their resources, a factor emphasised by the nomination of 1981 as International Year of Disabled People. As its contribution the Fund gave £272,961 to forty-five organisations which help disabled members of the RAF. Another reminder of the Fund's generous reputation as a donor was the presentation of £50,000 to the Royal Air Forces Association to endow three beds at Sussexdown in memory of Marshal of the Royal Air Force Sir John Slessor, a Vice-President; Air Marshal Sir William Coles, Controller from 1968 to 1975; and the Guinea Pig Club.

Statistics prepared for the chairman's 1982 report showed that welfare spending of almost £4 million out of a total expenditure of £4.85 million had almost doubled over four years, giving a deficit on ordinary income of £865,777. However, other income, including legacies, totalling £1.136 million — welcome but uncertain by their very nature — brought receipts of £6.36 million to provide a healthy surplus. Some measure of the burden carried by the dedicated welfare team of Air Commodore Roy Dutton and his assistant, Jean Ashton, can be appreciated from the chairman's acknowledgement on Dutton's retirement as Welfare Secretary that over eleven years he had administered the disbursement of more than £19.5 million.

Dutton's retirement and succession by Air Vice-Marshal Michael Robinson shortly preceded other retirements which indicated that age and service was gradually claiming members of the old guard, who seemed to have been at Portland Place forever. In 1983 Wing Commander Ted Holloway, who had implemented the Fund's financial policies for nearly seventeen years laid down that particularly onerous burden, while Wing Commander Freddie Tame who had looked after the Dependants Fund and Dependants (Income) Trust said goodbye after fourteen years. Long service is customary at the Fund and not only among its salaried staff. In Council the Duke of Kent, the President, thanked Catto for his fifteen years of service, especially for the past five years as chairman.

Figures prepared for 1983 by Holloway's successor, Wing Commander Jack Connell, showed welfare spending of over £4 million, but once again public support saved the Fund from what would otherwise have been a deficit of £700,000. It was noted that a new and expanding part of the Fund's work was the provision of accommodation through the acquisition of nominations for units with Housing Associations and provision of a comprehensive advisory service for needy applicants seeking somewhere suitable to live.

Looking ahead in the conclusion of his 1984 report, the chairman remarked that more than £5 million had been spent on the direct relief of distress and that demands made on resources showed no signs of abating. The Fund, he emphasised, must expect the numbers of welfare cases and the sums expended on them to increase until at least the turn of the century. He also stressed that some forty per cent of men who served with the RAF during the 1939-45 War were born between 1920 and 1924, creating an expectancy of a high level of claims for fifteen years or more.

With key members of the Fund's old guard belonging to the same generation, the year inevitably yielded further retirements. Wing Commander Allan Scott, Secretary, Homes and Princess Marina House, who had been at Portland Place since 1975, made way for Group Captain Don Starkey, and Paul Cutting handed over as Secretary, Administration, to Group Captain Ken Hebborn. Cutting's retirement after thirty-nine years with the Fund left a void impossible to fill. Sensibly, his successor recognised this and, while supported by the Cutting tradition, updated the role and set a new style compatible with the introduction of computer technology. Cutting, as will be recalled from an earlier chapter, was part of the Cordingley legend, an attribute which greatly assisted his task as editor of earlier editions of *The Debt We Owe*. He was awarded the OBE, a richly merited honour.

The chairman's financial fears for the future were confirmed by events in 1985. Welfare cases were 7.5 per cent up at 13,044, calling for expenditure of £7.13 million, an increase of more than thirty-two per cent. Total expenditure of £8.53 million exceeded income from donations and fund-raising, repayment of welfare loans and return on investments, which the Fund regards as dependable income, by £2.92 million. Legacies of £1.15 million, as ever unpredictable, failed to close the gap which was met by realisation of assets and reinvestment, leaving a net cash gain and minimising the need to erode capital.

The RAF coach crash in Germany affecting the lives of the families of many victims was a reminder that heavy calls on the Fund do not necessarily involve its ageing beneficiaries or aircrew families. During the year, 110 serving personnel died as a result of accident or illness. Inevitably, however the deaths of 1,756 former service people reminded Welfare of the ageing factor. Help was given when needed. It would, in the chairman's own words, have been 'unthinkable' not to have helped any case whether serving or non-serving. In response to the Fund's ever growing welfare commitment, two retirng Assistant Secretaries in the branch, Wing Commander E.L. Macro and Wing Commander H. T. Williams were immediately replaced by Air Commodore April Reed, a former Matron-in-Chief and Director of RAF Nursing Services, and Squadron Leader Sheila Joy, another former member of Princess Mary's Royal Air Force Nursing Service.

Surveying events of 1986 the chairman felt obliged to view the increasing scale and cost of the Fund's welfare activities 'with a sense both of satisfaction and apprehension'. The Fund was achieving its prime purpose of relieving distress, but in doing so was putting considerable strain on its financial resources. Profits had been 'creamed off' from the sale of investments, while maintaining the book value of the investment portfolio to bridge the gap yet again between income and expenditure. But the chairman warned that this could not go on and new sources of income would have to be explored.

Welfare spending rose to 'the staggering sum' of £8.16 million, a new record which signified the Fund's indebtedness to Air Chief

Marshal Sir David Lee, chairman of the Grants Committee. Certainly, its new members, Lady Harcourt-Smith, Air Vice-Marshal H. A. Caillard, Air Commodore D. F. Rixson, Lady Jones and the Polish Air Vice-Marshal, A. Maisner, had been plunged in at the deep end. Support from the Royal Air Forces Association and the Soldiers', Sailors' and Airmen's Families Association, frequently the link between the Fund and its beneficiaries, assisted it in dealing with forty per cent of cases and in disbursing the Fund's money. However, a change at the top of the Insurance Advisory Service when Wing Commander A. J. Webster, handed over after ten years to Group Captain C. S. Jackson, served as a reminder of its contribution to narrowing the long term drain on resources. Another departure was that of Group Captain S. J. Perkins who had served nearly eleven years as an Assistant Welfare Secretary and was replaced by Wing Commander A. J. Schollar.

Although the Fund fared better than many investors in the Stock Market crash of October 1987, a 19.6 per cent fall reduced its investments' market value to £24,282,816 and reinforced the chairman's call for new sources of income. But the Fund's escape from an investment fate that might have been far worse owed much to the counsel of Morgan Grenfell, its advisers, and its own cautious approach to risk, twenty-eight per cent of its investments being in gilts. Even so, at such a time, the importance of the £1,882,815 of self-help from the RAF's voluntary half-a-day's pay, and after fund raising, shone through the accounts, as did receipts from station and wives' functions, public support through the International Air Tattoo and other events and individual donations ranging from fifty pence to £25,000. All very necessary set against stock market volatility and the continuing rise in welfare spending. Up 4.8 per cent at £8,556,972, it set yet another new record and marked the retirement of Air Chief Marshal Sir David Lee after more than sixteen years as Chairman of the Grants Committee. He was succeeded by Air Chief Marshal Sir John Aiken.

Other retirements included two long serving Council members, Lord Ward, Honorary Treasurer from 1969 until the end of 1986 when he was succeeded by Mr F. W. Crawley, and Mr E. de Rougemont who had been involved with the Fund for forty years. With the death of Lord Trenchard, whose father had founded the Fund and who had been a Vice-President since 1970, the Fund lost another valued member of the Council and Finance and General Purposes Committee. Another distinguished Vice-President, Marshal of the Royal Air Force Sir William Dickson, died during the year.

But recruitment of Sir Kenneth Durham brought additional business expertise to the Council and Finance and General Purposes Committee. After a succession of changes in the Fund's staff in recent years, there was less movement in 1987, though Wing Commander Arthur Carvosso's retirement as manager at Princess Marina House, since managed by Group Captain E. J. Goodman, was a reminder of how much he had achieved there in fourteen years.

Once again, 1987 was a year in which self-help among the serving was such that it should not be seen to be eclipsed by the massive expenditure on welfare. Ninety-six per cent of service personnel subscribed ten pence a month to the Royal Air Force Dependants Fund which raised to £1,200 its immediate tax free grant made to nominated beneficiaries of subscribers who die while serving. In 1987, too, that other fine example of self-help, the Royal Air Force Dependants (Income) Trust, which pays an increasing tax free income to beneficiaries of subscribers — basic subscription £1.30 a month for an income of £440 a year until what would have been the subscriber's fifty-fifth birthday — paid out £380,000.

In 1988 there was a welcome deceleration in the rate of welfare expenditure, the total of £8.664 million being but one per cent up on 1987. Moreover, possibly reflecting an early result of Kennedy's 'tighter ship', of which more later, the rise, historically infinitesimal, was almost entirely accounted for by awards associated with donations to other organisations that assist the Fund in its welfare work. In view of long term concern over the call of the 1939-45 War 'bulge', it seems more likely that careful stewardship rather than reduction in demand was responsible. Financial support from the Service at £1.98 million, and £2.46 million from the public, was strongly boosted by a grant-in-aid of £418,000 from the Ministry of Defence. This related to a Retail Price Index-linked adjustment to pensions paid to Service pensioners and an outstandingly generous personal donation of more than £1 million from Mr J. W. Greening, one of the Fund's honorary helpers.

Evidence that over the years the Fund's costly help on housing was not always one-way can be found in figures featuring repayment of loans, and gains from the sale of Housing Trust properties no longer required by benificiaries. Taking in payments made by residents and guests at Princess Marina and Alastrean Houses and rentals from Housing Trust properties these amounted to more than £2.8 million. Total expenditure of £10.26 million against income of £11.59 million produced a welcome surplus, though but for Mr Greening's donation and the Ministry of Defence's grant-in-aid there would have been a small deficit. The Fund's three financial services, the Insurance Advisory Service, the Royal Air Force Dependants Fund and the Royal Air Force Dependants (Income) Trust, continued to flourish.

Among the exits and the entrances of the year, the Chairman in Council welcomed Steedman, the retiring Controller to its ranks and his successor, Kennedy, to the various committees on which the Controller sits. Among staff retirements, Air Commodore Mike Stanton's departure from Appeals lost the Fund its most talented fund-raiser ever — so much of the success of IAT and its burgeoning activities was due to his persistence — placing an onerous burden on his successor Air Vice-Marshal Freddie Hurrell, formerly Director-General of RAF Medical Services. With the Battle of Britain Appeal in preparation it was a challenging moment to become Appeals Director. In a year which saw a Controller's retirement it might seem impossible to match his departure in terms of service to the Fund, but such, uniquely, was the case with Jean Ashton, Deputy Director Welfare, who said goodbye after nearly forty-four years. As the Chairman noted, 'for much of that time the name of Jean Ashton has been almost synonymous with that of the Fund. Her compassion and wealth of experience endeared her to many and especially to her beloved Poles and Guinea Pig Club members'. Jean's devotion of a lifetime was earlier recognised with the award of an MBE.

Among other changes were Air Commodore D. F. Rixson's appointment as Deputy Chairman of the Main Grants Committee on the retirement of Wing Commander C. R. Griffiths after nearly eleven years on the committee. Almost as big a break with the past as Jean Ashton's retirement was occasioned by the resignation of Mrs R. E. Croome after thirty years' service as a Governor of Vanbrugh and the Duke of Kent Schools. In Edinburgh, Air Marshal Sir Richard Wakeford retired as Director of the Scottish Branch after more than ten years and from the Board of Management of Alastrean House. The Fund is indebted to him for all he did to bring about the establishment of Alastrean House. Air Vice-Marshal C. E. Simpson has taken over from him. There was a change, too, at Princess Marina House, where Lady Kyle, widow of Air Chief Marshal Sir Wallace 'Digger' Kyle, a former chairman, joined the Board.

Chapter 23
The Way Ahead

Kennedy — no sacred cows

The Fund, as has been explained earlier, has always been fortunate that each Controller has been the man for his time. Air Marshal Sir 'Jock' Kennedy arrived at Portland Place in the summer of 1988 with an appetite for change at the moment when change was essential to the task of finding the wherewithal to meet the needs of ageing 1939-45 War veterans.

An early example of Kennedy's tendency to turn existing practices on their heads was to give *greater priority* to inviting station commanders and others to Portland Place than to visiting their units, although this practice had been introduced by Coles and expanded by Steedman. Obviously, he accepts invitations to a range of functions to fly the flag, but he prefers to get station commanders and a variety of commissioned and non-commissioned officers round the long table in the Council room. This highly effective innovation has demonstrated beyond all doubt that, in the cause of bringing home the Fund's welfare record and activities, there is no substitute for sitting in on the Main Grants Committee and discussing the morning's decisions over an informal buffet lunch round the Council table. Serving officers and NCOs return to their units with a first hand view of the Fund at work and a source of stimulating talk, even gossip. Such occasions, Kennedy has found, are of particular value to Warrant Officers who provide an indispensable link with barrack life and the needs that inevitably arise among airmen and their families. One of Kennedy's chief concerns has been, with the help of Air Commodore Robert Barcilon, his Welfare Director, to dispel the ancient barrackroom and sergeants' mess myth that the Fund 'is something for officers, providing homes and a public school education'.

That Kennedy, like Steedman a Scot — Hawick High School and RAF College, Cranwell — is the first Controller without 1939-45 War service is of special value in getting the message across to so many who were contemporaries in the Service. However, absence of war service should not imply that he is any the less knowledgeable about operational and training conditions, as is confirmed by his AFC and

Bar, and experience in No. 27 Canberra Squadron, and command of No. 99, Britannia. And at the top he was only too aware of current problems as Air Member for Personnel.

Exceptionally, Kennedy is a Controller for whom there are no sacred cows. As he studies afresh so much that has been routine or ritual in the Portland Place rabbit warren of offices, corners and cubbyholes — the result of Cordingley's long and honourable record of counting the pennies — he regards each of the Fund's institutions as a candidate for reform or even the scrapheap; all this in the cause of enabling the Fund to meet its welfare responsibilities to the year 2000 and beyond. It is an indication of his single-mindedness on this score that, musing on the future, he can so much as hint that perhaps the time will come when the rationale and cost effectiveness of the Duke of Kent School should be reviewed — a view previously put to him by Steedman. Of course any such radical issues would rest with the Finance and General Purposes Committee and finally with the Council which, in the case of the Duke of Kent School, would have to assess the annual advantages of educating, say, forty Foundationers, against such a heavy investment. It could, for instance, be argued that a better return on the investment could be achieved to meet the requirements of educating eligible children.

In the Fund's seventieth anniversary year, the Controller, employing a nautical phrase as a reminder perhaps that in 1918 the RAF, and in 1919 its Memorial Fund, resulted from a merger of the Royal Naval Air Service and the Royal Flying Corps, emphasises the importance of running a 'tight ship' before asking the public for money. Certainly, comparison between the Lee and Steedman partnership's steerage of the Main Grants Committee and the current team of Aiken and Kennedy confirms their adhesion to this self-imposed discipline. No case is neglected or deprived in conformity with the Fund's abiding philosophy on the relief of distress, but each award is made with a strong sense of responsibility towards donors in mind and, with commemoration of the fiftieth anniversary of the Battle of Britain in the summer of 1990, in particular all those who support the Royal Air Force Benevolent Fund's massive £20 million Battle of Britain Salute fund-raising surge.

Since the prime objective of the £20 million appeal is to add to the capital and complement 'tight ship' efforts to plug the gap between income and expenditure, the Controller perceives a paramount need to strike a balance between going flat out for the appeal and carrying on the Fund's day-to-day routine work. He is also intensely aware that casualties suffered by Fighter Command in 1940 were, by the very nature of the victory of the 'Few', fractional compared with overall RAF losses in the 1939-45 War, the majority of which occurred in Bomber Command, burdened as it was with the long sustained offensive against Germany. Thus, while the appeal salutes the victory which enforced German abandonment of *Operation Sealion*, the invasion of Britain, it serves also as a reminder of the men and women, the survivors of whom as they grow older, will swell the 'bulge' of the coming decade.

To cause the least possible interruption of the Fund's normal routine, the Controller chairs a specially established company, The Battle of Britain Appeal Limited, the board of which is in turn advised by a Steering Group set up by Steedman in 1986 and headed by Sir Peter Masefield and a widely representative Appeals Committee, which has covenanted profits to the Fund. But such dedicated committee commitment, helped in its early stages by John Anstey, successor on his retirement to Peter Taylor as the Fund's public relations consultant and since deceased, would avail little without the work at the sharp end of Paul Bowen, Tim Prince and their staff at the International Air Tattoo Organisation. The proposed film première, air shows, special displays, concerts, sponsored sporting events, joint promotions, a *Son et Lumière* spectacular in blitzed London, a Guildhall celebration, many other national and regional events, not to mention publishing ventures for which Fairford is responsible, reflect the remarkable development of what has become the Fund's business arm, since Crowley-Milling established it in 1975.

Since then and throughout the 1980s the Tattoo Organisation — a company limited by guarantee under the Fund's First Development Trust — has established an international reputation, and Bowen and Prince are consulted on air shows from the Gulf to California and The Down Under Air Show in Australia. Lockheed has been so impressed by the IAT's operation that it has sought to transport Bowen and his entire team — it numbers 3,000 when volunteer helpers are included — to run its air show in America. Bowen felt obliged to decline the offer, feeling that it would be impossible for his volunteers to take time off from work simultaneoulsy.

Certainly, the IAT has progressed beyond all recognition from the business which began in Hut 91 at Greenham Common. Indeed, the success of the organisation's original function, the Tattoo, has been such that it now alternates with the Society of British Aerospace Companies' longer established air show at Farnborough as one of the world's leading aviation events. In what Bowen modestly describes as its 'fallow year', the IAT helps to stage such other biennial events as

TVS's Air Show South, an International Air Show at the Army Air Corps Centre, Middle Wallop, and the World Aerobatic Championships. Spreading its 'wings' further, it is taking responsibility for a variety of fund raising events and publications which not only attract income but also raise the profile of the Fund. Standing out among these is the Festival of Music given at the Royal Albert Hall by Massed Bands of the RAF; publication under former British Eagle air stewardess Claire Lock's unit at Fairford of souvenir programmes for its own and other events, including the Farnborough programme and RAF Year Book and its American companion, the United States Air Force in Europe Year Book; operation and display of a 'Huey' Argentinian Bell UH-1H helicopter captured in the Falklands, and also of a hot air balloon on behalf of the Nationwide Anglia Building Society. Another lucrative activity is the management on behalf of companies of their sponsorship events in the aviation field. And, as if all this was not enough to occupy Bowen and his staff of more than thirty people, there is the additional responsibility since 1985 for awarding and supervising nine disabled flying scholarships a year in memory of Group Captain Sir Douglas Bader, to whom, in 1983, the Tattoo accorded the honour of a flypast salute by twelve Spitfires. Such activities, including publication of the books *The Royal Air Force at War* and *A Lifetime of Service*, were driven along by Steedman and Stanton.

The generous support and active participation of King Hussein of Jordan, the Tattoo Patron, in this scheme has been noted earlier, but there have been occasions when the Controller has prayed for a little less dedication to it. Steedman recalls that possibly the most anxious moment of his entire career, either in the Service or at Portland Place, was standing on the edge of a runway as the King took off to check out the progress of a partly-trained seriously disabled woman at the controls.

Selection for a scholarship is made on the basis of a candidate's personal record and an essay, which is attached to the application. One such candidate was Simon Weston, the Welsh Guardsman who was so badly burnt and disfigured in the Falklands Campaign. Each scholarship provides thirty-nine hours' dual and solo flying during a six-week residential course at an approved flying school, books, and equipment, examinations, licence and landing fees, accommodation and meals and the candidate's travelling expenses. Some candidates are too disabled to be permitted a pilot's licence, but such disablement does not disbar. In 1988 the nine scholarship winners received their Certificates of Award from the leader of the Red

Arrows during the TV South Air Show organised by Bowen's team at Bournemouth.

The most notable success of the scheme has been the issue of a completely unrestricted licence to a paraplegic. What better memorial could there be to the legless ace whose spirited refusal to surrender to disablement offered so much inspiration to countless disabled people?

In the tradition estsblished by Crowley-Milling and carried on by Steedman, with Air Commodore Mike Stanton so much responsible for the growth of IAT, Kennedy rates the chairmanship of IAT as the most stimulating of his numerous responsibilities. He is supported by Fred Crawley, the deputy chairman who, as well as being Honorary Treasurer of the Royal Air Force Benevolent Fund, and a Council and Finance and General Purposes Committee member, brings his experience as former Deputy Chief Executive of Lloyds Bank to a whole variety of the Fund's activities. One of their chief preoccupations every other year is to agree the theme of the Tattoo at Fairford, ranging in previous years from Sea Search 81, an international reconnaissance, search and rescue gathering, to Strike, Attack and Reconnaissance in 1983, International In-flight Refuelling, 1985, and Skylift 87, the world's first Military Air Transport Meet. Since such themes are central to each air show, a key member of Bowen's team is the theme co-ordinator, currently Wing Commander E. J. A. Patterson.

Co-operation by air forces from around the world is essential and generally this is obtained by running the theme on the basis of a training exercise, making it possible for air commanders to justify the considerable costs of attending, but a good theme would, of course, be wasted were it not for media attention over a long warm-up period and looking after press, radio and television people throughout a show. Here John Lightfoot, a retired local police chief inspector, has a key role. Since he has a law degree and remains well connected with the local police, Lightfoot sorts out legal wrangles over trademarks and copyrights, and liaises with police on traffic, security and a host of matters which require his experience and expertise. Lost children and a crêche looked after by the Womens Royal Voluntary Service and the Tattoo's own radio station, Wings Radio, are also his responsibilities.

In 1989, despite the International Air Tattoo Organisation's major preoccupation with arrangements for the Battle of Britain Appeal, Bowen and Prince successfully planned a magnificent trailer tattoo for 1990 to celebrate NATO's fortieth anniversary, placing emphasis on the peace thus achieved in Europe.

Such large, mass attended, outdoor events should not, however, be allowed to eclipse the many and varied fund-raising efforts of RAF stations nor, in particular, the Royal Air Force Anniversary Concert at the Royal Festival Hall, the annual event which in the early spring opens the Appeals season. Jubilee years are, of course, of especial significance and the Fund has been fortunate in being privileged with Royal attendances on such occasions. In 1978, the Diamond Jubilee of the RAF, the Queen Mother, Patron since the death of her husband, King George VI in 1952, was present. Sadly it was Peake's last appearance in the Royal Box. When he died that, May the Fund, in expressing its appreciation of his services, noted that, during the eleven-year period of his chairmanship, it spent more than £13 million on the relief of distress among nearly 100,000 members of the RAF family. Air Commodore Dame Felicity Peake's long membership of the Council and Finance and General Purposes Committee maintains the family association, and their son, Andrew, attends the concert annually with her. The President, the Duke of Kent, extended an especially warm welcome to them at the 1989 concert which marked the seventieth anniversary of the founding of the Fund by Lord Trenchard.

Besides being a rousing musical occasion in which the Central Band of the Royal Air Force, conducted in 1989 by Wing Commander Barrie Hingley, Principal Director of Music, Royal Air Force, shared the honours with the Royal Philharmonic Orchestra, conducted by Louis Fremaux, it also included the annual presentation of the Fund's Wilkinson Sword in recognition of outstanding fund-raising achievement within the Service. The President presented the 1989 Sword during the interval to Wing Commander J. Whitston, the Officer Commanding, Royal Air Force, Manston. This small station, with an establishment of only 215 Service personnel, donated £20,000 to the Fund from the proceeds of its Open Day, and also brought in £13,000 from sales of the RAF Year Book.

On the threshold of the £20 million Battle of Britain Fiftieth Anniversary Appeal in 1990, the Fund remains acutely conscious of its year-in-year-out indebtedness to the spare time activities on its behalf of RAF families and all those others whose comparitively small offerings, the bread and butter of its Appeals Branch, help to swell the total available for the relief of distress.

Epilogue

Duke of Kent School, Princess Marina House, the International Air Tattoo and Alastrean House — these remain the Royal Air Force Benevolent Fund's chief enterprises. No doubt, as differing needs identify themselves, the President, Chairman and Council, Committees, staff and their successors will be as resourceful in meeting them in the selfless tradition which Trenchard introduced in 1919 when, proposing the Fund, he said: 'Lots of people will get into trouble and go looking for others to help them, but the finest men and women will not ask.'

After seventy years the Royal Air Force Memorial, which was Trenchard's inspiration, remains the focus of those who remember the Royal Flying Corps, Royal Naval Air Service and Royal Air Force dead. However, it is possibly symptomatic of the changes which have taken place in international relationships and in British society since the Prince of Wales unveiled the memorial in 1923 that British and West German Chiefs of Air Staff lay wreaths there jointly on suitable commemorative occasions. Perhaps the Japanese will follow.

Seventy years ago when the Royal Air Force Memorial was planned, the war to end war had been won and it seemed inconceivable that civilised nations might sink into such madness again. Fifty years ago they did and after hostilities had been resumed, in 1940 it seemed momentarily certain that a victorious enemy had forced a reversal of his previous defeat. Then in the summer of that year, the Royal Air Force saved Britain and her people from national oblivion, and the free-thinking world from subjugation.

'Never in the field of human conflict was so much owed by so many to so few', Winston Churchill said at the time and repeated his immortal phrase when, some years after leading Britain to victory, he made his broadcast appeal on behalf of the Fund. He continued, 'By 1945, alas, as our casualty lists told the tale: 'the Few' had become 'the Many.'

'The Royal Air Force Benevolent Fund,' Churchill concluded then, 'is part of the conscience of the British nation. A nation without a conscience is a nation without a soul. A nation without a soul is a nation that cannot live.'

This account of the Royal Air Force Benevolent Fund's first seventy years, which closes here, is offered in support of Sir Winston's testimony.

Appendix A

Patrons, Presidents, Founder, Life Vice-Presidents, Chairmen and Controllers

Patrons
  6 May 1936   His Majesty King George VI
  to 6 February 1952
  3 June 1952 to date   Her Majesty Queen Elizabeth II

Presidents
  6 November 1919   His Royal Highness The Duke of York
  to
  5 May 1936
  25 February 1937   His Royal Highness The Duke of Gloucester
  to
  6 October 1941
  11 March 1943   Her Royal Highness Princess Marina, Duchess
  to   of Kent
  27 August 1968
  January 1969 to date   His Royal Highness The Duke of Kent

Founder
Marshal of the Royal Air Force the Rt. Hon. The Viscount
  Trenchard GCB, OM, GCVO, DSO, DCL, LL D

Vice-Presidents
The Rt. Hon. Julian Amery MP
The Rt. Hon. The Lord Amulree PC, GBE, KC
The Rt. Hon. The Lord Ashfield PC, TD
The Duke of Atholl KT, GCVO, CB, DSO

His Excellency The Rt. Hon. J. A. Beasley PC
Marshal of the Royal Air Force Sir Michael Beetham GCB, CBE, DFC,
  AFC
Admiral of the Fleet The Earl Beatty OM, PC, GCB, GCVO, DSO
Wyndham Birch Esq. DSO, MBE
The Hon. Sir Reginald Andrew Blankenburg

Vice-Presidents (continued)

The Hon. Sir Edgar Rennie Bowring KCMG

Marshal of the Royal Air Force Sir Dermot Boyle GCB, KCVO, KBE, AFC

Lt. Colonel The Rt. Hon. Lord Brabazon of Tara GBE, MC, PC

The Rt. Hon. The Viscount Brentford PC, DL

The Rt. Hon. S. M. Bruce CH, MC

The Viscount Burnham CH, GCMG, LL D, D LITT, MA, JP

Marshal of the Royal Air Force The Lord Cameron of Balhousie GCB, CBE, DSO, DFC

The Most Hon. The Marquess of Cholmondeley GCVO

The Rt. Hon. Sir Winston Churchill KG, OM, CH, FRS

The Rt. Hon. Sir Joseph Cook GCMG

Air Vice-Marshal Sir John W. Cordingley KCB, KCVO, CBE

The Viscount Cowdray PC, GCVO, DL

Marshal of the Royal Air Force Sir David Craig GCB, OBE, ADC, MA

The Rt. Hon. The Viscount De L'Isle VC, KG, GCMG, GCVO, PC, FCA, FRIBA, LL D

Marshal of the Royal Air Force Sir William Dickson GCB, KBE, DSO, AFC

Marshal of the Royal Air Force Sir Edward Ellington GCB, CMG, CBE

Marshal of the Royal Air Force The Lord Elworthy KG, GCB, CBE, DSO, MVO, DFC, AFC, MA

The Hon. George Howard Ferguson KC, LL D, BA

The Rt. Hon. Andrew Fisher PC

The Rt. Hon. Hugh Fraser MBE, MP

Marshal of the Royal Air Force Sir John Grandy GCB, GCVO, KBE, DSO

The Rt. Hon. Frederick Guest CBE, DSO, MP

Dame Helen Gwynne-Vaughan CBE, LL D, D SC, FLS

Air Chief Marshal Sir Peter Harding GCB, CBIM, FRAeS

Air Chief Marshal Sir Lewis Hodges KCB, CBE, DSO, DFC

Marshal of the Royal Air Force Sir Andrew Humphrey GCB, OBE, DFC, AFC

His Excellency The Rt. Hon. Sir William Joseph Jordan KCMG, PC, LL D, LP (NZ)

Vice-Presidents (Continued)
The Rt. Hon. The Viscount Knollys GCMG, MBE, DFC

The Hon. Peter Charles Larkin
Air Chief Marshal Sir David Lee GBE, CB
The Most Hon. The Marquess of Londonderry KG, MVO

The Hon. Sir Thomas Mackenzie GCMG, JP, FRGS, MLC, LL D
The Rt. Hon. Harold Macmillan OM, FRS, DCL, LL D
The Rt. Hon Vincent Massey CH
Sir Charles McLeod, Bt.
The Lord Montagu of Beaulieu KCIE, CSI, CC, JP, VD, DL
The Rt. Hon. The Lord Mottistone PC, CB, CMG, DSO

Marshal of the Royal Air Force The Rt. Hon. The Lord Newall GCB,
    OM, GCMG, CBE, AM
The Rt. Hon. George Heaton Nicholls
The Viscount Northcliffe

Air Commodore Dame Felicity Peake DBE, JP, AE
The Hon. Sir James Parr KCMG
The Hon. Sir Charles Parsons OM, KCB, MA, LL D, D SC, FRS, JP
Sir Geoffrey Pattie MP
The Rt. Hon. Sir George Perley GCMG
Marshal of the Royal Air Force Sir Thomas Pike CGB, CBE, DFC
Marshal of the Royal Air Force The Rt. Hon. The Viscount Portal of
    Hungerford KC, CGB, OM, DSO, MC, DL, DCL, LL D
Joan, Viscountess Portal of Hungerford

The Rt. Hon. The Lord Quickswood PC, DL, LL D

Colonel The Hon. Deneys Reitz
The Rt. Hon. The Lord Rhyl OBE, PC
The Lord Riddell
The Rt. Hon. The Lord Riverdale CBE, LL D, JP
N. Robertson Esq.
The Viscount Rothermere PC
The Rt. Hon. The Lord Rowley QC, PC, MA, LL B
Major-General The Hon. Sir Granville Ryrie KCMG, CB, VD

Marshal of the Royal Air Force Sir John Salmond GCB, CMG, CVO,
    DSO, DCL, LL D
The Rt. Hon. The Lord Shackleton of Burley KG, PC, OBE,
    LL D, DSc, FBIM

Vice-Presidents (continued)

Marshal of the Royal Air Force Sir John Slessor GCB, DSO, MC, DL, JP, CC

Marshal of the Royal Air Force Sir Denis Spotswood GCB, CBE, DFC

The Rt. Hon. The Viscount Stansgate PC, DSO, DFC

Rear-Admiral Sir Murray Sueter CB

His Grace The Duke of Sutherland KT

The Rt. Hon. The Earl of Swinton GBE, CH, MC, DL, LL D, PC

The Lord Sydenham GCMG, GCIE, GCSI, GBE, FRS

Air Vice-Marshal The Rt. Hon. Sir Frederick Sykes CBE, GCSI, GCIE, KCB, CMG, PC

Marshal of the Royal Air Force The Rt. Hon. The Lord Tedder GCB, DCL, LL D

The Rt. Hon. The Viscount Templewood PC, GCSI, GBE, CMG, DCL, LL D, DL, JP

Brigadier-General The Lord Thomson PC, CBE, DSO

The Rt. Hon. The Viscount Thurso KT, CMG, PC, LL D, JP

Marshal of the Royal Air Force The Rt. Hon. The Viscount Trenchard GCB, OM, GCVO, DSO, DCL, LL D

The Rt. Hon. The Viscount Trenchard MC

Air Chief Marshal Sir Augustus Walker GCB, CBE, DSO, DFC, AFC, MA

The Hon. Sir Edgar Walton KCMG

The Rt. Hon. The Viscount Ward of Witley PC

C. T. te Water Esq.

The Hon. Sidney Frank Waterson

The Rt. Hon. The Viscount Weir PC, GCB, DL

Sir Thomas Wilford KCMG, KC

The Rt. Hon. Sir Kingsley Wood MP

Marshal of the Royal Air Force Sir Keith Williamson GCB, AFC

Chairmen

The Rt. Hon. Lord Hugh Cecil PC, MP	1919-1929
Sir Charles C. McLeod Bt.	1929-1934
The Viscount Wakefield of Hythe GCVO, CBE	1934-1940
His Royal Highness Prince George, Duke of Kent KG, KT, GCMG, GCVO	1941-1942
The Rt. Hon. The Lord Riverdale GBE, LL D, JP	1942-1952
The Rt. Hon. The Viscount Knollys GCMG, MBE, DFC	1953-1966
Sir Harald Peake AE	1967-1978
The Lord Catto of Cairncatto	1978 to date

Controllers

Air Vice-Marshal Sir Hazelton Nicholl KBE, CB	1944-1947
Air Vice-Marshal Sir John W. Cordingley	
KCB, KCVO, CBE	1947-1962
Air Marshal Sir John Whitley KBE, CB, DSO, AFC	1962-1968
Air Marshal Sir William Coles	
KBE, CB, DSO, DFC, AFC	1968-1975
Air Marshal Sir Denis Crowley-Milling	
KCB, CBE, DSO, DFC, AE	1975-1981
Air Chief Marshal Sir Alasdair Steedman	
GCB, CBE, DFC, FRAeS, CBIM	1981-1988
Air Chief Marshal Sir Thomas Kennedy	
GCB, AFC, DL	1988 to date

Appendix B

Fund Branches
and Agencies Overseas

Scottish Branch:
  20 Queen Street, Edinburgh EH2 1JX
  (Telephone: Edinburgh 031-225 6421)
  Chairman: Group Captain V. R. Murphy
    Director: Air Vice-Marshal C. E. Simpson MB, ChB, MSc, FFOM,
  MFCM

Republic of Ireland Branch:
  14 Merrion Square, Dublin
  (Telephone: Dublin 766205)
  Chairman: Air Commodore J. J. Murphy OBE FIMechE
    Hon. Secretary: Wing Commander J. H. Simpson DFC
    Assistant Secretary: Miss W. Sheerin MBE

Agencies

Australia	— The Returned Services League of Australia
Canada	— The Royal Canadian Legion
Jamaica	— The Jamaica Legion
New Zealand	— Air Staff Defence Headquarters, Wellington
United States	— British Defence Staffs, Royal Air Force Staff,
of America	Washington DC

Appendix C

The Fund's Work, 1919-1988

	Awards	Relief expenditure £		Awards	Relief expenditure £
1919	—	919	1954	20,240	557,316
1920			1955	17,465	523,916
1921	—	6,569	1956	17,199	568,564
1922	320	5,868	1957	16,475	579,118
1923	539	9,861	1958	15,912	520,478
1924	750	8,380	1959	14,986	495,500
1925	1,022	8,636	1960	12,585	527,979
1926	1,180	10,451	1961	12,157	580,087
1927	1,406	10,461	1962	12,727	593,717
1928	1,699	12,538	1963	13,570	634,667
1929	1,812	14,498	1964	12,389	675,024
1930	1,812	14,450	1965	11,635	859,392
1931	1,966	15,581	1966	11,590	890,272
1932	2,189	15,167	1967	11,368	803,885
1933	2,529	17,759	1968	10,240	845,155
1934	2,174	16,189	1969	9,552	905,199
1935	2,134	18,785	1970	10,302	935,441
1936	1,928	18,817	1971	10,038	1,005,598
1937	1,849	20,292	1972	9,557	1,071,380
1938	2,132	22,290	1973	8,190	1,293,264
1939	2,477	22,921	1974	7,663	1,619,738
1940	3,709	27,766	1975	7,368	1,494,033
1941	5,596	38,352	1976	7,859	1,759,626
1942	8,354	55,610	1977	6,916	1,486,402
1943	12,824	89,495	1978	7,852	2,023,322
1944	17,780	163,679	1979	7,088	2,048,078
1945	28,591	326,697	1980	8,128	2,709,005
1946	31,134	507,615	1981	8,906	3,041,828
1947	28,546	529,735	1982	9,480	3,973,847
1948	32,541	668,656	1983	10,778	4,063,643
1949	30,362	711,829	1984	12,138	5,340,060
1950	27,044	608,816	1985	13,044	7,135,469
1951	24,143	640,466	1986	14,742	8,164,663
1952	25,659	681,474	1987	14,777	8,556,972
1953	22,752	588,364	1988	15,880	8,641,262
			Totals	739,749	£82,832,886

Appendix D

Honours and Awards for Services to the Fund

Year	Name	Award
1944	Squadron Leader V. S. Erskine-Lindop	OBE
1945	Sir Bertram Rumble	Kt
1947	F. C. Hawkes Esq.	OBE
1947	Mrs F. Vesey Holt	OBE
1948	J. F. Linney Esq.	CBE
1951	F. Wilkins Esq.	OBE
1952	W. Wallace Withers Esq.	CBE
1956	Major (formerly Sqn. Ldr.) H. G. Vyse	OBE
1959	E. de Rougemont Esq.	CBE
1961	Mrs R. J. Sanceau	MBE
1962	Air Vice-Marshal Sir John W. Cordingley	KCVO
1964	P. F. du Sautoy Esq.	OBE
1965	Mrs G. Inglis	MBE
1968	Flight Lieutenant J. A. B. Cairns	MBE
1972	Mrs E. A. Page	MBE
1973	Harald Peake Esq.	Kt
1973	Flight Lieutenant G. C. Sykes	MBE
1974	John H. Corner	OBE
1975	Mrs K. R. Masters	MBE
1975	Lady Drummond	MBE
1976	Miss Helen McDougal	MBE
1980	Miss Jean Ashton	MBE
1983	Miss W. Sheerin	MBE
1985	P. M. Cutting Esq. DFC	OBE

Appendix E

Some of the Organisations and Schools with which the Fund has co-operated

Alexandra and Albert School, Reigate
Alexandra House, Newquay
Alzheimer's Disease Society
Army Benevolent Fund
Association of Jewish Ex-Servicemen and Women
Association to Combat Huntington's Chorea
ATS and WRAC Benevolent Funds

Barnardo's
Blond McIndoe Centre for Medical Research
Bournemouth War Memorial Homes
British Commonwealth Ex-Services League
British Hospital and Home for Incurables, Streatham
British Limbless Ex-Servicemen's Association

Calibre, Cassette Library
Care for Mentally Handicapped
Chaseley Trust for Disabled Ex-Servicemen, Eastbourne
Cheshire Foundation Homes for the Sick
Chest, Heart and Stroke Association
Christ's Hospital
Church Army
Church of England Children's Society
Clifton College, Bristol
Counsel and Care for the Elderly
Cranleigh School

Danson Clinic of the Incorporated Liverpool School of Tropical Medicine
Dean Close School, Cheltenham
Disabled Drivers' Association
Dolphin School, Newark

Douglas Haig Memorial Homes
Dresden House, Hove

Earl Haig Fund (Scotland)
East Lancashire Homes for Disabled Sailors, Soldiers and Airmen
   (Broughton House, Salford)
Ellesmere College
Ex-Royal Air Force Dependants' Severely Disabled Holiday Trust
Ex-Service Fellowship Centres
Ex-Services Mental Welfare Society
Ex-Services War Disabled Help Department of the Order of St. John
   and the British Red Cross Society
Eventide Homes, Brixham

Family Welfare Association
Far East Prisoners of War and Internees Fund
Finchale Training College for the Disabled, Durham
Forces Help Society and Lord Roberts Workshops

Gordon's School, Woking
Guild of Air Pilots' Benevolent Fund
Guinea Pig Club

Hanover Housing Association
Harcourt School, Andover
Help the Aged
Holiday Care Service
Home Farm Trust, Bristol
House Association for Officers' Families
Hurstpierpoint School, Hassocks

Invalid Children's Aid Association

King Alfred School, Somerset
King Edward VII's Hospital for Officers (Sister Agnes Foundation)
King Edward VII Convalescent Home for Officers, Isle of Wight
King George's Fund for Sailors
Kingham Hill School, Oxford
Kitchener Scholarships — The Lord Kitchener National Memorial
   Fund

League of Remembrance
'Lest We Forget' Association

Lilian Faithful Homes, Cheltenham
Lord Kitchener Memorial Holiday Centre
Lord Wandsworth College, Basingstoke

Malvern College
Marie Curie Memorial Foundation
Marlborough College
Mental After Care Association
Mill Hill School
Morden College Home, Blackheath
Motor Neurone Disease Association
Multiple Sclerosis Society

National Association for Mental Health
National Association of Swimming Clubs for the Handicapped
National Council for One-Parent Families
National Organisation for the Widowed and their Children (CRUSE)
National Society for Cancer Relief
'Not Forgotten' Association

Officers' Association
One Parent Families

Papworth and Enham Foundation
Park House Preparatory School, Paignton
Phyllis Tuckwell Memorial Hospice
Polish Air Force Benevolent Fund
Portland Training College for the Disabled, Mansfield
Princess Louise Scottish Hospital for Limbless Sailors, Soldiers
    and Airmen

Queen Alexandra Hospital Home, Gifford House, Worthing
Queen Elizabeth's Foundation for the Disabled, Leatherhead
Queen Victoria School, Dunblane

Reed's School, Cobham
Regular Forces Employment Association
Royal Air Forces Association, Richard Peck House, St.
    Annes-on-Sea; Sussexdown, Storrington; Dowding House, Moffat
Royal Association for Disability and Rehabilitation (RADAR)
Royal British Legion
Royal Caledonian Schools

Royal Homes for Officers' Widows and Daughters
Royal Hospital and Home, Putney
Royal National Institute for the Blind
Royal National Institute for the Deaf
Royal Naval Benevolent Society
Royal Naval Benevolent Trust
Royal Patriotic Fund Corporation
Royal Star and Garter Home, Richmond
Royal Surgical Aid Society, Homes for the Elderly
Royal United Kingdom Beneficent Association (RUKBA)
Royal Wanstead School
Royal Wolverhampton School

Salvation Army
Scottish National Institution for the War Blinded
Scottish Naval, Military and Air Force Veterans' Residences
Scottish Veterans' Garden City Association
Shaftesbury Homes and 'Arethusa'
Sir Beachcroft Towse Ex-Service Fund for the Blind
Sir Oswald Stoll Foundation
SOS Society
Soldiers', Sailors' and Airmen's Families Association (SSAFA)
SOUNDAROUND
Spinal Injuries Association
SSAFA Officers' Widows' Branch
St. Dunstan's
St. Edward's School, Oxford
St. Loye's College for the Disabled, Exeter
Sue Ryder Home, Nettlebed

Talking Books for the Handicapped
Tape Programmes for the Blind
Thistle Foundation, Edinburgh
Treloar Trust, Alton
Turning Point

Viscountess Barrington Homes

Wellington College, Crowthorne
Whitefoord House and Rosendael, Edinburgh
Winged Fellowship Trust
Women's Royal Naval Service Benevolent Trust

Index